INVENTINS
AND
PATENTS

the complete
manual on how
to make money
from your

INVENTIONS
AND
PATENTS

Steve S. Barbarich

Adams Media Corporation
Holbrook, Massachusetts

Published by
Adams Media Corporation
260 Center Street, Holbrook, MA 02343. U.S.A.
www.adamsmedia.com

ISBN: 1-58062-298-4

Printed in the United States of America.

J I H G F E D C B A

Library of Congress Cataloging-in-Publication data
Barbarich, Steve.
The complete manual on how to make money from your inventions and patents /
by Steve Barbarich.
p. cm.
1. Patents. 2. Inventions—Marketing. I. Title
T211 .B37   2000
608—dc21   00-038127

This publication is designed to provide accurate and authoritative information with regard to the subject matter covered. It is sold with the understanding that the publisher is not engaged in rendering legal, accounting, or other professional advice. If legal advice or other expert assistance is required, the services of a competent professional person should be sought.

— From a *Declaration of Principles* jointly adopted by a Committee of the American Bar Association and a Committee of Publishers and Associations

This book is available at quantity discounts for bulk purchases.
For information, call 1-800-872-5627.

Visit our exciting small business Web site: www.businesstown.com

Visit these exciting Web site for inventors:
www.inventorspublishing.com, and www.absolutelynew.com

Contents

Acknowledgments

Special thanks goes out to my mother, Anna Phelps, and patent attorney Milord Keshishzadeh (Los Angeles), for supporting the crusade toward creativity.

www.inventorsdigest.com

Milord Keshishzadeh, Patent
   Attorney, *patentmil@earthlink.net*

www.Patent-ideas.com

www.inventorfraud.com

www.patentityourself.com

www.patentpending.com

www.patentcafe.com

www.onebox.com

lawworks-iptoday.com/

www.patentsearcher.com

adesigner.com/invention

members.aol.com/t2design

C. Bart Sullivan, Licensed Patent
   Practitioner, Benicia, CA 94510

Robert Toczycki, Patent Attorney,
   www.members.aol.com/toczycki

www.patents.com

www.bobmerrick.com

www.thoughtstore.com

pages.prodigy.net/g_mccotter/
   mtech.htm

www.patent-site.com

www.mahiconsultant.com

www.InventorServices.com

Richard Maczan, PCE Patent
   Consulting Engineers,
   RMaczan@compuserve.com

www.InventAndGrowRicher.com

www.iplawusa.com

www.invent1.org

InventionCily.com

www.metaformusa.com

www.bugstik.com

www.icaninvent.com/

www.ideafinder.com

www.franceandassociates.net

www.MarketLaunchers.com

www.inventorsunion.com

www.inventions-australia.com.au

Introduction

There were more than 122,977 patents granted in the United States in 1997 out of about 237,045 applications filed. These 122,977 patents generated more than $1 trillion for those who use, sell, or buy intellectual property. As an author and an individual who has been through the process many times already, I am convinced that coming up with and selling original ideas is perhaps one of the easiest ways for an individual to get rich nowadays. Not only can it be done with low risk and little investment, and on a part-time basis, but you do not even need a technical background to carry out the process.

Selling or licensing out inventions may seem like a difficult and intimidating process at first, but you just need to learn which steps to follow. This easy-to-follow, yet highly thorough, step-by-step manual will show you how to *make big money from your patent*. Nowhere else will you find a book so devoted to helping you create large returns from your intellectual property.

Almost every single new idea that is marketable is either taken to the market by a new entrepreneur (a start-up company) or an already established entrepreneur (a large corporation). No matter how crazy, simple, or useful your invention may be, there is always someone out there who will take your invention to the market if they are *convinced that it will be profitable*. This manual shows you exactly how to find those "someones" and exactly how to convince them. It is written from pure experience and includes all the secrets and tactics that my colleagues and I have used religiously to secure dozens of large royalty contracts with major corporations.

Steps 1 through 5 explain the crucial process you must follow before you even contact potential companies. Steps 6 through 8 show you how to attract the large corporations to your product and attain the largest possible royalty returns from them. The last steps, 9 through 10, show you how to protect your investment further and to increase your profits fourfold by creating a whole product line from your one patent.

Now it's up to you. Once you start carrying out this step-by-step process, you will probably have your patent sold or licensed within a year. Note that this is an average time frame. You could sell out within just a couple of months or it might take you more than a year, depending on your particular invention and how well you implement the information in this book. Whatever the case, just remember that perseverance is the key to anything. Hang in there, and the fruits of success will be yours.

The Ins and Outs of Patents

This chapter will help you evaluate whether or not you have a patentable and marketable idea. It will also explain what steps you need to take to protect your intellectual property with the U.S. Patent and Trademark Office (PTO). (If you already have a patent, then you've completed the first step of many on your way to success. In this case, continue on to the next chapter, "Step 2," and the rest of the book.)

Evaluating Your Idea: Marketability vs. Patentability

Having a patentable idea doesn't necessarily mean you have a marketable idea. Some ideas are novel and interesting, yet it may not be worth going through the patent procedure if there is *no* market or there exists *significant barriers to entry* into the market for the invention. Before you spend the time and money to get a patent, you will want to do market research for your invention.

For instance, some important questions to ask yourself to verify marketability are:

1. Does my product get the job done quickly?
2. Does my product fulfill an unsatisfied need?
3. Can my product be manufactured at a reasonable cost?
4. Does it follow a current trend?
5. Does my invention stand out over competitive products?

You should be able to answer "Yes" to most of these questions, but there are also many other factors in judging the marketability of your invention. I will discuss this in more detail in Step 3.

The key is for you to do a little research in Step 3 to make sure there aren't any specific major barriers to entry into the market for your invention. In other words, before filing a patent application, you should at least know whether there are barriers to your invention's market, and if so, would they ruin or make difficult your future marketing efforts. For example, you may not want to pursue an invention if you find that your invention's field is a highly crowded art (many inventions very similar to yours) thereby making your future patent easy to work around and compete with. Or perhaps your idea is a new drug, or medical device that requires FDA approval, taking it up to 10 years for approval for release into the market. In that case, your personal decision may be to pursue other ideas. If your invention is so novel that the market for it doesn't exist, be prepared to spend many years culturing and developing your new market.

The good news is, as you can see, these *barriers to entry* that I've described are not insurmountable. Instead they are merely obstacles to varying degrees that you personally will need to overcome if you think they are worth pursuing. There is plenty of hope in regard to most situations. With the right marketing efforts, I believe you can sell just about anything to practically anyone.

The following "Marketing Factors Pyramid" can help you brainstorm the factors that may effect your marketability, sales, as well as the patentability of your invention. The most important factors are at the top of the pyramid, although the priority of some factors can vary depending on the type of invention you have. Make sure more of these factors are positives on your side, rather then negatives that will work against you. In addition, assure yourself that *no one* of these factors is so bad that it could render your invention "unmarketable." For example, if you've invented a new type of 22mm bullet with a diamond tip so that it could pierce through bones, its cost would be so high that it would outweigh its value to the customer. Step 3 includes detailed explanations of each of these marketing factors.

Speed
Cost
Market Size
Long-Existing
Need
Barriers to Market
Ease-of-Use Novelty
Computerized/
Mechanized Process
Appeal to the Senses
New Discovery or Technical
Advance
Safety-Improved Properties
Competition/Crowded Art Size
and Weight of Invention
Part of a Larger Existing Product
Can't Teach an Old Dog New Tricks
A Controversial Area or Hot Media Topic/
More Accuracy & Quality
Hip or "Faddy"/FDA Approval (i.e., Nuclear Medicine)/
New Market or Industry
High Growth Area/High Value or Low Overhead/Market Trends
Endorsement by Public Figures/Appeal to Organizations/
Reliability or Maintenance
Life of Product/Accessory and Product Spin-Off Potential/Green Products

Types of Patents

There are three types of patents: utility, design, and plant. The *utility patent* is the most common and meaningful patent class. It requires an invention to be innovative enough to pass several requirements of the PTO. Utility patents filed after June 7, 1995 have a term of 20 years, which is measured from the application filing date

The *design patent* is a much less complex patent. It only requires your invention to look or be shaped differently than anything else (i.e., it's purely ornamental). The term of a design patent is 14 years. A design patent does not protect the functionality of your invention.

The last patent, the *plant patent*, is offered due to the special considerations of inventing new varieties of plants that are asexually reproducible. The plant patent term follows the same rules as the utility patent except that plant patents have additional requirements that must be complied with.

Evaluating Your Idea for Patentability

Before you spend time and money on a patent application, you should consider whether your invention will meet the legal requirements for a patent set by the PTO, which has the following four criteria for patent approval.

Requirement 1: Statutory Class

This criterion requires that your patent fall into at least one of the five patent classes established by Congress: process, machine, manufacture, composition, or "new use" of any of the previous four. A *process* is an actual series of steps or a method in accomplishing a given outcome or producing a certain product. A *machine* is any device with moving parts, such as an automobile. A *manufacture* is anything that can be constructed or manufactured (many ideas fall into this bracket). A *composition* refers to a composition of matter or material, such as a new chemical or a biological formula for a new type of rubber. A *"new use"* patent must be a process-type patent. For example, you might use a known entity such as toothpaste for a new use, such as filling holes before painting.

Requirement 2: Utility

Utility refers to whether or not your invention is useful. Usually, an invention will easily pass the utility test. Occasionally, however, the PTO calls for further investigation into utility. Someone proposing a new chemical, for example, might need to show explicitly how it will be used. Under this criterion, inventions that are unsafe, whimsical, illegal, immoral, non-operable, nuclear, or classified as theoretical phenomena *fail* the utility test. Other items that are unpatentable are mathematical formulae ($E=mc^2$) and laws of nature. You cannot pass the utility test by stating that your invention can be used as a paperweight. Design patents and plant patents do not require utility.

Requirement 3: Novelty

The novelty requirements are set forth in Title 35 of the United States Code, Section 102. In order for your invention to pass the novelty test, amongst other requirements in Section 102, no single prior item can describe all the elements of your invention. If you find something exactly like your product on the market, the prevailing invention goes to the party who can prove its conception at the earliest date.

To prove the conception of your invention, you can use witnessed, signed, and dated records showing the conception, building, and/or testing of your invention.

One important rule to remember with novelty is the *"One Year Rule."* The "One Year Rule" states that if your product is publicly known or in public use or on sale for more than one year *in the United States*, neither you nor anybody else can obtain a patent on it. *Public use* includes public knowledge about your invention either through word of mouth or a published article, and also the sale or offer to sell your product, even though the sale may not have been finalized. "Public use" would generally not include experimental activity by a group closely supervised by the inventor and for the sole purpose of "completing" or ascertaining the utility of the invention.

Another important rule, *the foreign rule,* is a little bit more tricky, and it will also prohibit a U.S. patent in certain situations. Your invention is only novel in this country if it is not patented or described in a printed publication in a foreign country (or this country) before the earliest date of your conception. If millions of your inventions have been sold in a foreign country more than a year before you patent the invention in the United States, it is still acceptable as long as there was no detailed foreign publication about your invention. Section 102 also sets forth additional situations that will prevent patenting. You should review the statute or ask your attorney about the limitations.

Requirement 4: Unobvious

Is your product truly inventive? That is, would it be obvious to any technically competent person in your field or does it represent a real advance over existing technologies? To meet this requirement, your invention must have novel—or new—features and in some way perform better than similar devices or produce new, unexpected results. If it is derived from an earlier technology, it must also have been substantially modified to perform new, "unobviously" better results. Clearly, unobviousness is a very subjective matter that depends on a number of factors. In general, if you're making only small physical differences from an existing invention, your new, unexpected results must be relatively great. On the other hand, if you've made immense physical modifications to a particular concept, only small differences will be required to pass the unobvious test.

If you're not sure that your invention is unobvious enough, there are some common arguments that you can use in your patent to convince the PTO. If your patent satisfies one or more of the following conditions in addition to satisfying the three preceding PTO requirements, chances are favorable that the PTO will grant your patent.

Satisfies a long-existing need or solves an unrecognized problem. If your invention is different from prior art in that it satisfies a long-existing need, that's beneficial. (Prior art is defined as any invention that came before yours that is similar or that solves the same problem.) For example, in 1992 I patented a welding tool that mounts on your finger so you don't have to hold it. This frees up the rest of the hand to hold other items, making soldering easier.

Shows a small difference in crowded art. If the market for your invention is very crowded, such as the market for mountain bikes or computer central processing units, sometimes very small differences from a similar product will be enough to consider it unobvious.

Has proven market success. If you have sold a million units of your products before they consider your patent, this pulls much weight in your favor.

Demonstrates a novel modification of prior art. If you modify a prior patent in a way that was not described or suggested in the prior patent and produce new, unexpected results, this is patentable.

Successfully develops a product or concept where others have failed. The product or concept may be something that has long been dreamed of, but never successfully accomplished (e.g., the ability to fly). For centuries, people tried many schemes, but continuously failed to fly until the Wright brothers came along. Solving difficult schemes such as these carries much weight with the PTO.

Produces synergistic results. Synergy is when the sum of the parts is equal to more than the whole. For example, if you combine a common cigarette lighter and a childproof cap, the result is a lighter that is safe in children's hands. The safety advantage this provides (protection to children and prevention of accidental fires) is of great value as compared to lighters, caps, or covers as separate, uncombined elements.

Combines incompatible elements. If you've taken two previously incompatible elements, but modified them and put them together so that they now work together to provide some utility, this is a plus on your side.

Combines many elements and modifies the elements. The more elements from prior inventions you combine and the more you modify such elements, the better you are in satisfying the "unobvious" requirement. Using such combinatory "unobviousness" will only work if prior art does not describe or suggest such combinations. If your combination is mentioned in prior inventions, but is described as a nonworkable solution, this is good for you and should be mentioned in your patent arguments because your invention has overcome what was before held in regard as insoluble.

Doing a Patent Search

When you file a patent application, the PTO will automatically do a search as part of the application process. In spite of this, there are a few reasons why you should do a preliminary search *before you file*:

1. If you find that someone has already patented your invention, you'll have saved yourself a lot of time and money.

2. If you find that there isn't a patent on your invention, and you satisfy all the criteria in the previous section, you know that your chances for getting a patent are fairly good. Therefore, you can confidently continue with the development and marketing of your product. You can also use your patent search to convince potential corporations that your "patent pending" will most likely go through.

3. Executing a patent search also helps you get a grip on competitive products and the kind of jargon they use in your industry. Understanding your competition and markets are very important issues, and are covered at length in Step 3.

4. By researching prior art, you may discover that you have solved common problems with your new invention. In your patent application you can point out the downfalls of those existing inventions and convince the PTO that you have come up with a better solution. This technique is highly recommended and will carry much weight in your favor.

5. You may save the PTO time or have uncovered references that the PTO may accidentally miss. Doing a preliminary search also shows the examiner that you have conducted a search and still believe in the patentability of your invention.

Ways to Conduct the Search

Doing a search is a relatively easy process that anyone can do. Because of this, I recommend that people do searches on their own, rather than paying professionals to do it. Here are the possible ways to do a search, listed in order of fastest and cheapest to slowest and more expensive:

1. Visit a patent depository library and do a computer search.
2. Visit a patent depository library and do a microfiche search.
3. Do an online search at the IBM Web site (*ibm.com*) or the PTO Web site (*uspto.gov*).
4. Use a patent depository librarian who will do a search for a fee.
5. Use discount professional searchers (e.g., Inventors' Publishing & Research, LLC does searches for a wholesale price of $300: 1-800-MARKET2).
6. Use patent agents (listed in your telephone book).
7. Use a patent attorney (listed in your telephone book; to get a national list, look at the PTO publication *Attorneys and Agents Registered to Practice Before the U.S. Patent and Trademark Office*).
8. Contact the Main PTO office in Arlington Virginia, which will do searches for $300 or more.

One important point to mention here is that only a patent agent or attorney can give you an opinion of patentability (patent agents are non-attorneys who are licensed professionals when it comes to patents). With the other methods, you'll have to develop your own opinion of patentability from the criteria discussed in the first section of this chapter. In addition, keep in mind that online searches only date back to 1970.

The first four search-for-a-fee options are fairly straightforward methods that you might be interested in pursuing if a few hundred dollars isn't much to you, or if you don't have any free time. Otherwise, I definitely recommend the first three options since they are free, offer you a good experience, and can get you results just as soon as you start.

Computer Searches

Find out where your nearest patent depository library (PDL) is by asking a local patent attorney or agent, or checking the telephone directory of your state capital (typically, most states have a PDL at the capital). All depositories have on-line search capabilities where you can conduct a search through many categories, such as subject, patent number, patent title, issue year, classification, assignee name, and other general information. The typical computer search systems offer the title and abstract of patents, but not the complete patent text. (Separate computer systems are typically set up for this since full-text databases are enormous and require different software.) The abstracts given from the "quick search" systems should be adequate in describing how the prior art differs from your invention. If not, then you may have to search for the full text of the patent on a computer that is set up for "full-text" searches. Some libraries may not be that advanced, so you may be stuck with the traditional patent searching methods such as microfiche or paperback.

If it sounds a little complicated, don't worry. When you arrive at a PDL, the librarians will usually walk you through the process of using the computers and assist you in doing your search. In addition, many libraries have classes you can attend, or videos you can watch that will teach you the basics of searching.

Basics on Computer Searching: The PTO Classification System

Before you start your search, there are a few books that are available to help you classify your patent. These books can be accessed on-line for your convenience.

The first one, *The Index to the U.S. Patent Classification*, helps you come up with a broad spectrum of keywords and possible subject areas within which patents in your area might fall. Because there are more than five million patents, the PTO has made a class/subclass procedure that allows you to narrow down and locate your invention. There are about three hundred classes in all. Each class represents a very broad subject area. In each class, there are two hundred to three hundred subclasses to further narrow down a specific invention. Once you've come across some key subject words or class number/subclass number combinations, you can look in the *Manual of Classification* to narrow your search by subclass even further. For instance, you may want to find a particular patent in class/subclass 200/105, but to pinpoint the actual patent you may have to look in the *Manual of Classification* and find that under subclass 105 there is a further subclass 278, and an even further subclass of that subclass, 15, making the full classification 200/105/278/15 (a chain that gets narrower and narrower). However, for practical reasons, the PTO only references patents by their class/subclass. You have to keep track of where the individual patents are beyond the first subclass.

Now is the time to get started with your search efforts! You are equipped with many key/subject words, class/subclasses, and ideas of what to enter as a search mode. You can enter these items into the appropriate fields on the computer, and it will quickly bring up lists of patents that fall in the specific areas you are searching. You can then browse through the abstracts to learn more about the prior art. As a bonus, when you are searching patents, each patent record brought up on the screen will also include cross-references to other class/subclass combinations that you may not have thought of, thus possibly giving you even more tips of where to look for prior art inventions. Again, there are librarians and users' manuals at the libraries that will help you with the exact details of using these computer searches when you get there; most people get the hang of it in less than 30 minutes.

Here is a compilation of the most popular computer products that you're likely to run into at PDLs (Patent Depository Library) and an explanation of what they do:

CASSIS series/ASSIST. These computer search programs are produced by the government and are the most common search utilities. This database is updated every two months. The search can go back as far as 1969. Information included: titles, abstracts, classifications, patent number, issue years, status, assignee's name, address, total number of patents by assignee since 1969, assignment information, patent attorney names and information. You can obtain more information and order these computer search kits on CD-ROM disks from (703) 308-0322.

MicroPatent search system. This private company produces search programs much like CASSIS, except that they are more powerful and flexible as far as searching capabilities and the type of information received. These databases are updated on CD-ROM more often than the government products.

MicroPatent Image Search System. This is a computer look-up system that gives you the full text of all patents in history and allows you to print them out. It is made up of computer-scanned images of all the pages of every patent issued (through the *Official Gazette*) in history. If you have this at your disposal, you'll never have to use microfiche or paperback to search for the full text of any patent.

Additionally, if you have a home computer and a modem, you can access the PTO online and do searches of patents through the World Wide Web at *www.uspto.gov* or with *www.ibm.com*. You can also access an on-line searchable database with full text and graphics through *ibm.com* in its patent section.

When Your Search Is Complete

If you've done your search, and there's nothing exactly like your idea, use the criterion in the last section to get a feel for whether or not your idea is patentable. If you're really uncertain, you may want to take your search results to a patent attorney or agent and get an expert opinion. If you satisfy the patentability criteria but had to significantly narrow down your claims or add many small features (narrowing your scope) to differentiate your invention from prior art, it may not be worth getting a patent; your patent may be so weak that others can work around it. When you think your patent will be approved, move on to the next section, which discusses one more relatively quick and easy action that you can take before the actual lengthy patent application filing.

The Invention Disclosure Document— Save Your Spot!

How many times have you heard that someone's come up with an idea you know will make millions? Usually, the idea is so simple you can't believe you never thought of it yourself. It is probably also original and makes some sort of breakthrough or improvement.

If you *did* think of the idea but sat on it, you may kick yourself to know that someone else has gone ahead and capitalized on it!

Maybe you decided not to move forward with your idea because you thought it wasn't fully developed. Or you were too busy to devote enough time to the project. Perhaps you were afraid your idea was too big for you to handle. Or you thought some giant corporation would come along and steal it. Then again, maybe you just weren't sure what steps you could take to protect your idea.

Many people have been waylaid by all the same fears—and they're often the ones still crying over what might have been. What they should have done, and what *you* still can do, is file an *Invention Disclosure*. For a small fee paid to the PTO ($10), this simple piece of paper protects your idea for two years. Not only is filing a disclosure easy, but the Patent Office will confirm the date of your idea if somebody else tries to duplicate it. To file an invention disclosure, all you have to do is send the PTO a rough description of your idea. If you don't have the time, Inventors' Publishing & Research, LLC (IP&R) will file your disclosure for free (except for the $10 fee the government charges you). Call 1-800-MARKET2 (627-5382). You can save your idea the same day if you use IP&R's faxing procedure.

Be warned, though, that a disclosure document is *not* a substitute for a patent application. It does *not* take the place of any development or testing notes. Nor can you use it as a "grace period" to delay the filing of your patent application. Finally, it does *not* let you claim "Patent Pending Product" on your invention.

Here's how you can file a patent disclosure document:

1. Send a letter asking that your disclosure document be accepted under the legal right of the disclosure document program (follow the example in Figure 1-1). If possible, type all correspondence and forms; legible handwriting is also acceptable. It doesn't matter whether you use a professional, personal, or business letterhead. *Be sure to include a copy of the original letter, as well.*

2. Enclose a check for the proper fee (currently $10), payable to the "Commissioner of Patents and Trademarks, Washington, DC 20231."

3. Attach a copy of your disclosure document (see the sample form in Figure 1-2). *Keep the original for your files.*

4. Enclose a self-addressed, stamped envelope.

Figure 1-1. Sample letter requesting participation in the disclosure document program.

Date _____

Commissioner of Patents and Trademarks
Washington, District of Columbia 20231

Request for Participation in Disclosure Document Program:

Disclosure of _____ [Your Name Here] _____

Entitled ____ [Name of Document] ____

Sir:

Attached is a disclosure of the above entitled invention (consisting of _____ sheets of written description and _____ separate drawings or photos), a check for $ _____, a stamped, addressed return envelope, and a duplicate copy of this letter.

It is respectfully requested that this disclosure be accepted and retained for two years (or longer if it is later referred to in a paper filed in a patent application) under the Disclosure Document Program and that the enclosed duplicate of this letter be date stamped, numbered, and returned in the enveloped also enclosed.

The undersigned understands that (1) this disclosure document is neither a patent application nor a substitute for one, (2) its receipt date will not become the effective filing date of a later filed patent application, (3) it will be retained for two years and then destroyed unless it is referred to in a patent application, (4) this two-year retention period is not a "grace period" during which a patent application can be filed without loss of benefits, (5) in addition to this document, proof of diligence in building and testing the invention, and/or filing a patent application on the invention, may be vital in case of an interference, and in other situations, and (6) if such building and testing is done, signed and dated records of such should additionally be made and these should be witnessed and dated by disinterested individuals (not the PTO).

Very respectfully,

_____   _____

Signature of Inventor   Signatures of Joint Inventors

_____   _____

c/o (print name)   Print Name

_____   _____

Address   Address

Enclosures:

As stated above

Disclosure Document Format

A sample document is shown is Figure 1-2. In general, be sure to follow these instructions:

1. Print your name, address, telephone number, page number, title, and the words *disclosure document* as a footer. If you have more than one page, all signatures, the title of your invention, and a page number indicating the total number of pages (e.g., "Page 1 of 2") *must appear on each page.*

2. Sign and date the description of your invention. Then write in this statement: "The above confidential information is Witnessed and Understood," and have it signed and dated by at least two competent technological witnesses. It's best to find experts in your invention's field of design who are disinterested and unrelated to you.

3. In the heart of your document, provide as much detailed information as possible about your idea. More information is better.

4. There's no particular required format to the rest of the document, but as a guideline, you should try to include as many of the following that apply to you:

    a. How you came up with the idea

    b. Advantages

    c. A broad description and an informal sketch

    d. Ramifications

    e. Novel modifications or features

    f. Technical advances

    g. Potential applications

    h. Closest prior art known

Figure 1-2. Sample disclosure document

Invention Disclosure

Page _____ of_____

Inventor(s):   Steve Barbarich

Address(es):   1462 Folsom Way. Walnut Creek, KY 94508

Tel&Fax: (402) 871-2102 / (402) 871-2557

Title of Invention: FingerTip Soldering Iron

Idea Conception: I came up with the idea while working in my garage one day because I became a little frustrated trying to solder some jumper wires to a PC board.

Advantages of the Invention: The FingerTip Soldering Tool rests on top of any finger thereby freeing up the rest of the hand to hold other items, such as wire, solder, or any piece of interest. Other solder tools occupy the whole hand because they have handles. It gives fingertip control and quick maneuverability since it is attached to the end of your index finger. It is also small, light, and electrically efficient.

Description & Sketch: The FingerTip tool is made up of a fingertip soldering body that is secured above the human finger. Within the fingertip soldering body is a soldering tip heating element. See sketch that follows:

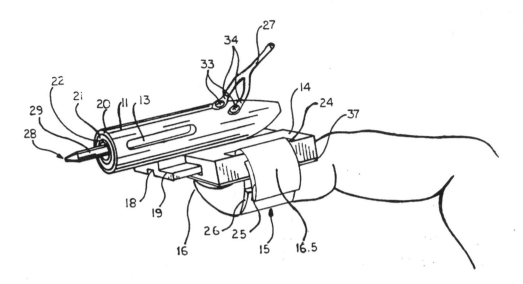

Illustration of FingerTip Soldering Tool on finger.

Ramifications: As a result of this product, users not only have one extra hand to work with, but they also have a lighter, more maneuverable soldering tool to work with. Hence it provides the most efficient soldering tool known to date.

Closest Known Prior Art: I have found nothing close to my idea. All the other soldering tools have handle assemblies. These references are Sauer 228/57 and Sylvester 219/236.

Inventor(s):   Steve Barbarich

Date of Signature: 1990 December 15

The above confidential information is Witnessed and Understood:

Jim Dancy 90/Dec/17

Tom Jefferson 90/Dec/23

Keeping a Journal

Another good way to protect your idea is to keep a bound journal of the building and testing of your invention. In a court of law, your inventor's journal may even prove more credible than an invention disclosure because witnesses can testify to more than just the *conception* of your idea. For example, by reviewing the construction and testing information in your journal, they can testify to how you got your idea. To be of any use, your journal must contain frequent endorsement by witnesses who sign off on your project. Make sure you choose witnesses who have the technical expertise to understand your invention completely, such as a professor in your field, a businessperson in the same area, or a knowledgeable friend. Because your witness may need to testify later on, do not pick someone who is elderly or ill. Also, you should *not* use relatives, co-inventors, or financially interested parties as your witnesses.

Filing Your Patent Application

Getting Started

If you are serious about following through on your idea, plan to file a patent application. There are two types of applications: a *regular patent application* and a *provisional patent application.* The provisional patent application is a new type of "pseudo" application resulting from 1995 legislation. It essentially serves as a "mini" patent application, but it has very special limitations. A provisional patent application *does not* take the place of a regular patent application, but rather saves your date of conception, much like an Invention Disclosure. A discussion of what a provisional patent application can do for you appears on page 23.

A regular, "classical" patent application is your most meaningful filing; it is what ultimately issues into a patent. Invention disclosures and provisional patent applications are only temporary spot holders that expire if you don't follow up with a regular patent application.

You can file your regular patent application in two ways. Either you can have an attorney or agent do the work, which typically costs between $3,000 and $6,000. Or you can file your patent application yourself. Since doing it on your own usually costs between $1,000 to $1,400 ($375 filing fee + $625 issue fee + the cost of required professional drawings), you can save quite a bit of money. But here again, a word of warning is in order: If you don't have any experience with patents, don't understand the legal work involved, or don't know how to take advantage of a pending patent, this process is too complicated for you! Don't risk losing a lot of money after your patent has been approved; get a good patent attorney or patent agent to start with. Even if you write your own patent application, you should have a patent attorney review your application.

Design patents and plant patents are much simpler in design such that almost anyone can complete them. The cost of a design patent usually ranges between $370 and $770 ($155 application fee + $215 issue fee + drawings). The cost of a plant patent will run you $570 to $970 ($255 application fee + $315 issue fee + drawings).

Your *patent term* lasts until 20 years after the filing date of your application. The time in between the application filing date and the issue date is considered the "Patent Pending" phase. During this phase you do not yet have any rights to your invention since it hasn't been approved yet. You may still earn royalties while your patent is pending, but you can only enforce your patent, by suing others for infringement, after it issues.

If you do plan to file your own patent, go to your local library or bookstore and find *Patent It Yourself* by David Pressman; it's a wallet-saver. If you need representation, you may want to consider using a patent attorney from my firm, Inventors' Publishing & Research (IP&R). The firm gets all of its patents at half price because it generates a consistent volume. Call 1-800-MARKET2 (627-5382) if you wish to take advantage of these discount services.

If you think your invention might sell outside the United States, you should either file an application in each country where you seek patent protection, or you can file under the Patent Cooperation Treaty. See your patent attorney about this. And remember that not only European but also newly industrialized nations can have tremendous market potential. You must file your international patent application within a year of your U.S. patent *filing* date or provisional patent *filing* date.

Writing the Patent Yourself

Don't attempt to write a patent if you consider yourself a lousy writer. The wording of your patent application is very important; not only does it affect whether your patent is granted, but it also affects the strength of your patent if it is so granted. If you write a lousy patent that still gets accepted, you may find that the resultant patent may be easily worked around by attentive competitors.

If you do consider yourself a decent writer, pick up a copy of *Patent It Yourself* by David Pressmen and learn the many details about the process. I believe inventors know their own inventions best, and can do the most convincing job in drafting such an application. Again, however, you should at least have your claims reviewed by a patent attorney to ensure the broadest protection for your invention.

Utility Patent Applications

This section describes the main parts of a utility patent application.

Field of invention. In this section, you must briefly state the field of your invention.

Discussion of prior art. In this section, you essentially utilize the searching and research you have done to try to "bash" the disadvantages of prior art inventions as much as possible. Try to maintain a respectful fashion. Make sure you're only bashing the disadvantageous attributes that your product improves or corrects. Lay down your arguments one by one in as descriptive and eloquent terms as you can.

Objects and advantages of the invention. In this section you lay down the objects, or main advantages, of your invention. They should go hand in hand with solving the problems you stated in the discussion of prior art.

Drawing figure descriptions. You must include some brief tables that cross-reference your reference codes on your drawings with a name or short description.

Detailed description of invention and its embodiments. This section must be very meticulous and lay out every single part or aspect of the preferred embodiment of your invention. It must also describe how all such parts interact or lay together. Be sure to include some brief descriptions or possibilities for any other possible embodiments you can conjure up. The idea here is to hit on every possible detail that may be included in your preferred and envisioned embodiments. Writing this section is usually easier for those who are technically oriented (e.g., engineers).

Legal Claims. This may be the most important and yet the most difficult section to write out of all the sections because there is a requirement to use legal patent jargon in claiming your invention. As opposed to the last section, which should be as long and detailed as possible, the shorter and more broad the legal claims, the more *scope* you attain for your invention. In other words, the less you mention, the more coverage you get. The more that you go on about the features and attributes of your invention, the further you narrow the scope. You should only mention the minimum physical or procedural characteristics (in the case of a process patent) that you can get away with in describing the invention. If all your minimum characteristics are the same as some other prior art's minimum characteristics, then you naturally will have to add more to your claims to differentiate your invention over the prior art.

Abstract. This is a short, all-encompassing description of your invention (250 words or less).

Drawings. Drawings of your invention must follow very specific PTO guidelines and must be professionally done. If you only have two or three views to show, you may be able to get a freelance artist to do your drawings for $100 or so. Be sure to give the artist the PTO guidelines and a few examples of drawings from other patents. A professional patent artist will cost $300 and up, but you'll be guaranteed a high standard of quality.

Design Applications

The design application only requires a descriptive title, an optional description, one and only one claim, a description of figures/drawings, and drawings showing the object from all possible angles.

Plant Applications

The plant application requires a title, a specification (description of plant characteristics, related plants, proof of asexual production), one and only one claim, and two color depictions (if color distinguishes your plant).

Sending the Application

When you've completed the application, you will have to mail two copies of the application with a few additional required forms to the PTO with an application fee (keep a third copy for yourself). Within a week or two, you should get a receipt from the PTO of your application with an attached application number (you are now *patent pending*). The rest of the patent pending phase can be complicated because you may get rejections on various items that must be overcome by you (or your patent attorney). If no rejections are encountered, or they are all overcome, your application will be *allowed*. At this point the PTO is ready to *grant* (also called *issue*) the patent for your invention. All they usually require at this point is an issue fee payment and sometimes a few small changes or additional cursory modifications. Once you take care of the issuance requirements, shortly after (within three months), you will get a *granted* patent with an associated *issue date* and *patent number*.

The Provisional Patent Application

The last type of "pseudo" patent application that can be optionally filed is called a *provisional patent application* (PPA). The purpose of the PPA is to give inventors who may not have the time to build/test their invention or file a regular patent application a quick and easy way to temporarily protect their invention.

This is sort of a "mini," temporary patent application that can only be useful if you file a regular patent application within a year from your provisional patent filing date. PPAs are not examined and do not issue into patents; so it's crucial that you file a regular patent application within one year of the PPA filing. Your actual patent term will still start from your regular application filing date and terminate 20 years later. When you file your PPA, make certain that it's thorough because you will not be allowed to add new matter later to the regular application.

Your possible royalty period doesn't change either. This period runs from the patent issuance date until 20 years after the filing date of the regular application. If used correctly, the PPA can be used to increase your royalties! The extra year doesn't directly effect you in regard to increasing your patent or royalty terms, but it does protect you in cases of infringement much like the Document Disclosure program discussed earlier.

For example, let's say you come up with a fantastic idea, file a PPA, and then follow through a year later with a regular application. Later you find out that someone else filed a patent application for the same invention (but no PPA) three months before your regular patent application. Given this exact scenario, you will be the first inventor, and assuming your patent will be granted, you will gain a priority date of the earlier PPA. So gaining the priority date of the PPA serves a similar purpose as an Invention Disclosure in the Document Disclosure program, except that it is stronger proof because your regular application will actual carry on the PPA's filing date. Any infringers will see this earlier date as the real, official date of conception of your invention. In contrast, an invention won't really be looked at until you are in an infringement case and need to prove that you came up with the idea before an infringer's patent application filing date. In addition, a PPA requires an exact description of your invention (more binding), whereas an invention disclosure can contain a more incomplete, casual description of your invention.

Writing a PPA

A PPA is stronger proof that you came up with the idea first. The Invention Disclosure Program is a quick and dirty way of saving your spot, but a PPA is stronger proof of invention. In turn, a regular patent application is the strongest final proof. The stronger the proof, the better chances there are you will win a dispute later if two people came up with the same invention and are trying to prove who came up with it first.

You should always follow up with a PPA or a regular patent after using the Document Disclosure Program. If you have the time and money to get a PPA or Provisional, skip the Document Disclosure Program. Taking good notes, witnessed by third parties (signed), who aren't your friends or family, is just as strong proof of conception as filing with the Document Disclosure Program. When you file with the USPTO the Document Disclosure Program, they don't even look at it. They just file your information and date it to prove that you conceived the idea at that time. But they will throw it out after two years exactly if you don't follow up with filing a PPA or regular patent application. Also, if you file a PPA or regular application after you file the Document Disclosure Program, you don't get to retain the original date of the Document Disclosure Program. The original date will only come up if some day you find yourself in court disputing with another invention and you have to prove that you came up with your invention even though your PPA or regular patent filing date came after a second inventors filing date for their PPA or regular patent. Then they will go back and look at the Document Disclosure Program date of any other signed and witnessed "paper trail" to ultimately see which inventor actually invented the item first. PPA or regular filing is better because the date you file these will actually be printed on the final patent.

Basically, in the U.S., the law says whoever is "first to invent" owns the invention. It's not who files a PPA or regular patent first. The Document Disclosure Program was designed to help inventors prove they actually came up with the invention first even though someone else may have filed before them.

The time to write a PPA falls halfway between writing a cursory invention disclosure and writing the time-consuming regular patent application. The PPA must be very thorough in the sense that it requires a complete and meticulous description and drawings of the preferred embodiment of your invention (much like a regular patent application). You will not be able to add new features beyond the scope of your PPA when filing your regular application, so you better be thorough in your description. What you don't have to include in the PPA that a patent application does require are the claims, "description of prior art" section, "objects and advantages" section, and the abstract. In essence, it's about half of the work of a real application and costs less than $100 to file. *Just keep in mind that you must later file the regular application within a year or your PPA will be trashed!*

PPA Forms

All forms you may need for completing your patent application can be acquired through the PTO: (703) 308-HELP. You can also fax your orders to (703) 305-7786.

Reaping the Rewards of Protecting Your Idea

It's important to realize that the PTO keeps your application confidential until it issues your patent. Then—and only then—does it grant your patent and disclose it publicly. During this highly confidential "patent pending" phase, other companies may—without knowing it—develop, manufacture, or sell a product like your own invention. If you already are producing your product during this time, you may want to mark your product "Patent Pending" to discourage such companies.

One important point about this: *Another company is not liable for infringement if it makes and sells your product during this pending phase.* You only get your monopoly rights starting from when your patent is granted (after the issue date). After your patent is granted, you then have the right to halt any infringing company's dealings with your patented product. Because of this, companies that discover or notice that your product is "Patent Pending" before the grant will usually not take the risk of setting up expensive tooling and marketing of your product only to have it halted in the near future. If you believe that the competing company is making a product within the scope of your patent, and they already know that your product is "Patent Pending," you may want to try to convince them into signing an early royalty license agreement with you. That way, they are assured that you will not stop their production when the patent issues, and you'll be reaping "pre-patent grant" royalties in addition to the years you will receive royalties after it officially issues.

After your patent has been granted, if you haven't worked with the company that seems to be infringing on your patent, you should file a civil claim against that company. Your attorney will then have to prove that your patent prevails, by showing that your conception date is the earliest. Here, things can get tricky, because a disclosure document only helps your case if you filed it before the other party filed its patent application. If the other party filed its patent application first, your best hopes are if you transferred your invention disclosure to your patent application, were diligent in your reduction to practice, kept witnessed notebooks/conception records ready and on hand, or claimed priority on an earlier provisional patent application (if you have filed one).

If your attorney proves your case and the court holds the other company liable, you could be in for a windfall if they've been selling your product during the infringement period! The infringement period doesn't automatically start from the date of patent issuance/grant. This is only true if your product or product's packaging had a label such as Patent #4,506,503 (or whatever number applies). If you have no such label on your product, or you haven't been producing your product yet, the infringement period only starts after you've sent the infringing company a cease and desist letter by certified mail. Hand off a written notification to the infringer proving and explaining your beliefs. You may also want to contact the infringer's legal representatives via telephone. If you win the infringement case, the other company may be ordered to pay you royalties back to the time you first contacted it (after patent issuance date) or back to the actual patent issuance date if you were already producing your product and included on it: "Patent <number>". In addition, through your lawyer, you can require the infringing company to stop production and negotiate with you on your terms.

One inventor, a couple years back, found that GM was using his patented "intermittent windshield wipers" for their cars. He ended up suing for damages of close to $20 million in back-royalties (5 percent of net sales each year for several years)!

Incidentally, there is a time limitation on damages if you contact the infringing company too late. The law says "no recovery shall be had for any infringement committed more than six years prior to the filing of the complaint or counterclaim for infringement in the action" (35USC286). Also, if you're having problems contacting the infringing company because it is a foreign company importing your product or pieces of it into the United States, you can have the importation stopped by getting a proceeding before the International Trade Commission.

If you have been granted a patent, and find out about another patented product that is strikingly similar to yours, you may want to determine which patent *dominates* over the other. In this odd case, if your patent legally dominates over the other patent because it is broader in scope, the competitive product will be required to pay you royalties on its sales. Furthermore, even if your patent dominates another, if you want to make the invention described in the *subservient* patent, you must also pay royalties to that patent since they have the right to *exclude* others from producing their invention. This kind of dominant-subservient clash is a little unusual since typically when invention patent applications are that similar, the later filed is rejected. Such scenarios usually lead to *cross-licensing* agreements that allow both parties to manufacture each other's inventions.

Choosing the Most Profitable Path

How do you plan on marketing your invention? As an inventor, you can't afford to take this decision lightly. If you make the wrong marketing choice, you will *never* profit greatly from your invention, no matter how great an idea you think it is. Depending on where your time constraints, savings, ambitions, strengths, and weaknesses lie, there are a number of possible routes to choose from. Not all of them are equally profitable, of course, and only one may be suited to your particular needs. An important question to ask yourself is whether the amount of money you plan on making from your invention is realistic or just based on wishful thinking. Step 2 will show you which marketing course you and your invention best fit into.

Route 1: Use a Brokerage Firm

These companies have so-called "expert marketing" brokers who claim they will find you both manufacturing and distribution outfits and negotiate agreements on your behalf. Of course, this means that they do all the work for you, but the catch is you'll have to pay a stiff price for such work. We're talking in the neighborhood of tens of thousands of dollars that you'll be required to pay.

You may want to consider using a broker if:
- You don't have the time to efficiently promote your invention.
- You don't have the business skills to deal with large corporations.
- You don't have connections to the business world or at least the confidence to try to open new doors.
- You don't have experience in negotiating or licensing.
- You don't have much experience with promoting products or inventions.

Most brokers charge up-front fees—which means you can be paying an awful lot of money but see no results to show for it. Be careful! In many cases, brokerages that require up-front fees are the ones you want to stay away from. Some brokers work on a *straight* contingency fee, but these are very selective of the inventions they take. A contingency fee is basically a percentage of your future royalties *if they* sell or license your invention. Other firms, such as my firm, Inventors' Publishing and Research, LLC (IP&R), work on a contingency if your invention satisfies certain criteria. Otherwise, they also require a minimum work fee to cover their marketing overhead and support staff.

Brokerage firms quickly develop reputations based on their performances; it's rare you find one that's honest, reputable, and provides a legitimate service for a fair price. In fact, there have been many reports showing that the total amount of money many of these firms charge inventors is more than the total amount of money that they make for inventors! You should steer clear of invention brokerage firms that claim to have a high success rate or "guarantee" your invention's sale (this is impractical). Statistics show that only one out of one hundred inventions (1 percent) ever make it to the marketplace. The brokerage firm you choose should have a success rate of at least 10 times that.

You should also avoid those large invention firms that usually advertise on T.V. One of those firms, Invention Submission Corp. of Pittsburgh, admits that out of 5,291 inventors they signed from 1995 to 1997, only eight inventors actually received more money than they paid for the services. This is only one-tenth of 1 percent profitable success! You'd be better off doing the job yourself. Invention Submission Corp. paid $1.2 million to the Federal Trade Commission to settle charges that it misrepresented "the nature, quality, and success rate" of its services.

If you read, learn, and use the information in this book, you will have acquired all the tools and special knowledge you need to turn your patent into a money-making success. Save yourself from handing over a percentage of your royalties by learning the process and following through with it yourself. This is not a full-time job; it can be done on a part-time basis, step by step right out of your home.

If you are going to go with a broker, and if they charge up-front fees, make sure they have the references and successful track record to back it up. Be wary of firms that charge less than $900 and claim that they will try to find a possible manufacturer for your invention by creating and submitting a description of your invention. Typically these firms will write up a brief, unappealing description of your invention, and then send out a "blind" mailing to a list of manufacturers. Once again, these firms achieve very low success rates. It takes much more time and effort (as described in this book) to license your invention than this kind of impersonal mailing will do for you.

Other firms claim they will evaluate your invention for "market potential," and still others claim they will present your invention at "invention tradeshows." Save your money by avoiding these scams and rip-offs. In actuality, if you were going to have a fee-based broker really help you, it would cost you thousands of dollars due to the amount of quality time and effort that needs to be spent in trying to sell or license a patent. Obviously, if you put in the time and effort yourself, you can greatly minimize your costs.

You should also avoid any broker with a licensing success rate of 5 percent or less. These are frauds. You can ask your broker directly what their success rate is; they are obliged to tell you. Also, be leary of any broker that does not want to take a lifetime interest in your invention. This shows that they are not really interested in making money from your invention, but would rather make money from you! Moreover, most products don't really peak in royalties until well into their patent term (after five to 10 years).

To recap, these are the brokers you should avoid:
- Very large firms that tend to advertise heavily on television
- Brokers with a licensing success rate of 5 percent or less
- Brokers that do mass mailings to manufacturers for a fee of a few hundred dollars
- Brokers that only ask to take a share of your invention for five years or less

If you do decide to go through a broker, be careful not to lose your invention rights through theft or inadvertently signing them away, either of which can happen more easily than you might think. Since your patent is confidential while it's pending, an unscrupulous broker can simply pass your invention off as his or her own. The broker can sell or license it directly to a company without even letting you know. Or the broker can write out a contract with such wording that takes the invention away from you and transfers it to the broker. So, again, make sure you check your broker's track record as well as the fine print of any agreement. You can lose a great deal of money and time trying to win back your rights in court.

A good broker should:
- Find potential manufacturers and distributors
- Help build and test your idea if you haven't done so already
- Give demonstrations of your product to interested companies
- Continually work "live contacts" from interested companies
- Negotiate an agreement with a manufacturer for you
- Make sure that the agreement (license or sale) is in your best interest
- Set a deadline for the successful handling of your product

Considering that only one out of one hundred inventions (1 percent) ever make it to the marketplace, a broker with a success rate of 10 percent or greater is actually quite good. This is 10 times better than what the average inventor can do for him or herself.

If you do choose a broker and after a year you see little result, start looking for a new broker. Just make sure that all rights, research, development products, models, presentation materials, and lists of contacts revert to you.

Route 2: The Broker Finds You a Manufacturer and Distributor but You Negotiate Your Own Agreements

In this case, you use a broker only to find manufacturers and distributors. When it comes to negotiating agreements you take over, retaining for yourself the power to shape your own contracts. You might want to take this route if:
- You consider yourself a good negotiator.
- Only you can truly appreciate and explain your product's potential.

- You think you can present your product so convincingly that no one else will dare challenge your product.
- You're not willing to trust your important financial decisions to someone else.
- The nature of your product could involve especially careful consideration, beyond what's typical for inventions.
- You must use extreme caution and work your contract in a way that fully protects you in case of invention mishaps.
- You're concerned that the broker, out of self-interest, would not comply with all your negotiation requests.

That's an awful lots of "ifs," but if they apply to your situation, by all means negotiate the contract yourself! You're likely to encounter one problem though: Many contingency-fee brokers initially won't accept this type of agreement. It would mean that they would get a smaller percentage of your royalty. If they refuse, simply point out that you'll take your business to their competitors.

In general, though, negotiating requires a lot of experience. I would recommend considering a professional before trying it yourself.

Route 3: Find a Manufacturer and Distributor, and You Negotiate Your Own Agreements

This approach requires hard work, but the benefit of all that work is almost entirely yours. It does take perseverance to do the job yourself, and diligence and boldness to approach large companies and interest them in your invention, but the personal satisfaction, experience, and profitability of this route by far makes it the most appealing. Furthermore, finding a company yourself may not be as hard as you think.

Depending on your invention and on how much free time you have to work on it, this process typically lasts anywhere from three months to four years. If you have a full-time job, you should count on anywhere from five to 20 hours a week. In a sense, you can think of it as moonlighting, except that the potential payoffs stemming from your effort could allow you to quit your regular job one day! In the meantime, during the patent-selling process, you will find that your regular income will become helpful in financing your invention's developmental costs.

I recommend this approach over any other route. Probably your main goal is to secure a large profit, which makes it in your best interest to negotiate your own agreement and let another company take over your manufacturing and distributing—especially if you have other money-making projects on your agenda. Since you won't have to pay a broker's fees, you and the company only will split the profits from your product. If you're tempted to do it *all* by yourself, consider how much time, planning, preparation, heartache, and capital it would take not only to manufacture but also to distribute your own product. Unless you have the time, dedication, and startup capital to invest, you should let another company do the work and assume the expense. Furthermore, if, for whatever reason, your invention flops, the thousands of dollars in production costs will be the company's loss, not yours.

Routes That Require You to Start a Business

Of course, routes that require you to start a business are more time-consuming and risky than the prior mentioned routes, but the advantage of course is a greater return from your invention, if successful. Most of these steps will require a full-time dedication from you and a little bit of start-up capital, so holding a separate full-time job in these cases would be impractical. If you're not interested in such a commitment, Route 3 in the last section is our recommended course of action.

Route 4: Have the Product Made for You and Find a Company to Distribute It

While this fourth approach can work well, it's often costly. The time and money you save by not making the product yourself must be weighed against the amount you'll pay someone else to make it for you. Your new business might find it hard to meet manufacturing costs, especially in periods of low cash flow.

There are two basic problems you could run into here. The first is the high initial tooling/molding/setup costs of producing your product that you'll have to give the manufacturer. The second is your specific agreement with the distributor. Should you sell your product outright to a distributor for immediate profit? Or do you want your profits to represent a *percentage of total sales*—or gross sales—of the distributor from your product?

If you use a small local manufacturer, production costs will be high. However, you may have no choice. Since your own business is probably small and your budget probably limited your production orders will probably be for small lots, maybe two hundred to five hundred units at a time. It's hard to get a price break when you're dealing with a small manufacturing company and, because your budget is likely to be limited, you may not be able to take advantage of a large manufacturer's production discounts, which require orders in the tens of thousands.

If you cannot afford the initial tooling or molding involved in making your product, you may have to have your product manually made at first (see "Step 4: Prototyping"). Manually constructing your product will preclude the need for initial tooling, but it will severely raise the cost of your product—probably up to five times.

Distributors Who Buy Outright

When you are dealing with distributors who buy your products outright, your selling price to the distributor is your total cost plus a little bit extra to make a profit. Typically, the distributor will then double your price and sell the product in their distribution network for the final *retail* price. This is because of the relatively high overhead costs involved in maintaining a large distribution network.

You will run into problems trying to get larger distribution companies to take your product if you are an individual or small company because they typically will only deal with larger companies with proven product lines and relatively good track records. In addition, in some cases you will have to spend a few thousand dollars just to apply for access to some distribution companies. On top of all that, your application may not even be accepted. Large distributors don't want to take the risk of buying an unproven product from an unproven small company. It seems like a Catch-22, but with enough persistence, eventually you get your first product in, and then the second and third and so on get easier and easier.

Distributors Who Buy on Special Agreements

While your product is still in the "unproven" state, you may initially be forced to go with distributors who will make a special agreement with you. If you sell your product outright to a distribution company, you may be able to live with high manufacturing costs. The problem is that a distributor may be reluctant to buy your product outright. It may want you to meet it halfway by working on a contingency or consignment-fee basis. That's fine if your product sells, because both of you profit. If your product does not sell, however, both you and the distributor lose—and you lose even more because you're stuck with inventory and unpaid costs! In that event, things can get sticky. So consider whether you're more likely to benefit from a *percentage* of the *total projected sales* or an *expected margin rate of profit* (the relationship of gross profit to net sales).

To figure your margin rate of profit, first determine your net sales by subtracting *returns* and *allowances* of gross sales. Then subtract the *cost of goods sold* from your net to arrive at your *gross profit*. Subtract your *gross profit* from your *net sales* to get your *profit margin*.

Clearly, a *percentage of total sales* arrangement can offer more benefit than a *profit margin* if the percentage is right. Avoiding a percent-of-profit-margin agreement becomes even more attractive when you take into consideration additional high production costs. You can use these high production costs as a bargaining point when negotiating an agreement with a distributor, who often will push for a profit margin arrangement.

Route 5: Use an Agent to Sell/Distribute Your Invention

Finding a good agent to sell your invention can be tough. You'll have to use your own common sense in judging whether or not the agent is trustworthy, reputable, and reliable. There are a few points to understand about sales agents. First, in the beginning, you should generally offer an agent a high percentage of the sales (40 to 60 percent depending on your cost). Remember, most agents work on commission only, and they have to pull out of their pockets in the beginning before they make any sales. If you think 50 percent is a high percentage to give away, total up how much of your product you're selling currently, and compare that to what you'd be making with someone representing you and selling a few hundred units each month.

You should make an arrangement such that as the agent's sales go up, his or her percentage goes down. Don't ever drop the percentage sharply though; this will take away the incentive for the sales agent. Outline a schedule in which the drops in percentage are gradual and continuous over quantity of product sold. By this time, if the sales of your small business went up to 100,000 units/year, even having a commission of 1 percent may be making the agent more than $100,000/year. With volumes this high, you'll probably not have much of a problem finding several agents who will be enthusiastic about selling your product.

Another important aspect to monitor when using an agent is performance. If you see no results (sales) after three or four months, it is probably time to find a new agent.

To find a sales agent, you can advertise in one of the following magazines, which are read by sales reps who are always looking for new products to handle. Ask for a free copy of these to get a feel for them:

Rep World. P.O. Box 2087, Sinking Spring, PA 19608. Editor: Thomas C. Reinhart. (215) 768-3361.

Agency Sales. Manufacturer's Agents National Association (MANA), P.O. Box 3467, 23016 Mill Creek Rd., Laguna Hills, CA 92654. Editor: Bert Holtje.

Salesman's Opportunity Magazine.1460 John Hancock Center, Chicago, IL 60611.

Route 6: Have the Product Made for You, and You Distribute It

Getting involved in the distribution of your product puts you in a whole new line of work. Distributing any product means starting a small business that entails much more than "dumping" your product off onto a buyer. As a distributor, you'll be responsible for organizing your business to facilitate all means of distribution—and the ease with which you can move the product will determine whether your company fails, breaks even, or makes a profit.

For this route you'll need to make a detailed business plan, bearing in mind that the distribution business is part hard work, part heartache, and part research. Distributors also must adjust to continually changing markets—ones that are growing, dying, and transforming. You'll have to anticipate these changes to make logical, profitable decisions.

Try to imagine yourself five years into the distribution business. How will you transport large supplies of your product reliably? A distribution company should be organized around several steps:

- To receive the product from the manufacturer
- To take inventory of the product received
- To package the product
- To arrange and divide the product for deliveries
- To ship the product off to commercial sellers

Another important part of any distribution business is building good relationships with retailers. You'll need to handle returns, defects, and allowances as well as deal with payment delays, bankruptcies, and capricious order changes.

Think of a distribution company as a three-way relationship among the manufacturer, the distributor (yourself), and commercial retailers. Any drastic change by either of the other two could cause your business to go into the red or even collapse. In addition, the legal requirements on distributors can lead to prohibitive costs.

The big question about undertaking distribution yourself, then, is whether your sales will exceed your manufacturing costs and your distribution costs put together. You'll have to sell in high volume and keep distribution costs to a minimum to come out ahead.

Route 7: Manufacture Your Own Product but Another Company Distributes It

This route takes the opposite approach to the previous one. Here you'll be in the manufacturing business, producing your own product, and letting someone else do the distributing. While this marketing method calls for good organization and intense effort, it has certain advantages. First, as a manufacturer, you won't have to deal directly with retailers, which can save you a great deal of aggravation. Your manufacturing company will also have the potential to expand into new products, accessories, novelties, or breakthrough technologies. Plus it will cost you less to manufacture your product than to pay someone else to do it (excluding initial fixed capital investments, of course).

A manufacturing company is no bowl of cherries, however. Tremendous work is required: This is no place for half-hearted efforts! If you don't organize, develop, and build your manufacturing company skillfully, you could end up facing financial disaster.

The basic organization of a manufacturing company includes:

- Design
- Production
- Equipment maintenance
- Quality assurance
- Packaging
- Legal work

Depending on your product and how you plan to grow your company, your initial costs could be huge. Still, if you have to choose between manufacturing or distributing your own product, I recommend manufacturing. Your profit objectives can be clearer, easier, and more realistic—and your business could be a liquid asset worth millions if you decide later to sell it.

Route 8: Manufacture and Distribute Your Product

If you're planning to go this route, you should know that you've chosen the most difficult path. For all the reasons already described, both activities require experience, planning, capital, perseverance, skilled management, teamwork, and most important, a full-time commitment from you.

If you do plan to start a manufacturing and distributing company, I strongly recommend that you find out as much as you can in advance about how to operate this kind of business. One good source of information is your local Small Business Administration office. Don't just request printed materials; also seek the advice of its experts. Study the reasons why other manufacturing and distributing companies have failed. Remember: Even if you don't make a single mistake running your business, outside forces could still cause you to go under.

The Patent Marketing Plan

Developing a Successful Patent Marketing Plan

Without a marketing plan, your hopes for ever turning a profit from your invention are just that—only hopes. A patent marketing plan is quite similar to a business plan, except that it will not have to include nonapplicable parts such as sections on employee guidelines or company assets. A business plan is typically made to convince investors to invest in a promising new business. Likewise, a patent marketing plan needs to be made to entice potential companies to invest in your product by ultimately purchasing the rights to your patent. Not only will your patent marketing plan guide you, it will also convince companies in the area of your invention that they can make money from your invention. Whatever your invention might be, a solid patent market plan is essential for it to make money.

Consider the example of an inventor who came to me in 1995. Borris Khudenko, owner of 12 U.S. patents, was frustrated when a potential manufacturer would not take enough interest in his work. After I helped Borris complete a patent marketing plan, as outlined in this book, he presented it to the potential manufacturer in a personal meeting. Soon thereafter, declaring undying gratefulness, Borris called me to say that the presentation of the marketing plan was a hit and it turned everything completely around! They agreed on a deal of almost $1 million for his patents due to this presentation.

There are a number of benefits that you should derive from completing a patent marketing plan. First, you should take advantage of all the market research done in recent years; this information is an invaluable resource when you are bringing a new product into the industry. Such research can show you whether your invention falls into a nonexistent, low-, or high-profit market. If the market for your product proves disappointing, don't panic; all hope may not yet be lost. You may be able to find a way to turn a poor market into a thriving one. How can you improve your product's market? Look at the market's negative aspects and try to make them positive by changing, adding, or introducing a new element.

The second reason to create a marketing plan is that it will take you through the entrepreneurial process of learning, identifying, and assembling many of the determinants for success. Primarily, you will learn which companies manufacture and produce competitive or similar products. Analyzing the market potential of these companies will become important later on, when you decide which companies to approach to sell or license your invention, and in predicting how much money you expect to make from your invention.

How else can a patent marketing plan help you? It draws a clear picture for others involved with your invention, establishing agreement, cooperation, and unity of format. It also creates working evidence of your invention, which you can reproduce and show to several companies of your choice. Thus, your plan will let you explain your invention more thoroughly than if you only gave a brief description in person or over the phone. It also provides a working starting point, from which progress can be made while still allowing you to go back and re-examine, change, correct, or add to particular sections as necessary. Factual and complete, it becomes a negotiating tool that carries more weight and is harder to challenge than spoken plans or promises. As evidence of your product's potential, it should be taken seriously by all parties and used to encourage their commitment. It is a working set of blueprints indispensable to its builder. It works as a checklist, reminding you to carry through on all parts of your plan. Because of all these advantages, a market plan greatly enhances your chances of success.

If you're too busy to do the research and create the plan, this is one of the few times in the book in which I can recommend a firm, Inventors' Research Division, which is associated with Inventors' Publishing.

The trick to developing an effective patent marketing plan is this: *Keep it simple.* A market plan can be a huge project. It's not uncommon to see 1,000 pages or more. So don't get carried away with unnecessary, trivial, or academic information that only makes your plan look impressive without adding any truly useful data. You don't want to end up with a document that is confusing, redundant, or out of focus. What you *do* want is a market plan thorough enough to answer the major, most commonly asked questions about your invention. For example, take a look at my original patent marketing plan as shown at the end of this chapter. It's also a good idea, in general, to follow a format similar to the one outlined here. Bear in mind, of course, that every invention is by definition different, so only you—the inventor—can ultimately decide which determinants you want to use in your market plan.

Executive Summary

By way of introduction, the executive summary presents a brief description of your entire marketing plan. Your summary should contain three broad elements:

1. The *product description*, which includes the description of your invention and/or your company, and of its purposes and goals

2. The *competition and target market analysis*, which demonstrates why your invention should turn a large profit by evaluating the data and determinants in your industry

3. The *market plan/action statement*, which explains how your company will be able to carry out its objectives, outlining your execution strategy within your industry.

Background to Your Market

This section makes up the heart of your marketing plan. It develops, explains, and analyzes more specifically the *product description* and the *competition and target market analysis*. For instance, you might break your *product description* model down to describe the size, weight, classification, sketch, mode design, materials, shape, color, texture, chemicals, odor, taste, and other properties of your invention.

Under *product purposes*, you might discuss such aspects as main advantages:
- Composition/size/design of your product
- Control-maneuverability
- Reliability factors

- Safety features
- Warranty and money-back guarantee
- Special/unique product features
- Accessories/perks
- Testing requirements satisfied
- Instructions/manual
- Compatibility with other equipment
- Dependability/life span
- Enhanced product materials
- Consumer demand/marketability
- Practicality of product
- Positive/impressive demonstrations/examples of product
- Product achievement awards

Under *competition* and *target market analysis*, you should provide evidence of your product's ability to turn a profit, using a variety of data such as:

- Competition/range of competition (domestic/international)
- Classification of product (breakthrough technology, similar, competitive, accessory/perks)
- Method of sales (catalogs, stores, sales representatives, magazines, trade shows, direct mail, electronic mail, auctions, personnel sales)
- Market share among competition (companies involved, revenue of companies/pie-graph, total annual sales, strategic opportunities, advantages your product has over competition, competitive position, barriers to entry, market description, market size, market trends, market prediction, market growth rate, market GNP, evidence/surveys, target customers, company performance)
- Breakthrough technology, executives, management structure, quick product/diversification, revolutionary, creativity, funding, history, and customer/company feedback

Figure 3-1 shows some additional sales pitches you can use (if they apply to you) when selling your product over the competition. An explanation of each level of the pyramid follows:

Figure 3-1. Marketability factors pyramid

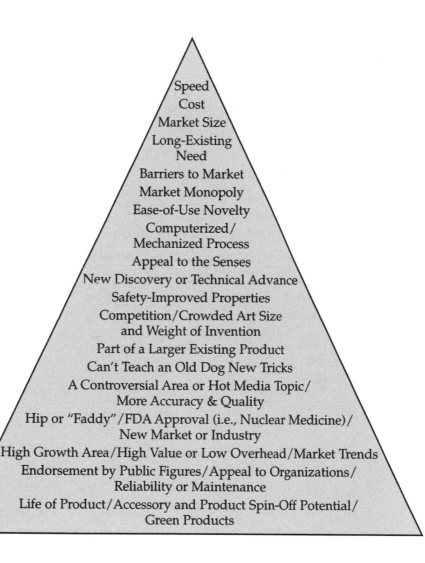

Speed. If your invention is more efficient or does the job more efficiently, this will probably be your key selling point.

Cost. If the cost of your invention outweighs its perceived customer value, then obviously it will be impossible to make money from it.

Market size. Obviously the bigger the market for your invention, the higher the volume and hence royalties that will come to you. Computers, automobiles, and medicine are good areas to make a fortune quickly.

Long-existing need. If you've satisfied a long-existing or unrecognized need through your invention, you will definitely find a large customer base.

Barriers to market. Barriers to market can make your product temporarily or permanently "unmarketable." Some barriers to entry may be federal laws, FDA approval for drugs and medical devices, Nuclear Commission approval, or a public disapproval of certain kinds of products.

Market monopoly. The market in which you want to enter may be completely dominated or monopolized by one or only a few competitors. For example, an inventor/entrepreneur named Tucker tried to create a new automobile in the 1950s, but no matter how good his car was, he could not counter the pressure and threats coming from the Big Three (Ford, GM, Chevrolet). On the other hand, if you can sell your invention to such a monopolizing company, you'll probably be rolling in the dough.

Ease of use. If you've redesigned something such that it is easier to use, this will give you an advantage over your competition and make your product easier to market.

Novelty. Ideas that are innovative and completely new often excite and inspire curiosity from people. For example, if you invent a new dieting method that's very different from all the other dieting methods and scams out there, many dieters who have given up on the other processes may try yours because it's innovative.

"Computerized/mechanized" a human process. If you have, through your technology, replaced some activity that could only be performed by human labor, this will save people time and money. Garage door openers, computer database manipulation, and the electric can-opener are all examples of this. Lazy people especially will appreciate this kind of breakthrough.

Appeal to the senses (taste, touch, smell, hearing, sight, ESP). Making your invention appeal to as many human senses as possible will pull much weight on the market. Examples include an exercise machine that has a comfortable support seat, stickers that have a scent (scratch-n-sniff), or automobiles that have an automated voice system that kindly reminds you to attach your seat-belt. Any product that you can visually or cosmetically make more appealing would be a perfect candidate for a good design patent.

New discovery or technical advance. Scientific discoveries or significant technical advances can be the biggest royalty winners. For example, going from the vacuum tube to the transistor instantly translated into hundreds of millions for the inventor. Recently, another inventor came up with a special alloy that has amazing thermal dissipation characteristics. With the thin sheet-metal form, you can put a blowtorch to one side of it, yet comfortably place your hand upon the other side without feeling any heat. Aerojet offered the inventor $17 million outright for his patent; purportedly, the inventor didn't accept it because it wasn't a good enough offer.

Safety. If your invention deals in an area where human life is an issue (e.g., firearms, explosives, fire department aids, etc.), you may have a hard time finding a manufacturer. Product liability insurance rates for that particular invention may be very expensive.

Improved properties. If you can improve the important characteristics of your invention, such as strength, hardness, corrosion resistance, shock resistance, and formability, all these translate into a value customers look for when shopping around for the best product.

Competition/crowded art. The more competitive or crowded your field is, the less market share your product can expect to acquire. Moreover, your invention can be worked around and legally copied more easily in crowded markets.

Size and weight of invention. The size and weight of your invention are typically important features. Lighter and smaller products are usually more convenient and easier to use, and therefore they tend to sell better.

Part of a larger existing product. If your invention is a small piece of a much larger invention that already has success in the market, then you're assured of success if you can convince manufacturers to use your part in the production of the larger product. On the other hand, this isn't a plus if the product you are relying on is approaching the end of its production life.

Can't teach an old dog new tricks. If you've invented something that, though more efficient, requires that a significant portion of the population has to relearn the process, this could work against you. For instance, let's say you've invented a new type of foot clutch that allows you to rest your foot on the ground and just push up with your toes instead of pushing all the way down with your foot. Your new invention may be easier and more efficient, but people will find it bothersome to have to relearn the use of the clutch. (This is why the design hasn't changed in so many years!!)

A controversial area or hot media topic. Hot media areas that fade in and out of the public eye can be good invention areas for those who are opportunistic. For instance, I know one inventor who invented a powdered nonprescription drug that helps prevent colon cancer. He did this during the media hype coverage of President Reagan's colon cancer operation.

More accuracy and quality. An invention that improves *the accuracy or quality* of anything usually translates into big market sellers. One area that is currently going through growing pains is the business of printing. Printers are constantly being developed and sold at different market entry points to improve the quality or resolution of originals.

Hip or "Faddy." Ideas that are "fashion hip" or suggestively faddy will work in your favor toward increased sales. No one likes to be out of date or behind the times, especially younger generations. Swatch watch designs in the early 1980s made fortunes, and even an accessory called the "Swatch Guard" (a little protective band that covered the watch) turned out some respectable royalties for its inventor.

FDA - Legal - Nuclear approval. Some inventions may not be marketable due to restrictions in the law and federal regulations. If you've invented a medical device or drug, the FDA (Food and Drug Administration) must approve it. Likewise, inventions that could be viewed as nuclear weapons in the eyes of government officials would most likely have problems going through Nuclear Commissions approval.

New market or industry. If your idea is so original that there isn't even a market for it yet, you'll have to spend a few years developing and creating a viable market for it. You'll find it tough to convince potential manufacturers that your product will sell unless there is already a rich, healthy market for it. Or you can be the pioneer of something that may become huge.

High growth area. Naturally, if your invention falls in a high-growth area such as computers or educational services, your potential sales will also grow at that same rate.

High value/Low overhead. If your product has improved value or is cheaper to make than its competition, it will inherently sell easier. For instance, you may have designed a new computer mouse that is small enough that it only requires your index finger to control it. Not only will your computer mouse be easy to control, but it will require less material to build it.

Market trends. If your product lies right smack in the middle of an increasing "trend," this can only pull for the sales of your invention. On the other hand, be careful not to go into areas that are being phased out (such as inventions that deal with cigarette smokers).

Endorsement by public figures/appeal to organizations. If your invention lends itself to the popularity of major organizations or key public figures, this alone could double your potential sales. For instance, "The C.L.U.B." commercials are personally endorsed by an ex–chief police commissioner as a fail-safe way of protecting your car from theft. Any drug that you can have approved by the Surgeon General would also ring in sales because of a key public figure endorsement.

Reliability/maintenance. If you've improved a process or product in a way that it lasts longer, has a lower failure rate, or requires less upkeep than its competition, customers will naturally be attracted to the proclaimed reliability of your product.

Life of product. If the life of your product (product cycle) is less than your patent term, then you can expect dwindling sales of your product toward the end of your patent royalty term. For instance, portable computers have a life expectancy of only five years before they are phased out and replaced with entirely new models.

Accessory and product spin-off potential. Sales due to your patent may be strong for many years if your patent has many foreseeable spin-offs or accessory add-ons. These new combinations keep customers coming back for years to buy your "new improved" or modified products.

Green products. Making your invention environmentally sound is a popular trend that will lead consumers to your product.

Market Plan/Action Statement

This last section represents your plan of action—how you, together with an interested manufacturer, could execute your plan. Specifically, it describes what steps you can take to push, sell, and profit from introducing your product in its field. It's important that your marketing plan show potential companies who may buy your patented invention that they can go into or expand their business with your invention. You want to specifically outline unique steps that, potentially, any normal business would have to conjure up and follow if it was planning on bringing your patented product onto the market (this is quite analogous to the classic "business plan").

In this section, you should figure in close detail the amount of revenues and costs the sponsoring company of your product could expect to generate through sales and production. Be careful not to underestimate or overestimate your expected profit, and do not exaggerate yours plans for accomplishing your goals. Even if the first two sections of your market/business plan are thorough and convincing, your action statement may be met with skepticism. That's to be expected, since it deals entirely with financial projections. Be sure that your estimations are specific and accurate, leaving no room for controversy.

You want to make it easy for potential companies interested in your patent to imagine what it would be like adding your patented product to their product line. Your action plan should include a schedule of events, market strategy, early company strategy, execution of sales, product promotion, advertising tactics, psychology/incentives, and market segmentation. It should also contain a projected annual income statement broken down by month, which details your income, operating expenses, general/administration expenses, total operating expenses, and net income after taxes. Finally, it should provide an estimated five-year income statement, broken down annually, with information on royalties, long-term profit growth, and any necessary appendices. In the next section, I will discuss the research you'll need to do in order to complete your plan.

Doing the Research for Your Patent Marketing Plan

Before you can develop your marketing plan, of course, you must research your market *thoroughly*. But don't be intimidated by the tools listed in this section, you will be able to do such research within a week's time by spending just a few hours each night at your public library.

There are many approaches to doing research. The U.S. Department of Commerce and other branches of the federal and state government provide dozens of books, booklets, and reports that you might find useful. Trade associations also have many articles that could help with your research. Or you may be able to find a researcher who has already done the study you've envisioned. Committees or small groups of experts—such as church organizations, government associations, media, and independent market opinion services—may be able to answer many of your questions.

If you don't have time for research, research services will do the work for you. They perform a variety of tasks, from data and report preparation to personal, on-site business management. Audit services also collect and provide accurate, detailed information on company sales, which you can use to understand your particular market and where it's heading.

My advice—as usual—is: *don't just fall back on "experts"; try to do the work yourself!* The only exception might be computer database research. Unless you're completely familiar with on-line services and have free university access to databases in your search area, your research efforts could drag on for days before you even get the rhythm of how the network operates, let alone retrieve any information. In that case, you might want to hire a professional.

To obtain market information thoroughly, quickly, cheaply, and easily, your best research option is my comprehensive, efficient library guide provided here. It should help you find all the specific marketing information you could ever need.

Business Research Guide

Your first duty should be to find companies that deal with your product or invention, so you know how much money you can expect to make—(the total market share of your particular product). This also shows you who to contact if you later decide to sell or license your invention. Once you have established which companies deal with your product, you should then do extensive data research on the largest companies of your field. When you have found a company that deals with your idea, make sure it is in the same (or closest possible) category as your invention. It's also important to realize how many different markets your invention might cover. For instance, if your invention has to do with cycling, there are several different markets that might cover your invention: bikes for kids, mountain bikes, cross-training bikes, road bikes, and so forth. Different companies specialize in each area, so make sure you contact the right company for your particular invention.

After you've researched the companies of your interest, call them and simply ask for any information—particularly new information, which is difficult to research—they might have about the company itself. Calling a company can help you find that "missing link" in your research quest. Secretaries often are proud of high company sales and might get caught up in the moment and spill major important information, such as if and when the company is planning to merge with another corporation. On the other hand, if the person you talk to sounds reluctant to answer questions, mention that you're interested in buying several thousand dollars worth of stock and need more information to make your decision. Sometimes this will open the door.

Directions for Using This Research Guide

If you already know whether the company you're researching is public or private, skip to the section "Directory Information on Private and Public Companies," and begin your research there. After you have obtained the information, supplement your research quest by reading the sections "Periodical Information on Private and Public Companies" and "Finding Business and Industrial Ratios." If you don't know whether the company you're researching is public or private, start at the following section and proceed from there.

Finding Information on Privately or Publicly Owned Companies

Unlike public companies, whose stock is publicly traded and who are required to file reports disclosing their financial situation with the United States Securities and Exchange Commission and issue annual reports to their shareholders, private companies are more difficult to research because they do not publicly trade their stock and consequently are not required to disclose their financial situation. To find out if the company you're interested in is public or private, or a subsidiary of another company, follow these steps.

Step 1: Analyzing

Look up the company in the SEC filing *Companies*. This volume provides a listing of companies that file reports with the Securities and Exchange Commission (SEC) and are therefore publicly held companies. If your company does not appear on this list, it may be either private or a subsidiary of another company. In that case, go to the next step.

Step 2: Troubleshooting

Look for the company in the *Directory of Corporate Affiliations*. This source shows who owns whom. It allows you to study the family tree of many major corporations in the United States, both public and private. Your company may be a subsidiary of a parent company (public or private). If your company is owned by another company, you will need to research the parent company to find information on the subsidiary. The following volumes can help you with this.

Subsidiary Information on Corporate Family Trees

America's Corporate Families. Volume I lists U.S. parent companies and their subsidiaries and divisions. Volume II links parent companies with foreign subsidiaries and, conversely, foreign companies with their U.S. subsidiaries. Geographical and industry indexes are also provided.

Ward's Business Directory of U.S. Private and Public Companies. Lists 90,000 companies, including information on type of company, such as division or subsidiary.

Predicasts. F&S Company Thesaurus. List of company names indicating parent-affiliate relationship.

International Directory of Corporate Affiliates. Shows who owns whom, and provides the family tree of major corporations in the world.

Who Owns Whom: North America. Lists parent companies in alphabetical order by company name. An alphabetical index to subsidiaries and associates shows their parent companies. Other similar companion volumes are:

Who Owns Whom: Australia and the Far East

Who Owns Whom: Continental Europe

Who Owns Whom: United Kingdom and the Republic of Ireland

Predicasts. F&S Index of Corporate Change. A guide to name changes, new companies, reorganizations, bankruptcies, etc.

Mergers and Acquisitions. The M&A Roster section of this bimonthly publication reports merger, acquisition, and divestiture activity of U.S. firms.

Directory of Obsolete Securities. Contains brief information on companies whose original identity has been lost due to name change, merger/acquisition, dissolution, reorganization, or bankruptcy.

Periodical Indexes that List Articles About Subsidiaries

Business Periodicals Index

Predicasts F&S Index: United States

Predicasts F&S Index: Europe

Predicasts F&S Index: International

Predicasts F&S Index of Corporate Change

Wall Street Journal Index

Directory Information on Private and Public Companies

Ward's Business Directory of U.S. Private and Public Companies. Lists 90,000 companies. Includes rankings, number of employees, type of company, and sales figures.

Dun's Million Dollar Directory. This annual provides information for some 160,000 public and private corporations with a net worth of $500,000 or more. Companies are arranged alphabetically, geographically, and by industry (Standard Industry Classification).

Inc. "The Inc. 500." A yearly report, published in the December issue, on America's fastest growing private companies. These might not always be the largest, but they are the ones likely to be of interest. The information given on the "500" includes sales growth, sales, number of employees, and a brief business description.

Standard & Poor's Register of Corporations, Directors and Executives. Information on 40,000 public and private corporations with a biographical section on directors and executives.

Thomas Register of American Manufacturers. Lists products and services of U.S. manufacturers.

Dun's Directory of Service Companies. Lists businesses covered by Standard Industry Classification (SIC) codes 70–81, 83, 89, alphabetically, geographically and by SIC.

Moody's Manuals. Information on corporations traded on the New York, American, regional, and over-the-counter (OTC) exchanges is included in these annual volumes. Information contains history, business/products, income statement and balance sheets, and financial ratios. Moody's has divided the companies by type of business into separate series: Bank and Finance Manual; Industrial Manual; International Manual; Municipal and Government Manual; OTC Industrial Manual; OTC Unlisted Manual; Public Utility Manual; Transportation Manual.

Standard & Poor's Corporation Record. A financial service including such information as corporate background, stock data, earnings, consolidated annual report, and balance sheet. For updates, check the *"Daily News"* volume.

Standard and Poor's Stock Reports: NYSE, AMEX, OTC. This series offers one page of information on all companies listed on the two major exchanges and 1,000 OTC companies. It provides a brief financial analysis and investment advice, and 10 years of financial data for each company.

Moody's Handbook of Common Stock. Provides price charts, summary description, and investment advice for some 900 companies.

OTC Handbook. One-page reports on some 700 OTC companies. Reports include price ranges, P-E ratio, dividends, orders, summary, new developments, financial summary, and per-share data.

Value Line Investment Survey. Data on about 1,700 companies, including a 10-year statistical history on key investment factors. A Value Line rating is also available.

Standard & Poor's Corporation. The Outlook. A weekly common stock investment advisory service. Has summary of stock market trends, current outlook, and information on companies in the news.

Periodical Indexes that List Articles About Private and Public Companies

Business Periodicals Index. An index to articles in more than 300 business-oriented periodicals geared toward finance and management. This index is organized by company name, product, industry, and business topic.

The Wall Street Journal Index. This index is divided into two sections: Articles about companies are listed in the "Corporate News" sections, and general business articles are listed in the "General News" sections.

Predicasts F&S Index: United States. An excellent source for industry, product, and company information. Two companion volumes are: *Predicasts F&S Index: Europe* and *Predicasts F&S Index: International.*

Predicasts F&S Index of Corporate Change. Index to journal articles citing corporate organizational developments. Journal articles may be found by company, by industry, or by type of organizational change: new companies, joint ventures, bankruptcies, name changes.

Predicasts Basebook. Indicators of market activity for products and industries. At least six years of data are given. Arrangement is by SIC numbers.

Predicasts Forecasts. Compiles forecasts on products, markets, industries, and economic aggregates for the United States and North America as reported in the trade and business press. Data are presented by SIC numbers.

Predicasts Worldcasts. Compiles forecasts on products, markets, industry, and economic aggregates as reported in the business press. Data are accessible by region, country, or SIC number.

Personnel Management Abstracts. Lists articles from academic and trade journals that deal with the management of people and organizational behavior.

Work Related Abstracts. An index to articles in more than 250 management, labor, government, professional, and academic periodicals.

Accountants Index. An author/subject index to English language periodicals in the field of accounting.

PARIS International in Print. An index to books, pamphlets, government documents, reports, and periodical articles relating to business, economic and social conditions, public administration, and international relations.

Special Issues Index. Specialized contents analysis of business, industrial, and consumer journals.

Guide to Industry Special Issues. Analysis of special issue feature in leading trade journals.

Sources for Business and Industrial Financial Ratios

Almanac of Business and Industrial Financial Ratios. Financial and operating ratios are listed for 1,150 companies. Featured in the January issue of *Forbes* magazine.

Robert Morris Associates. *Annual Statement Studies.* Financial and operating ratios for about 300 lines of business.

Financial Studies of Small Business. Individual analysis by asset size within industries and overall industry analysis that contains a "typical" composite balance sheet and income statement followed by 16 ratios arranged in order of liquidity leverage, activity, and profitability.

Forbes 500. Basic ratios are given for each of the Forbes 500 companies. This data is profiled in the April issue of *Forbes* magazine.

Dun and Bradstreet. *Industry Norms and Key Business Ratios.* Financial and operating ratios of more than 800 lines of business.

Schonfeld and Associates, Inc. *IRS Corporate Financial Ratios.* Financial ratios based on the income statement and balance sheet data compiled by the Internal Revenue Service.

Troy. *The Partnership Almanac: A Sourcebook on Financial Data, Trends, and Performance Ratios.*

U.S. Department of Commerce. *Quarterly Financial Report for Manufacturing, Mining, and Trade Corporations.* Presents estimated statements of income and retained earnings, balance sheets, and related financial and operating ratios for all manufacturing corporations and large mining and trade corporations. Data are classified by industry and by asset size.

Standard & Poor's Industry Surveys. Each of the industries profiled has a section called "Composite Industry Data" in which performance and financial ratios can be found.

U.S. Bank Performance Profile. Presents 70 benchmark performance ratios for all banks by state, by resource class, and for the nation as a whole.

Industry Information: Why It's Important and How to Find It

Knowing how a particular industry is doing lets you gauge the market potential of your product. If your market has not been profitable, you may be able to determine which factors were to blame. If so, you may even be able to come up with a creative solution that turns an unprofitable market into a profitable one.

Most of the information generated on American industries is produced by two sources: the agencies of the federal government, and the private companies that serve the nation's large investment community. Most information published is about those economic sectors dominated by large publicly traded companies. There is less data available for the new rising industries. However, the following sources will help you research the established industries and spot the newcomers.

Industry Information

U.S. Industrial Outlook. A yearly publication subtitled "Prospects of Over 350 Manufacturing and Service Industries." It serves as an index to the vast information produced by the federal government. Each industry discussed includes a current situation and outlook, illustrated with charts and graphs. The references at the end of each article lead to other sources produced by the government and by private publishers.

Moody's Industry Review. Some 4,000 companies are arranged into 145 industry groups. The comparative statistics include price ranges, earnings, dividends, and stockholder's equity. The companies are also ranked by eight criteria.

Standard and Poor's Industry Surveys. The survey divides American industry into 22 categories. Each industry features a basic and current analysis that discusses its prospects, trends, and problems. The text is illustrated with graphs and charts. There is a list of industry references included in each discussion.

Value Line Investment Service. Presents an analysis for each of 92 industry groups. The one- or two-page narratives offer a succinct characterization of the state and outlook of the industry.

Forbes. *Annual Report of American Industry.* A special January issue, this report covers some 40 industries and 80 subgroups. There is a brief discussion of each industry with financial data on the leading publicly traded companies in the industry and subgroups.

Industry Week. The March issue, "Financial Analysis of Industry," presents a special report on industries.

Quarterly Business Failures. This record is compiled from bankruptcy filings. It does not reflect business failures that do not go through the courts. Closings are arranged by SIC code allowing you to study the status of an industry over time.

International Directories That Provide Information on International Companies

Moody's International Manual. This manual includes company history, business/products, income statements, balance sheets, and financial ratios.

Macmillan Directory of Multinationals. Profiles the world's 450 largest industrial corporations with sales over $1 billion, and significant international investments.

Principal International Businesses. Directory-type information on 55,000 companies in 133 countries. Indexed by company name, by geographic area and by SIC code.

The Times 1,000. This is a review of the world's leading industrial and financial companies.

The International Corporate 1,000. A directory of who runs the world's leading corporations. A directory type information with officers and management.

International Directory of Corporate Affiliations. Who owns whom—the family tree of major corporations, public and private companies across the world.

America's Corporate Families and International Affiliates. Lists U.S. multinational parent companies and their foreign subsidiaries; U.S. subsidiaries of Canadian and other foreign ultimate parents; all U.S. and foreign multinational family members by geographic area or industry.

Directory of American Firms Operating in Foreign Countries. Lists more than 3,000 U.S. corporations that have more than 22,000 subsidiaries and affiliates in 122 foreign countries.

Directory of Foreign Firms Operating in the United States. Lists approximately 1,300 foreign business firms in 36 countries that own or have substantially invested in some 2,200 American firms.

International Directory of Company Histories. Information on the historical development of 1,250 of the world's largest and most influential companies.

Regional Directories That Provide Information on International Companies

Asia's Largest Companies

Eastern European Business Directory

Europe's 15,000 Largest Companies

Kelly's Business Directory

Major Companies of Argentina, Brazil, Mexico, and Venezuela

Major Companies of the Far East

Soviet Trade Directory

Country Directories That Provide Information on International Companies

The Financial Post Survey of Industrials

Canadian Trade Index

Annals of Chinese Enterprise Register

Business Directory of Hong Kong

Directory of Hong Kong

Industries Directory of Japan's Affiliated Companies in the USA and Canada

Standard Trade Index of Japan

Korean Business Directory

Business Korea Yearbook

Times Directory of Singapore

Taiwan Buyers' Guide

Periodical Indexes That Provide Information on International Companies

Predicasts F&S: Europe. Covers Business activity in the European Community, Scandinavia, other regions of Western Europe, the Commonwealth of Independent Nations, East/Central Europe. It's organized by company name, product, and industry as well as by geographical area.

Predicasts F&S: International. Covers business activities in Latin America, the Middle East, Canada, Africa, Asia, and Oceania.

Sample Patent Marketing Plan

Executive Summary

Inventor's Philosophy and Product Description

The "FingerTip Soldering Tool" concept contains within it a vision to revolutionize the "idea stagnant" manual soldering/desoldering industry. The concept provides much higher efficiency to electronic manufacturing, prototyping, and electronic repair industries with its new fingertip control concepts. The inventor of the FingerTip Soldering Tool (FTST) believes that as fast as technology changes, so too should the tools used to develop these be created. In an industry where the tools haven't significantly changed in several decades, the inventor is combining creativity with customer feedback in an effort to create electronic soldering tools that are imaginatively distinct, more efficient, and more compact.

The Market

The target is an $82 million/year manual soldering market with a people customer basis of more than two million. Over two dozen companies employ a total of more than one thousand employees in this market. The soldering/desoldering products are sold nationally through stores, catalogs, and sales representatives.

Competitive Position

In this market, there are over two dozen companies competing nationally, but barriers are low due to low start-up costs (<$150,000) and ease of manufacturing. Moreover, market research shows that with the ever shrinking electronic components and the long-existing need to hold multiple parts/wires in human hands in addition to the actual solder, customers have been finding it increasingly difficult to perform manual solder/desoldering. The company that markets the FTST will be highly competitive because it has designed the very smallest and lightest of all irons to accommodate shrinking components. In addition, it has fulfilled the customers' need of removing the awkwardness out of soldering with its new patented, hand-saving fingertip design.

Market Share of Competition

Actual Revenues of Above Companies:

Ungar	=	35 M
Ok Industries	=	6 M
Wahl	=	6 M
GC Electronics	=	5 M
Master Appliance	=	4.5 M
SPC Technology	=	4 M
Hexicon Electric	=	3 M
Amer. Tech. Inc.	=	2 M
Edsyn	=	2 M
Esico-Triton	=	2 M
Amer. Elect. Htr.	=	2 M
Antex	=	1.5 M
Leads Metal	=	1.5 M
Solder Rem. Co.	=	1 M
Other	=	6 M

(Ersa, Techni-Tool, ISMECA,
Allied Electronics, Century Electr.,Wellman, Vanier)

TOTAL   82 Million Dollar Industry
Approximately 1-1.5 Million Units (Soldering/Desoldering) Sold Yearly.

Product Description

The FingerTip soldering iron is a unique miniaturized manual soldering tool, as seen in Fig. 1, which straps around the index finger of a human hand. The iron is a one-of-a-kind product with significant advantages, listed below.

Main Advantages

a. *Structure.* It is known that all current soldering iron and irons designed in the past have handles that must be held by one hand at all times when soldering. Having a handle on a soldering tool gives rise to the classical problem of not being able to hold the wires, solder, and/or piece of interest in the same hand while trying to solder. There is only one other hand to hold such items. This problem is frustrating and is an awkwardness that has existed in soldering tools since they were first conceived. The concept of the handle has been eliminated with the implementation of the new FingerTip Soldering Iron. The advantage is that the whole iron is above the finger on one of the fingers of the hand. This frees up that same entire hand to hold wires, solder, and/or the piece of interest. This greatly helps to eliminate awkwardness and difficulty as can be seen from current iron designs. This long-existing need to free up the hand will also eliminate the need to use clamping devices and aids to set up for the soldering of a single joint.

b. *Size.* Structural design of most currently sold soldering irons precludes the possibility of putting such assemblies above the finger because of their rather large sizes due to their large tubular members (up to 1" in diameter), long heating elements, and handles. The FingerTip Soldering Iron, "on the other hand," is the smallest, lightest soldering tool ever designed, being approximately 1" to 2" cubed in volume. The small assembly that secures the soldering tip allows easy, comfortable maneuverability amongst tangled wires or cluttered peripheral environments. This is in contrast to current products' bulkiness and limited scope characteristics. A cover on the present design about one-half the length of the tip gives way to exposure of less than .75" of the heating element at all times. A finger strap attached to the bottom of the iron's body and assembly firmly secures the finger, enhancing the feasibility of fitting the tool into very small places. Moreover, the smallness of the present FingerTip Soldering Iron makes it marketable to space-limited and small-component-surface-mount engineers/technicians as well as general hobbyists.

c. *Fingertip Control.* As another main object of the invention, the iron provides "fingertip control" and precision in soldering. Since the point of soldering contact is close to the actual human fingertip (.5"- 1.5" and insulated well from the finger), the user has the advantage of natural precision that goes along with having the heating element near the fingertip. With current soldering irons on the market, holding the soldering iron tool at a distance far away from the actual soldering tip (where the soldering is done) gives less control and often a shaky experience that requires much practice to become skillful at. The naturalness of having the soldering at the control of a nearby fingertip is analogous to using a pencil to write. For example, in order to get ample precision and speed in writing with a pencil, the fingertips of the hand must be very close to where the actual lead hits the paper. Holding the hand away from the tip gives rise to an unbalanced, "wobbly" effect. The fingertip iron allows beginners to learn much more quickly and experts to solder more effortlessly and efficiently. A protective cover around the tip, along with different layers of heat-resistant material and a finger strap, insulate and protect the hot iron tip from the human finger.

d. *Safety.* Almost all other competitors have long, undesirable tubular heating cores (>300F in temperature) exposed to the surroundings. This can be unsafe for obvious reasons (although still accepted by Underwriters Laboratories). As far as the inventor knows, the FingerTip Soldering Iron exposes the smallest amount of surface area of "hot" metal than any other soldering iron. This is accomplished by having a very small heating tip and further covering half of it with a protective cover.

Figure 1

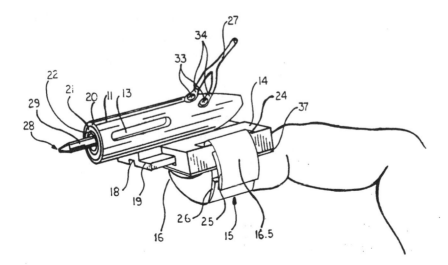

Other Product Features

The product is also adjustable for finger thickness by using a Velcro overlap strap and is adjustable for finger length by having a slider that moves up and down the base of the cylinder unit. Turning a set screw on the bottom of the unit tightens the slider down. There is a safety stop on the base of the unit to prevent the cylinder and tip from sliding forward off the base of the unit. The iron contains an efficient power supply, which simply consists of an A/C transformer, a switch/LED, and a casing that plugs into standard A/C outlets. The unit consumes about 10 watts.

The Competition

Competing companies in FTST's target market (hobbyists, electronic repairers and technicians, and electronic manufacturers) include more than two dozen national companies, which can be found in the *Thomas Register* under "Soldering Irons/Equipment." These companies either manufacture their soldering tools in house or farm it out (in the cases of smaller compa-

FingerTip Soldering Tool from original patent. (artist unknown)

nies). One important feature to notice about these soldering companies is that they all have full product lines for soldering/desoldering. For example, Weller/Ungar sells several soldering irons, desoldering irons, sponges, heat guns, and fluxes. To be serious in competing, quick diversification in the product line is necessary. The competitions' base headquarters are dispersed all over the U.S., but their distribution channels around the nation are what bring in most sales. The most common distribution channels of these companies, listed in order of highest sales intake, are:

- National distributors (catalogs such as Newark and Mousser)
- Electronic resale stores
- Sales representatives

Advantages over Competition

The advantages the FTST can bring to a company in comparison to other competitors are:

- A conceptually new patented product that provides an unprecedented ease in soldering
- A creative concept that allows for diversification
- A product tuned into constant customer feedback
- A product that is very value added in nature (low costs but with high price tag)
- Expansion of a new patented idea into a full product line of high-end, temperature controlled, DOD-standard-meeting fingertip soldering and desoldering tools.

Competitive Position

Weller/Ungar is the strongest competitor (Weller and Ungar merged in May of 1992) due to their rather large diversification of product lines, wide access to distribution and marketing channels, solid reputation (in business for over 30 years), and financial resources since they are a subsidiary of a billion-dollar parent company, Cooper Industries. However, as diverse as their product lines are, significant changes to the actual design of the soldering iron has not developed in any of the major competitors in more than sixty years (since the first manual soldering iron was invented back in the 1930s). All current designs still consist of a basic handle, tub and/or tip configurations.

With the constant shrinking of electronic components and with the need to hold multiple parts/wires in human hands in addition to the actual solder, customers have been finding it increasingly difficult to perform manual soldering/desoldering due to the bulkiness of handle-type soldering irons. These companies do make higher-end, expensive soldering iron units ($400–$1000), but do not solve the problems of soldering iron bulkiness or awkwardness in use. Rather, they add on fancy electronic features, such as temperature control units with digital displays or sturdy stands that make the unit appear more stable and large.

Any company that acquires the FTST will be highly competitive because it has designed the very smallest and lightest of all irons to accommodate shrinking electronic components. In addition, it has fulfilled the customers' unsatisfied needs of removing the awkwardness out of soldering with its new patented, hand-saving fingertip design.

Barriers to Entry

It is not very difficult for new competitors to enter the industry. The trades of production and manufacturing are not very complex, and small competitors have been entering the industry with low start-up costs (less than $150,000). Along with the top competitor, Weller/Ungar, there are more than two dozen other companies, some of which are very small yet still making a profit. However, because of the industry leader's popularity and large market share (50 percent), it is relatively difficult to obtain a significant market share. Having revolutionary new ideas such as the FTST will definitely lower these barriers to entry on the market. The FTST is aiming to replace older technology with a newer technology. Studying the competition, the inventor of the FTST believes the optimum strategy for a start-up company to acquire the maximal amount of market share in the next two years is to:

- Quickly acquire wide distribution channels across the U.S.
- Within the first year, develop two new products to differentiate the product line (develop one high-end electronic iron in addition to the original low-end fingertip iron, and also develop a fingertip desoldering iron).
- Provide adequate start-up financing ($200,000) to cover initial first-year costs.
- Focus on heavy advertisement/quality image. A company needs to create the illusion of being a well-established company with a breakthrough product. Financing will be critical here in order to obtain market share quickly.

Strategic Opportunities

The manual soldering industry has been an "idea stagnant" industry for several decades. The insertion of new ideas and designs into the present market is highly prudent and competitive.

Target Market Analysis

The target market is aimed at engineers/electronic technicians or hobbyists ages 20 and up with incomes ranging from $20,000 and up. This market of individuals can be separated into three categories:

1. Major electronic manufacturing/testing companies (45%)
2. Electronic repair technicians and associated companies (30%)
3. Technical hobbyists (25%)

With the first category, sales are often secured through technically apt company sales representatives who purchase needed equipment for their companies.

The method in which soldering equipment is currently sold to the above market groups is estimated as follows:
*   50% through national catalogs (distributors)
*   25% through sales representatives
*   25% through direct sales from national and local electronic supply stores

Market Size and Trends

In the United States, more than two million people are employed in electronic type companies or dabble in the field of electronics (according to Standard and Poor's). From these figures and total revenues of current manual soldering/desoldering equipment companies, estimated total revenues for the industry is approximately $80 million/year.

Electronic tooling companies, especially soldering equipment companies, follow the high growth rates of the general electronics industry. While the U.S. GNP grew 2.9 percent in 1988, 2.5 percent in 1989, and 1.5 percent in 1990, U.S. electronics production increased 7 percent, 4 percent, and 4 percent respectively. This means electronic soldering company growth is in general at least 2 percent above GNP growth. Even recently with recessionary times of 1990–1991, capital spending on semiconductor companies only declined less than 1 percent. "This health is reflected in the importance of products incorporating new technology to produce new generation semi-conductors. . . . Rapid growth is expected after 1991 with essentially flat sales in 1991" (*Standard & Poor's Industry Surveys*, July 1991). In fact, late in 1991, electronics growth and its associated tooling is now estimated to be as high as 8 percent.

Target Customers

The target sales are directed toward these industries:

- Semiconductor/computers
- Telecommunications
- Military
- Automotive
- Colleges and universities
- Electronic repair (TV, VCR, etc.)
- Home electronic hobbyists
- Vast array of consumer electronic companies

With a 1 to 1.5 million unit pool of soldering/desoldering iron sales from these industries, many company representatives can be found making internal equipment sales for their own private companies (45 percent of sales are made this way). Company sales representatives who make internal purchases for their large companies/corporations are generally more sensitive to quality and efficiency in a product and less sensitive to high price.

Price becomes more of an issue with smaller companies (such as electronic repair companies). On the other side of price vs. quality sensitivities, the home hobbyists are generally more sensitive to price than quality due to their frugal spending habits. In lieu of the widely varying price vs. quality sensitivities of our target customers, the original FingerTip Soldering Iron will be priced in a compromising position. For example, cheap soldering irons run as low as $10 while expensive models may be as high as $600 (other iron prices fall anywhere between those prices). Our iron would seat midway with a price of about $90 dollars with fairly good manufacturing quality. This would allow the FTST manufacturing company to capture the interest of all possible customers until the FTST can be further differentiated into a whole product line of cheaper to more expensive, high quality FingerTip Soldering/Desoldering units.

Strategic Opportunities

Since the electronic soldering tool market is full of engineers who design themselves, the market respects innovative ideas on technical products. Even though the soldering/desoldering industry has grown at high rates with the general electronics industry, the structural and conceptual design of manual tools has not changed enough to accommodate the shrinking electronic components and printed circuit boards. There is an ever increasing frustration among customers using the soldering tools because of the tools' large size and inconvenient handling relative to the soldering of very small electronic components. In the very near future, it is inevitable that a large portion of today's current manual soldering tools will be phased out of production because of their ineptitude and awkwardness on the small scale circuitry level (which currently accounts for almost 50 percent of all printed circuit boards). The FTST concept, the smallest and lightest hand-saving tool, is removing the frustration from this shrinking electronics industry. The FTST product line will turn over a 40-year-old stagnant industry and satisfy the growing needs of a large customer base.

Marketing/Action Plan

Any manufacturing or start-up company that acquires the FTST patents should have a genuine interest in providing customers with the highest technology and quality in electronic tooling in the current industry. Such company should be tied to customer feedback as it promises its customers changes in its future product lines to accommodate their needs.

Capturing the Market

Since the market size that can be reached for manual soldering tools is approximately 50 percent through company representatives of large technology type companies and the other 50 percent through direct sales to individuals through catalogs and stores, any company marketing the FTST should appropriate its resources accordingly. Sales employees are involved with outside relations by pitching to the larger high-tech company representatives, and marketing employees will be involved in marketing to individual and private party customers by securing company sales through national distributors (such as Newark & Mousser) and stores (such as Marshall Electronics). The marketing employees should also realize possible untapped markets for the sales employees to advance upon. The main emphasis of having sales reps initially is primarily to popularize the FingerTip product name in the industry.

The initial costs of these reps will outweigh their sales, but when the product becomes popularized enough through their national exposure of it and through the profits from the marketing people's efforts, the sales reps will reach a break-even point and will profit from thereon. Greatest sales of the FTST are anticipated to come from (respectively in order from most to least):

- Sales through national distributors (catalogs)
- Sales through national stores
- Sales through sales representatives efforts
- Sales due to advertising in national magazines
- Sales due to circulation of product line brochures
- Sales due to realizing new untapped markets (in the future)

Advertising will be based on the slogan "control at your fingertips," which stresses the advantages of having higher control and proficiency. The ease of soldering will also be emphasized by catch phrases like: "above the finger design," "taking the awkwardness out of soldering," and "realize a third hand in soldering."

Early Company Strategy

The fastest and earliest sales will be secured through marketing efforts to release the product for sales in as many national catalog distributors and stores as practical. The rest of the market, which is through major electronic company reps (50 percent), may take two or three years of effort to finally realize profitability since sales reps travel/success expense ratio will be high because the FTST product line will be relatively unknown in the industry for the first couple of years. The slack in profit from the sales representatives will be offset by the sales to individuals through national stores, catalogs, and direct orders from company headquarters.

The sales representative efforts in the beginning stages is an essential investment (though a loss at first) in gaining market share, and will eventually lead to future large company repeat sales due to customer loyalty. After two to three years, due to large company repeat sales and company name recognition, the sales force's efforts will break even due to increasing market share, and from thereon, profitability through their efforts will naturally accelerate.

By this time also, the marketing network will be secured. With the combination of a strong sales and marketing force, sales from all possible existing customer sources will be attained.

Incentives

All company personnel (of the company that carries the FTST) are considered members of the sales team and will receive commissions if their efforts lead to sales. A 5 percent commission goes to sales reps and 2 percent goes to marketing reps who may give indirect leads to the sales reps (this is also for the encouragement of intercommunication between marketing and sales employees).

Direct Mail

Direct mail is an integrated part of the sales team efforts to reach large company customers with color brochures of the FTST products. Large company contacts are located through the *Who's Who in Engineering* and through *Standard and Poor's Register of Corporations/Thomas Register*. Ten thousand of these brochures will be sent out each year to supplement the ongoing on-site visits that the sales teams will be making to potential large company customers.

In addition to those sales made through national catalogs and stores, and those secured by sales reps through on-site visits and direct mail, sales will also be taken by a secretary at the main office. Sales in this manner result from the FTST company's magazine advertising and general customer-to-customer word of mouth.

Building a Prototype

However spectacular your idea, it won't attract the attention it deserves without a working model. Even if your patent sketches look fabulous and you can answer the most difficult product design questions, any company worth doing business with will approach your idea with a healthy degree of skepticism. Simply put, companies have heard it all. They deal with hundreds of "great" new inventions every year, many of which turn out to be bogus and bad investments.

Many times, even if you do have a product, they don't believe your product will work or they are skeptical your product will work as well as you claim. Most patented inventions are so new and different that many people have to get a "real" physical feel for them to appreciate their advantages. Most people put more stock in what they can see—and touch. A prototype is worth a thousand sketches. It gives you a tangible product to show other people, something they can hold in their hands and get excited about.

At a trade show, for instance, I became discouraged by the lack of response to one of my inventions. I thought I had done everything in my power to make my idea attractive to a large company. My diagrams, research, and sketches were top rate. I expected them to impress any company and allow me to sell my invention immediately. Instead, I met with disappointment. One major corporate executive in the field of my invention even called it worthless. Hundreds of scouts from different companies walked right by my booth without giving my diagrams a second look.

I left the trade show that day disheartened, with my dreams and ambitions for my invention fading fast. All of my work had led nowhere. All of my time had been wasted on a useless product that had sparked no interest—a product joke. I was overcome by a feeling of failure: I had let down everyone

one who'd believed in my talents and loaned me money. I also felt that I failed myself—and it was a personal failure I couldn't accept. I wanted to be recognized for who I was—a talented entrepreneur.

Then I realized I couldn't let myself be defeated by the poor response at the trade show. I still believed in myself and the product I had invented, and that was enough to move forward with my idea despite criticism. Going back to the drawing board, I decided to build a prototype. For one month, I worked diligently on it. After I'd finished my prototype, I took it to another trade show to see what would happen. I felt nervous, and I didn't know what to expect. Would my invention flop again, despite my prototype? Or would it draw more attention? I set up my booth, and, with the physical working prototype in hand, I started to give a demonstration. What happened next destroyed any of my remaining doubts about my product forever.

In a matter of moments, reps from several leading international companies were in a frenzy over my product, circling my invention like hungry sharks. They couldn't take their hands off my prototype! The reps were pushing each other out of the way to try my product. They exclaimed over my "great invention." Retired millionaires walked by to see what all the fuss was about. Several people took one look at my invention, shook their heads in astonishment, and with big grins and thumbs-up signs said, "Steve, your invention is going to make millions. It's going to be a runaway success." Before I knew it, I had the attention of several companies at the trade show. Company reps were dropping their usual caution and running to get corporate managers and presidents to take a look at my prototype. Representatives from one company in particular saw in my fingertip soldering iron the breakthrough technology they needed for their new-improved product line.

By the end of the day, I found himself besieged by representatives from various leading companies in the industry, each of whom wanted me to sign an exclusive agreement. I knew, of course, that I now had the negotiating edge, given the competition for my product. Not bad, considering that my invention had been deemed worthless only a year earlier!

By now, you should have learned several things about prototypes from my example. First, don't even bother getting discouraged until you have a working model. Second, people respond better when they have something real to manipulate that goes beyond pictures and abstract ideas. Your prototype will let others see for themselves how your invention works and arrive at their own conclusions about its potential.

Also, as the saying goes, nothing succeeds like success—and prototypes are no exception. Once one scout becomes interested in your invention, others may follow, until you find yourself with a bidding war on your hands.

Bear in mind, though, that your prototype is only a working model, and expect it to need improvement. Every person you show it to is likely to make suggestions. Consider their input seriously, since their suggestions were the result of actually trying your invention.

Building Your Prototype: General Guidelines

There are seven steps to building a prototype, and you should complete each before moving on to the next. It's important to follow these steps, because skipping any of them can result in a disastrous prototyping experience. If a company becomes interested in your invention before you finish your prototype, it may help you complete your working model. You may also be able to convince a company to sponsor you in building your prototype—try! Here's a brief overview of the seven steps:

- *Phase 1: Project Plan.* This step includes the technical equipment you need for prototyping (e.g., getting access to milling machines or molding facilities). This phase should help you evaluate whether your project is feasible. You should also set a working schedule for making your prototype and estimate all costs.

- *Phase 2: System Description.* Here you must meet any required specifications in your product area, such as safety features and quality assurance. This step calls for checking with local, state, and federal agencies to see if any regulations apply to your invention.

- *Phase 3: Preliminary Design.* In this phase, you begin sketching your prototype. Your goal should be to overcome broad design concerns by coming up with specific physical solutions.

- *Phase 4: Comprehensive Design.* This step refines the process begun in Phase 3. It includes drawing a complete set of specifications for each separate part of your working model. If you are not confident in designing the details, engineering consultants can do the work for you.

- *Phase 5: Implementation.* With this phase, you're ready to build, test, and evaluate the performance of your prototype. Try to find a friend or retiree with experience in your product line who can help you avoid time-consuming, expensive mistakes.

- *Phase 6: Modification.* Never expect your first working model to be your last. Just the opposite: Plan to go through several generations of your prototype before you have a model that satisfies you and that you can present to companies.

- *Phase 7: Conversion.* By the time you've reached this step, you've already convinced a company of your product's potential. That company should take over the manufacturing, replacing your rough prototype with a more polished product. The company may also seek your help if it runs into stumbling blocks in the process of refining your original design.

Choosing the Right Material for Your Prototype

When you are ready to choose materials, you will have to look at the many different properties specific and unique to each one. Qualitatively and quantitatively weighing the different properties of materials is a highly technical exercise that I wouldn't recommend to you unless you are fairly well-versed in engineering. No need to worry, though! You can narrow down your preferred prototyping materials accurately from the information in this section. Once you've gotten an idea of several materials that may work for you, the tough part will then be to choose the *best and most suitable* material within that range of possible materials. Of course, you will have to do this for each part of your invention that requires a different material. Here are some tips that will help you go from a few possible materials in mind to *one exact* material:

1. Ask prototypers and material suppliers what they would recommend. Most will give you free advice in choosing materials if you show interest in buying their products and services.

2. Find out what the competition's products are made with.

3. Look at other products that fit the requirements, conditions, and stresses similar to your invention. Investigate the materials that these products are made from. (I've listed some in Tables 2 through 5).

4. Obtain samples of the materials that you think may work, and test them in the environment that your actual prototype may have to perform under (e.g., test for conditions such as temperature, corrosion, shock, strength, and stiffness).

Choosing a Major Class of Materials

It should be easy for you to define which major class your part could be made from (metals, ceramics, polymers, and composites). Table 1 shows some common properties of the major classes of materials:

Classes of Material	Good Properties	Poor Properties
Metals	Stiff Ductile Tough High melting points Thermal shock resistance	Yield Hardness Fatigue strength Corrosion resistance
Polymers	Ductile and formable Corrosion resistant Low density	Low stiffness Yield Low glass temperature Toughness often low
Ceramics	Stiff Very high yield, hardness High melting point Corrosion resistant Moderate density	Very low toughness Thermal shock resistance Formability-powder methods
Composites	Stiff Strong Tough Fatigue resistant Corrosion resistant Low Density	Formability Cost Creep

Table 1. Common properties of materials

Narrowing Your Choice to an Exact Material

Now that you have a good idea which general classes your material falls into (metals, polymers, ceramics, or composites), you can narrow your choice to an exact type of commercial material (see Tables 2 through 5).

Within the four general classes listed in Table 1 are a number of specific common materials that give you a wide variety of engineering attributes and qualities that you'll have to match up with your prototyping needs. Depending on your invention's environment and application, you'll have to select the material or materials that most closely suit your needs. Tables 2 through 5 provide a summary of common types of polymers, metals, ceramics, and composites respectively. Examples of how each material is commonly used and its practical advantages or disadvantages are listed for your convenience.

Polymers (plastics)	Examples	Advantages	Disadvantages
ABS (Acrylonitrile-Butadiene-Styrene)	telephones, sports gear, automotive grills, electronic instrument housing, furniture	tough, hard, rigid, adequate chemical, weathering, and electrical characteristics, resistance to hot/cold cycles, low water absorption, low price	not high performance
Acetal	gears, pawls, latches, cams, cranks, plumbing parts	exceptional resistance to abrasion, heat, chemicals, creep, and fatigue, low friction	not good around acids or oxidizing agents; can be expensive
Acrylic	exterior material on optical lenses, taillights, signs, nameplates, coatings for pool steps and plumbing fixtures	high optical clarity, best weatherability, broadest color range and hardest surface of all thermoplastics, cheap	average thermal and impact properties
Alkyds (Thermoset)	pavement markings	easy to mold, high heat resistance, excellent electrical performance	light colored
Allyl Resin "DAP" (Thermoset)	connectors, switches, relays, circuit breakers, terminal strips, coil bobbins	high heat and moisture resistance, superior retention of insulating properties in hot and humid environments	brittle, slow cure rates
Cellulosics	tool handles, control knobs, eyeglass frames	tough, transparent, hard, or flexible	tend to dry out and deform with exposure to light, heat, weather, and aging

Table 2. Polymers (plastics)

Polymers (plastics)	Examples	Advantages	Disadvantages
Epoxy (Thermoset)	adhesives, laminating, circuit boards, electrical potting repair kits, castings	hi-po of all thermoset plastics; high strength, tension, compression; low shrink, hard, good ability to stick	not good for low friction applications; prices vary amongst types
Fluoroplastics (Variations include PTFE, FEP, PFA, CTFE, ECTFE, ETFE, and PVDF)	bearings, valves, pumps handling corrosive chemicals, skillet linings, implants	superior heat and chemical resistance and electrical properties, flexibility	only moderate strength; highest cost of all plastics
Foams	packaging, furniture, bedding	soft, resilient, easy to process	low melting; no resistance to chemicals or weathering
Nylon	terminal strips, connectors, relays, bearings, cams, handles, sliding parts, heat insulation	tough, slippery, good electrical properties, very high temperatures (to 400 F)	hygroscopic, lower dimensional stability, water absorption ruins properties, harder to mold
PEEK	wire and cable for aerospace, military, and nuclear; high performance applications	good at very high temperatures (450 F); good fire, abrasion, and load resistance	expensive, limited colors
Phenolic (rocket nozzles, hi-temp)	rocket nozzles, high-temperature applications, opaque handles for cookware, knobs, toaster ends, electrical components	low cost, good chemical and weather resistance; excellent heat resistance	limited colors, change colors with heat, very rigid, notch sensitive

Table 2. Polymers (plastics) *continued*

Polymers (plastics)	Examples	Advantages	Disadvantages
Phenylene Oxide Based (PPO) Resin	top choice for electrical applications, housing for computers and appliances, auto wheel covers, pool plumbing, electronic parts	superior moisture resistance, dimensional stability	mediocre weather and chemical resistance
Polybutalene or "Duraflex"	water piping, food packaging	flexibility, toughness; resistance to cracking, wet abrasion, chemicals, puncture, impact	slow processing rate, low temperature brittleness
Polycarbonate	bullet-protecting glazing for vehicles/buildings, coffeemakers, food blenders, safety helmets, lenses	tough, good shock property, withstands boiling water	scratches and weathers easier than acrylics, notch sensitive, poor solvent resistance in stressed parts
Polychloroprene	neoprene wet suits	flexible, strong, good elasticity, good moisture resistance	low melting
Polyesters (Thermoplastic and Thermoset)	boats, aircraft parts, autos, under-the-hood electrical and mechanical parts, beverage bottles (thermoplastic form)	good balance of properties, resists moisture, creep, fire, and oils, good impact strength	marginal chemical resistance, high molding shrinkage and warpage
Polyethylene, PE	containers, bottles, boxes, buckets, trash bags	inexpensive (most used plastic), easy to process, strong, flexible, high chemical resistance	not transparent, difficult to cement or paint, low temperature, low stiffness

Table 2. Polymers (plastics) *continued*

Polymers (plastics)	Examples	Advantages	Disadvantages
Polyethermide or "Ultem"	printed circuit boards, heater housings, electrical components	superior strength; heat, flame, and UV resistance	expensive
Polyimide	critical engineering parts in aerospace, automotive (racing engines), and electronics; parts in corrosive environments	heat and fire resistance to 500 F, good corrosion resistance, low coefficient of friction	expensive
Polyisoprene	rubber products	good stick; good flexibility and elasticity	low melting, not stiff
Polyphenylene Sulfide/PPS	critical under-the-hood auto parts, hair dryers, cooking appliances	good at high temperatures (450 F), low warpage, good dimensional stability	expensive
Polypropylene	packaging, auto interiors, dishwashers, pumps, tubs, filters for laundry, sterilizable medical tools	superior resistance to flexural fatigue and cracking; excellent chemical and electrical properties; popular; low cost	poor low temp properties, flammability, low melt strength

Table 2. Polymers (plastics) *continued*

Polymers (plastics)	Examples	Advantages	Disadvantages
Polystyrene	tinted drinking glasses, blender jars, water pitchers, appliances, business machines, lenses	low cost–high volume, clarity, low water absorption	brittle, low heat and chemical resistance, poor weather resistance
Polysulfone or "Udel"/"Mindel"	medical equipment, solar-heating applications	flame retardance, auto-clavability, transparency, strong, stiff	notch sensitivity, attacked by many chemicals, poor UV resistance, expensive
Polyurethane (Thermoset or Thermoplastic)	auto exterior parts, tubing, cords, shoe soles, ski boots, roller skate wheels, tires, floor coatings, auto bumpers, upholstery	excellent wear resistance, cut strength resistance, strength, range from soft to glass hard, resistance to fuels and oils	Low heat resistance (250 F)
Polyvinylchloride/PVC	piping, bottles, jugs, siding, window profiles, disposable medical products, vinyls	high-volume–low cost, good chemical, weather, and flame resistance, tough, flexible or rigid, good surface appearance	low temperatures, difficult to process, poor resistance to ketones and chlorinated hydrocarbons

Table 2. Polymers (plastics) *continued*

Metals	Examples	Advantages	Disadvantages
Alumirum	power transmission lines, aircraft skins, cooking pans, drink cans, window frames, casting	good conductor, excellent corrosion resistance, low density, light	not strong (though can be hardened), 10 times more expensive then steel
Brasses	water fittings, screws, electrical components	good corrosion resistance, like copper except stronger	bendable, weak, expensive
Bronzes	bearings, ships' propellers, bells, art	good corrosion resistance (except can dezincify after long time in water), easy to machine, like copper except stronger	bendable, weak, expensive
Copper	wiring, coinage, water pipes, screws, electrical components, boilers	good conductor, corrosion resistant in water, ductile, thermally conducive	bendable, weak, expensive, turns green with water corrosion
Iron and steels	construction steel, nuts, bolts, tools, dies, high-stress pressure vessels, aircraft parts, high-temperature applications	high-stress, strength, pressure, temperature; good for all-purpose machinery	heavy, can rust, plastics easier to produce

Table 3. Metals

Metals	Examples	Advantages	Disadvantages
Lead-Tin	storage batteries, cable-sheathing, piping, roofing, acid-handling equipment	inexpensive, good corrosion resistance	heavy, low strength, high specific gravity
Monels	heat-exchange tubes	strong, corrosion resistant	expensive
Nickel	coinage, steam engines	very corrosion resistant, much stronger than copper, good strength, thermal, and electrical conductivity	bendable, expensive
Superalloys	furnace parts, turbine blades and discs	creep and oxidation resistant, strong	more expensive than monels
Titanium	turbo-fans, airframes, hip implants	hi-po material, strong as steel, corrosion resistant, half the weight of steel	expensive
Zinc	die-casting, valve parts, dies, bearings	good corrosion and wear resistance, high strength, low cost	poor shock resistance, need to be well lubricated in moving parts

Table 3. Metals *continued*

Ceramics/Glasses	Examples	Advantages	Disadvantages
Alumina	cutting tools, wear-resistant surfaces, bearings, cutlery grips	high-temperature, hard, wear resistant, high resistivity, low dielectric loss, excellent acid resistance	poor thermal shock resistance, brittle, expensive
Borosilicate glass	Pyrex, cooking and chemical glassware	inexpensive, easy to form and shape, clarity, thermal resistant, high-temperature strength, doesn't expand with temperature, good thermal shock	breakable, brittle, low impact shock
Brick	construction, refractory uses	inexpensive, easy to work with, visually appealing	breakable, corrodes, cracks
Cement	walkways, general construction	ease of manufacturing and inexpensive	brittle, cracks, low shock and corrosion resistance
China	artware and tableware tiles	easy to form, glossy, thermally resistant	breakable, brittle
Cubic Zirconia	jewelry, heat insulator, oxygen meters in boilers (limited applications)	hard, shiny, good heat insulator, inexpensive	poor shock resistance, weak, low hardness and stiffness (as compared to alumina)

Table 1. Ceramic/Glass Materials

Ceramics/Glasses	Examples	Advantages	Disadvantages
Porcelain	electrical insulators, plates	easy to form, glossy, thermally resistant	breakable, brittle
Pottery	tiles, artware, bowls, plates	easy to form, inexpensive, thermally resistant	breakable, heavy
Sialons	similar to silicon nitrides	same as below	same as below
Silicon carbide/nitrides	medical implants, engine and turbine parts, armor	high thermal conductivity, very hard, excellent shock resistance, many ways to manufacture nitrides	only moderate strength
Soda-lime, glass	windows, bottles, lenses	very inexpensive, clarity, easy to form and shape	breakable, heavy, plastics now more economical in many cases, low shock

Table 4. Ceramic/Glass Materials *continued*

Composites	Examples	Advantages	Disadvantages
BFRP (Boron-Fibre)	military aircraft parts, space shuttle, stiffening golf shafts, tennis rackets, bike frames	adequate strength, high-stiffness, light, high temperature resistance	brittle, expensive, hard to process, structural discontinuities form (the weaker of the fibers)
CFRP (Carbon-Fibre Reinforced Polymers)	rocket nozzles, hi-po bike frames, aircraft and aerospace parts, turbine, windmill blades, flywheels, implants	stronger than steel yet lighter than aluminum (the lightest fiber); high temperature resistance	very expensive
GFRP (Fiberglass)	aircraft, or ground transport vehicle parts, boats, window frames, tanks, bathroom units, pipes, ducts	light yet very strong, inexpensive, comes in a variety of forms	more breakable and more susceptible to static fatigue (high loads for long periods), moderate cost
Kevlar	bulletproof vests, shin-guards, aircraft parts, flaps and tail on planes	highest strength of all the composites, tough, flexible	heavier than CFRP, GFRP, moderate cost

Table 5. Composites

Choosing the Right Manufacturing Process for Your Prototype

Choosing how you want to make your prototype can be tough. Some factors that effect your process choice are: material, accuracy needed, quantity needed, size, cosmetics, shape, and thickness of walls. If you are just starting out and your part is not too complex, the classical method of manual machining is probably good enough for you. If your part cannot be easily machined or you are interested in creating more than a handful of prototypes, this section also discusses 32 other very common methods of prototyping in the industry.

Many prototyping companies use a variety of the methods described here and can quote you for quantities if you send them an engineering drawing of your piece(s). Of course, their price quote will depend on how well their particular manufacturing methods are suited to making your particular piece. They will generally tend to pick the cheapest method or combination of methods they have for your piece in order to give you the most competitive quote. For processes that require a set-up or mold fabrication time, manufacturers will often amortize the cost of the mold into the piece prices. So as you order more and more quantities, you will see the price of your piece dramatically go down (as the price of the mold pays off). Theoretically though, there is a fixed material and labor cost for each piece that you can inquire about if you want to know the actual piece costs *after* any set-up or mold fabrication.

Tooling Costs vs. Price-Per-Piece Costs

I've listed the prototyping methods in the next section, "Contemporary Methods and Processes of Prototyping," in order of increasing tooling costs. The first several methods have no initial tooling/mold costs, and the last few have the highest tooling mold costs. I recommend the first several "no tooling" methods for those of you just starting out. I've also included many other more sophisticated methods for those of you with more aggressive prototyping or production efforts.

A *tool* (also *mold*) is any working cavity that has to be initially fabricated before any prototypes can be made. Such a tool or mold is generally the inverse shape of your actual part. *The general rule is: As your tooling cost goes up, the life of your tool goes up, your price per prototype goes down, and the time to make the part goes down.* I've separated the prototyping methods into three categories based on how costly the initial tooling/molds will be:

1. *Methods that require no tooling/molds.* These methods are for producing quantities in the range of one to 100. Price per piece will be the most expensive. These methods are the ones you want to look at when you're first starting out.

2. *Methods that require "soft-tooling."* These methods build parts from temporary molds that can be used for making runs of between 100 and 5,000 parts until the mold becomes unusable. Price-per-piece and tooling/mold costs will be mid-range (see Table 6). You will be interested in this method if you want to do some test marketing and promotion of your patented product (see the next chapter, "Step 5," on test marketing your product).

3. *Methods that require injection or permanent tooling/molds.* These methods are for full-fledged production of thousands to even millions of parts per year. You probably won't be interested in this unless you're interested in starting a business with your patent. Price per piece will be very cheap yet mold costs will be very expensive (see Table 6). It is possible that some of these methods can fall into the "soft tooling" category if the tooling/molds are made out of weaker materials such as aluminum or rubber.

Note that some methods can be used with both "soft-tooling" and "permanent-tooling." By varying the material of the tool or mold, some of the methods are becoming more flexible in manufacturing needs. Aluminum molds are becoming commonplace in replacing steel molds in an effort to reduce tooling/mold costs. These weaker material molds break down much earlier, yet are cheaper to build (which is good for prototyping applications!).

Contemporary Methods and Processes of Prototyping

Here is a list of popular prototyping methods to guide you in your search for a prototyper who is right for your particular invention. Consult Table 6 after this list to compare the costs and quantity considerations of each method. Further consult Table 7 to see which processes work for which materials.

No Tooling Required

1. *Machining.* Traditionally, this has been the most common way of prototyping. From Computer Assisted Design (CAD) drawings, you can have a machinist manually carve your pieces out for you. This is economical at very low quantities.

2. *CNC (Computer Numeric Controlled) Machining.* CNC machining is replacing manual machining; a computer, through a milling machine, actually carves out a part from stock based on a computer CAD–CNC file. There is an initial set-up fee because the machinist has to program the computer initially to perform the same actions and use the same tools as an actual machinist would if done manually.

3. *Screw Machines.* Screw machines are one of the simplest ways to pound out machined parts fairly cheaply. A screw machine is cheaper than manual machining because a particular machine is set-up to pick up several tools and make several different cuts in a specified fixed manner. Once a screw machine is set-up, it can only produce one exact particular part. The limitation to a screw machine is that it can only be used for fairly simple parts and geometries.

4. *Stereolithography.* This type of prototyping falls under a very new branch of manufacturing called "rapid prototyping." From a 3-D computer model, the stereolithography machine actually creates and builds a three-dimensional prototype of any shape. It creates the object layer by layer from wax or resin by essentially melting and hardening the material into the desired shape. The more complex the part, the better, although actual machining is currently more accurate than this process. The process has a quick turn-around time and is typically used to get a feel for the actual designed part before continuing with full-fledged mold manufacturing. The cost of building prototypes with

this method as compared to other methods is fairly high unless your part is very complex (see Table 6). An expert in the field told me that machining is a cheaper method than this unless your machined part is more than $1,000 per piece (the crossover point).

5. *Selective Laser Sintering (SLS).* This type of prototyping also falls under a very new branch of manufacturing called "rapid prototyping." From a 3-D computer model, the SLS machine actually creates and builds a three-dimensional prototype of any shape. A modulated laser beam selectively describes the object's geometry by melting a powder. This process is faster than stereolithography. Materials that can be used currently are nylon and polycarbonate, but soon metals and many other materials will be possible.

6. *LOM (Laminated Object Manufacturing).* This type of prototyping also falls under a very new branch of manufacturing called "rapid proto-typing." It is like the previous methods, except it uses paper or wood to build 3-D models.

7. *FDM (Fused Deposition Modeling).* A slight derivative of LOM.

8. *Fastening.* If you can make your prototype out of already existing parts, you can use fasteners to build the complete part. Fasteners include screws, nuts, washers, bolts, cable wire, ties, clips, crimps, clamps, glue, and so forth.

9. *Sculpting.* If your piece is made out of wood, or other non-technical materials, there are sculptors who, for a stiff price, can carve out just about anything.

Soft Tooling Required

10. *Powder Compaction/Molds.* With powder molds, powdered material is actually placed into a die cavity and pressed into the desired shape through high pressure. Such molds are made out of aluminum and are made for medium-range quantities (see Table 6). The piece of interest must be ejectable from the die and have a surface area below 20 in². Walls must not be thinner than 0.05 inches, and height-to-diameter ratios of over 7 to 1 and sharp corners should be avoided.

11. *Blow Molding.* In blow molding, hollow products are formed by extruding a heated thermoplastic tube into a mold, and, under air pressure, expanding the tube to match the inner contours of the mold. This method is good for making hollow, thin-walled containers such as plastic bottles, milk containers, bleach bottles, detergent containers, fuel tanks, and surfboards. This method can be used with most plastic materials.

12. *Investment Casting.* This is a process in which molten metal is poured into a preheated mold, producing a ceramic casting that may have intricate internal and external features with little or no draft. Investment casting is commonly used in conjunction with rapid prototyping methods to get temporary molds for short runs. For example, one prototype can be built with a stereolithography machine, and then an investment casting can be made around that prototype (the female side). Then the investment casting actually can be used as a mold to create more parts. This process produces intricate detail and close dimensional accuracy.

13. *Compression Molding.* In this method, a thermoset plastic material is introduced directly into a heated metal mold, is softened by heat, and is forced to conform to the shape of the mold cavity as the mold closes. The advantages are that it requires no gates or runners, and metallic inserts may be molded into the product. One disadvantage is that the shape must have undercuts. In this process, tools tend to be cheap, and parts more expensive (see Table 6). This process is typically good for parts up to 12 inches in any dimension.

14. *Sand Casting.* This process involves an assembly of various mold sections or cores to form a casting mold. Cores made of sand and composites vary greatly in size and complexity. With cored sand casting, shapes not obtainable through other casting processes can be produced. A complex part such as an engine block is a good sand-casting prospect.

15. *Rotational Molding.* Rotational molding is a forming process in which melted plastic disperses over the inner surface of a rotating split mold, resulting in a hollow or open-ended part. Hollow chocolate candies were once made with this process. Tanks, portable outhouses,

packaging, garbage containers, and toys are some other applications. Common materials used in this process are polyethylene, polypropylene, PVC, and polybutylene. Tooling for rotational molds are relatively cheap compared to other molding processes (see Table 6). Complex design criteria such as undercuts, intricate contours, and molded-in-inserts are commonplace in rotational molding. This method is slow compared to other methods.

16. *Thermoform Molding.* This is a shaping process in which a thermoplastic sheet or film, heated to its softening point, is pressed against the contours of a mold and allowed to cool until it retains the shape of the mold. Typical products best made by this process are trays, plastic packaging, bowls, plastic cups, and other similar items. Thermoforming can be used with practically all plastics at more or less different difficulty levels. Molds for thermoforming tend to be cheaper and are often made out of wood, ceramic, or metal (see Table 6). Extremely small parts are typically not economical for thermoform molding because this process requires some post-handling and trimming. Parts with undercuts and negative draft are commonly produced with this method.

17. *Vacuum Forming.* Vacuum forming essentially sucks the plastic material down into the particular shape of a mold. This process is the most popular form of thermoform molding and is typically used in producing products with thin walls or shells. Vacuum forming is typically used for making plastic or cardboard like packaging.

18. *Transfer Molding or Resin Transfer Molding (RTM).* Transfer molding is a shaping process in which a pre-measured quantity of thermoset plastic is softened in a heated chamber and forced into a closed mold cavity, where it conforms to the shape of the cavity and is cured. (Resin is injected to harden it.) Common products made from this method are utensil handles, electric appliance parts, and connectors. With transfer molding, you can safely mold fragile inserts into the part. Transfer molding is good for parts up to 12 inches in any dimension. This process, along with thermoset materials, is particularly inexpensive per part when making multi-cavity molds.

19. *Room Temperature Vulcanization (RTV) and Rubber Silicone Tooling.* This process produces inexpensive molds made out of rubber by forming the mold around a model and then curing it. Once the vulcanized mold is cured, it is typically used to create urethane plastic models. Urethane is a material that looks and acts a lot like rubber.

20. *Reaction Injection Molding (RIM).* RIM is an injection process in which two chemical reactants are released under high pressure to form chemical linkages, producing solid or block polymers. Most common materials used in this process are polyurethanes, nylons, and epoxies. This process is typically used to manufacture very large parts such as automotive body parts, bumper covers, quarter panels, and dashboard units. This product is more economically competitive for larger parts. It produces relatively soft molds for small-quantity, detailed parts.

21. *Composite Tooling.* Composite tooling produces inexpensive molding such as RTV, except the mold is made out of urethane and the parts produced from it can be made out of common ABS. See Table 6 for a comparison to other soft-tooling methods.

22. *Dipping.* This process simply dips a softened rubber around a shaping mold. It is commonly used to produce products such as rubber gloves, balloons, and condoms.

23. *Pouring/Casting.* This is a classically simple method of building prototypes by essentially pouring molten material into a low-cost mold and later adding resin to harden and cure the material. Generally, only materials with low melting points can be used for pouring, and dimensional accuracy is hard to maintain. Urethanes, foams, and thermosetting plastic materials would be good materials for this type of process. The part may not have less than three-millimeter walls due to the fact that many liquids will not pour into such small cracks (due to their viscosity). Some typical applications for pouring/casting are frames for wall clocks or mirrors, figurines, or other complex shapes. The process is the simplest of molding processes, yet it is time-consuming and messy. It becomes economical for higher volume production.

24. *Low-pressure Molding*. This type of molding can mean a lot of things. Some ceramics are economically made in this manner. The material can be injected, heated, cured, and then cooled to finish the part. The molds are cheaper since they don't require fortified materials, but the parts are more expensive than straight injection molding due to the extra curing steps necessary.

Permanent Tooling/Molds Required

25. *Hot/Cold Die Casting*. Die casting is a metal shaping process in which molten metal is forced into a reusable mold and held under pressure until solidification occurs. Of all the casting processes, die casting is considered the fastest. With cold casting, this process requires only minimal machining, but does leave ejector pin marks. It produces good dimensional accuracy, yet may produce small amounts of flash marks around the edges. Casting is for metals only (see Table 3). Hot casting is more specifically used for lower-melting-point alloys and has a higher production rate than cold casting.

26. *Injection Molding*. Injection molding is the most common molding process if you are interested in going into production (high quantities). It is a shaping process in which thermoplastic material is fed into a heated barrel, mixed, and forced into a mold cavity, where it cools and hardens to the configuration of the mold cavity. Molds are very costly, but in most can be used with the cheapest materials (see Table 3). Thermoplastic, thermoset, and even ceramics can be injection molded. Injection molding's per-piece prices are economical for simple as well as complex parts.

27. *Extrusion*. Extrusion is a plastic and thermoset shaping process in which only a continuous workpiece is produced by forcing molten plastic material through a shaped die orifice. As the hot plastic workpiece is carried along a conveyor, it is cooled and cut to the desired length. In essence, you can shape the X & Y directions, but the Z direction must be cut to length somewhere. Simple shapes, such as round pipes and square extrusions, are common for this method. More complex parts made by extrusions are tracks and profiles (binding for

holding down office wires). Extrusion is a very quick process, getting outputs as much as 180 lbs/hour of plastic material.

28. *Filament Winding.* Filament winding is a laminating process wherein pre-coated strands of roving woven tape, glass, graphite, or boron are wound over a mandrel and then heated and cured. The resulting composite part utilizes various winding patterns to create workpieces of exceptional strength-to-weight ratio. Some products such as airplane wings or pressure vessels are made by this method. It is an expensive method due to the winding and curing processes.

29. *Permanent Mold Casting.* This is a metal shaping process in which molten metal is introduced into a permanent (reusable) mold, under gravity or low pressure, and held until solidification occurs. Castings with this method have good strength, low porosity, and good dimensional accuracy. This method is not good for complex or irregular shapes. Complex shapes require considerable expense in mold design and fabrication. Casting tool costs in general are very high, which is similar to the cost of injection molding for plastics.

30. *Stamping.* Stamping essentially produces thin-walled (from 0.01 to 0.4 inches) metal shapes by physically punching and then rolling a piece of sheet metal around a particular mold. Molds as well as finished pieces from stamping are relatively cheap compared to other processes. The downfall is that your metal part must be thin-walled and not too complex. Examples of items that may be stamped are oil pans and soldering tool tips. Stamping works best for hollow or flat objects.

31. *Cold Heading.* This is a metal forging process used for rapidly producing enlarged (upset) portions on a piece of rod or wire held in a die. For example, the head of a bolt can be created by pounding a rod several times into a female-shaped cavity. No heating is used in this process. Because of their heads, bolts, rivets, and engine valves are made in this method.

32. *Deep Drawing.* This is another cold forming process in which a flat blank of sheet metal is shaped by the action of a punch forcing the metal into a die cavity. Deep drawing is a derivative of the stamping process. Boxes or cylindrical containers can be easily made from this method.

33. *Impact Extrusion.* This is a forming process that produces shapes by striking a cold slug of metal contained in a die cavity. The metal slug is forced to flow around a punch by a single high-speed blow. Toothpaste tubes, nozzles, and aluminum cans are commonly made from this method.

Cost of Prototyping Methods/Processes

Table 6 shows typical prices of parts and tooling for the methods I've just discussed. Another important factor to consider is the life of the mold. How long will it last before another one has to be made? As mentioned before, the price of molds and parts varies greatly based on many different factors. Because of this, I've given ballpark ranges so you can get a feel for the costs of such methods. You'll have to send your drawings to the manufacturers to get exact quotes.

All tooling/molding estimates included in the table are based on one-cavity (one-part) molds for making a piece about the size and shape of a large plastic screwdriver handle (*6" x 2" x 2" max*). Note that methods and prices may vary depending on your object's material, the accuracy needed, the quantity needed, the size, the cosmetics, the complexity of shape, the material of mold, and the thickness of walls. I'm also assuming that no exotic, expensive materials are being used.

Table 6. Cost of processes

Process	Price per Piece	Tool/Mold Cost (protoyping quantities)	Life of Tool/ Mold (in pieces made)
1. Machining	$100–$500	n/a	n/a
2. CNC Machining	$15–$100	set-up fee $1–2K	(for >5 pieces)
3. Screw Machines	$10–$100	set-up fee $1–2K	(for >5 pieces)
4. Stereolithography	$1000–$4000	n/a	n/a
5. Laser Sintering	$1000–$3500	n/a	n/a
6. LOM	$1000–$3500	n/a	n/a
7. FDM	$500–$1500	n/a	n/a
8. Fastening	<$100	n/a	n/a
9. Sculpting	>$200	n/a	n/a
10. Powder Compaction/ Molds	$1–$10	$5K–$10K	10–20K
11. Blow Molding	$.1–$10	$1K–$10K	<10K, or >100K[A]
12. Investment Casting	$5–$15	$1K–$5K	<100
13. Compression Molds	$.1–$10	$1K–$10K	<5K, or >100K[A]
14. Sand Casting	$5–$15	$1K–$5K	<100
15. Rotational Molding	$10–$30	$500–$5K	>20K
16. Thermoform Molding	$10–$30	$500–$5K	<5K, or >20K[A]
17. Vacuum Forming	$10–$30	$500–$5K	<5K, or >20K[A]
18. RTM	$.1–$10	$1K–$10K	<5K, or >100K[A]
19. RTV	$10–$30	$500–$5K	<100
20. RIM	$5–$15	$2K–$20K	>100K, or >1M[A]
21. Composite Tooling	$15–$30	$5K–$10K	<1K
22. Dipping	$.1–$2	$1K–$2K	<10K
23. Pouring/Casting	$5–$15	$500–$5K	<5K, or >100K[A]
24. Low Pressure Molding	$5–$15	$500–$5K	<5K
25. Hot/Cold Die Casting	$.1–$5	$15K–$40K	>50K
26. Injection Molding	$.1–$5	$15K–$40K	>50K
27. Extrusion	$.1–$5	$1K–$5K	>50K
28. Filament Winding	$5–$15	$15K–$40K	<20K
29. Permanent Mold Casting	$.1–$5	$15K–$40K	>20K
30. Stamping	$.1–$5	$5–$10K or 10–30K[A]	<5K or >40K[A]
31. Cold Heading	$.1–$5	$15–$40K	>20K
32. Deep Drawing	$.1–$5	$15–$40K	>20K
33. Impact Extrusion	$.1–$5	$15–$40K	>20K

[A] In many processes, the material or the application of the mold or tool can vary. Stronger molds will cost more to produce (multiply the "Tool/Mold" Cost two to three times), but produce these larger quantities. Weaker molds or manual applications of a mold may be much cheaper, yet produce fewer pieces before they erode.

Choosing the Processes That Work with Your Material

Table 7 contains a listing of materials and the processes that can be applied to each material. Many processes are specifically made for only certain materials. The numbers in the table correspond with the previous list.

Table 7. Processes for materials

Materials	Prototyping Processes Possible
Metals and alloys	1–3, 4–5 (soon), 8, 10, 12, 14, 25, 26, 29, 30–33
Polymers	1–5, 7–11, 13, 15–24, 26, 27
Ceramics and glasses	1–3, 8–10, 24, 26
Composites	1 (limited), 28

Good News About Materials and Prototyping Processes

As you can probably see from the last few sections, making any "perfect" decision on materials and prototyping methods can be a tough one. Your best bet is to make the most prudent decisions you can in consideration of your knowledge, wallet size, and time limitations. Don't panic; many products work fine with many different materials and prototyping methods. Also remember that you are only building a prototype. It doesn't have to work perfectly or even be to scale (although this is preferred). The main goal is to have a working model so people can feel something in their hands and get excited about it. Through my own past experience, after I sold my inventions, the manufacturing companies almost always *changed the materials and the design* of my original prototypes in preparation for full production. Of course, such changes are usually within the scope of the original patent.

Finding Prototyping Houses: Getting It Built for You

Now that you have a good idea of what materials and prototyping processes can work for you, it shouldn't be too difficult locating a prototype house that can do a quality job for you. If you have some money to spend, your design is complete, and you aren't capable of building your invention yourself, there are a wealth of companies that make prototypes and models of just about any-thing. To find a list of prototyping houses, look under the "Prototyping" heading in the *Thomas Register of American Manufacturers*. Inventors' Publishing & Research, LLC. (in the back of the book) can help you design and build a low-cost prototype if you need help.

The cost of prototyping, because of its manual nature, can be from 10 to 20 times more than production pieces made from high production molds (see Table 6), so be ready to spend between a few hundred dollars and a few thou-sand dollars depending on how complicated your part is. For example, if you were to prototype a plastic toy Power Ranger (7 inches tall) through the method of "machining," this would cost anywhere between $500 and $1,000 per item depending on the detail and quantity involved. However, if you have a piece that is simple, small, and symmetrical (for example, a metal protective cap for a BB gun), it may only cost you $100/piece. Shop rates (labor rates) for prototyping houses run anywhere from $40 to $70 per hour (this includes their profit), not including any set-up time that may be involved.

To get an estimate of how much a prototype will cost, prototyping houses multiply the shop rate by the estimated labor time for one piece. If you have any set-up or mold or tooling prices for the particular prototyping method you're interested in, the company will usually amortize these costs into the price per piece for the quantity you desire. Ask them to separate the set-up or tooling costs so you can get a good idea of the actual cost of the labor for the particular prototyping process. This way you'll be able to compare the effi-ciency and cost-effectiveness of various prototyping methods for your partic-ular invention, quantity, and materials involved. If you send them detailed drawings of your piece, they can usually fax you quotes within a day or so.

To ensure quality, prototyping houses guarantee their work to the specifi-cations and drawings that you provide. You will find that the necessity of having a prototype to show potential corporations outweighs the high labor costs of prototyping houses, especially if you don't have the know-how to personally build your invention yourself.

One final note: It's often important not only to build a prototype but also to test market it. For the purposes of this chapter, these strategies have been treated separately; but you should bear in mind that they frequently go hand in hand. For a full discussion of test marketing, see the next chapter, "Step 5."

Building Your Invention Yourself

If you consider yourself fairly knowledgeable in the area of your invention and you are not afraid to work with your hands, you should consider building it yourself. Most inventions have solid parts unique to its shapes and can be "carved" out with the proper machinery (the "machining" method discussed in the previous section). Whether the unique parts are made out of plastic, metal, foam, sheet metal, wood, or other solids, there exists a wealth of machinery in the world to carve out such parts. In actual production, such parts would typically be made from a mold that could be used over and over again for high volume. In prototyping however, such parts are typically handmade due to the high initial expense of molds and the volatile state of early invention design. If your invention falls in the common category that requires the construction of carvable parts, you can learn how to use the applicable machinery and build the prototypes yourself. This would most likely save you hundreds of dollars, and additionally keep you in close touch with your invention.

Types of Prototyping Machinery

Lathes

The lathe is a very common machine that allows you to carve out symmetrical parts. On a lathe, your raw piece of plastic (or whatever material you may be working with) is secured in a spindle device and rotates. You can then very accurately carve the spinning piece from the outside or inside with stationary cutting devices mounted separately. Incongruent pieces or more complicated pieces will typically require the use of milling machines. Anyone can learn how to use the lathe, but the actual carving process will take much patience and care.

Access: local universities, private businesses, machinery rentals.

Cost: If you want to buy your own lathe, the average cost of an industrial lathe is around $5,000 to $10,000. You can find smaller, used units for around $1,000 that you can work with in a garage.

Mills

The mill is another common carving machine that allows you to design practically any shape imaginable. It handles the incongruent parts that a lathe does not. In a mill, the actual cutting tools rotate (like a drill press). The raw piece is placed in a clamping device, which can be moved in X, Y, and Z directions while being cut by the rotating cutting tools. It requires more time and skill than a lathe, but is capable of producing perfect results.

Access: local universities, private businesses, machinery rentals.

Cost: If you want to buy your own mill, the average cost of an industrial mill is around $5,000 to $15,000, but you can find smaller, used units for around $1,000 that you can work with in a garage.

CNC Mills

CNC mills are computer-controlled mills that automatically carve parts from a sequence of computer instructions programmed into the internal computer. It takes good understanding of milling and the tools to program the CNC mill, yet the payback is an automatic capability of producing many prototype pieces.

Access: private companies who use them.

Cost: Minimum $20,000.

Wood Shop

There are many carving and crafting tools that are available to cut wood. Unfortunately, wood is probably one of the more difficult materials to work with. Wood easily chips and burns, and it takes much skill to carve out wood in detail. Machines that are common in working with wood are skill saws, belt sanders, band saws, files, wood lathes, and many other hand-held tools.

Access: high schools, colleges, friends, private companies, machinery rentals.

Cost: Wood machinery can run anywhere from $200 to $1,000 depending on how upscale the machinery is. Hand-held tools used to carve wood are fairly cheap, ranging from $20 to $60.

Sheet Metal/Welding

If your invention includes pieces made out of very thin metal, there are a number of devices for sheet metal manipulation: benders, clippers, cutters, hole punchers, and spot welding machines. Such machinery is very easy to use and does not require a lot of skill or training.

Access: high schools, colleges, private companies, machinery rentals.

Cost: Sheet metal machinery, such as benders and large cutters, are fairly expensive: greater than $1,000. Hand-held clippers and other such devices are cheaper, running less than $100.

Reproducing Electronic Circuit Boards

One technology that allows you to reproduce circuit boards is called *silk screening*. Silk-screening kits are very inexpensive ($20 to $100), and essentially allow you to reproduce prototype circuit boards. After you've made copies of the circuit boards, you then have to solder all the necessary devices manually onto the circuit boards. If you're going to make many circuit board prototypes, you may want to acquire a "pick and place" machine to mount the devices on the board, but such machinery will run you a minimum of $2,000. If you don't have time to manually solder all the devices on the board, there are PCB houses that can do the job for you at shop rates of about $50 to $60/hour.

Test Marketing and Customer Feedback

The Advantages of Test Marketing

Even after you've finished your prototype, it still may not be enough to convince a company that your product will be a smash hit in the marketplace. You may also have to satisfy a company of your invention's potential by test-marketing the product yourself. Companies will want you to prove that there's a high demand for your product—and, therefore, that it will sell. Before buying into your product, a company will consider two things: Will the world be the richer for this product, or will the company be the poorer? The aim of your test marketing is to prompt a tentative "yes" to the first question, and a firm "no" to the second. No smart company is going to turn down a product that makes it see a growing dollar sign. However, they will be reluctant to spend money on a product they think might flop. It's your job to convince them that won't happen.

Remember how I turned my luck around after the first trade show by taking my idea one step further and building a prototype? Well, that wasn't my only clever tactic. I also brought proof of my invention's sales potential to the next trade show. Like me, you must eliminate every possible excuse a company could have for rejecting your invention. The point of testing the market yourself is to demonstrate (1) that your product draws *positive customer feedback*, and (2) that people don't just find your product exciting—they *buy* it.

The Best Test-Marketing Method for You

There are essentially two ways to test a market: the *traditional* approach, and the *simulated* approach. The traditional approach replicates nationwide distribution by launching the test product on a large scale, such as in a particular city or group of cities (the "target markets"). A target-market plan can enhance consumer demand for the test product, just as it would for a "real" product. A thorough plan of this sort requires substantial research because it must be revised and updated continually to improve sales. This approach also allows a company to analyze and predict a good deal about your product's performance than it could otherwise. Moreover, because a traditional approach is the most comprehensive way to test your product's market, it best addresses key considerations such as:

- Market segmentation
- Purchasing and buying patterns
- Means of distribution
- Advertising availability

On the other hand, advocates of the second test-marketing method, simulated test marketing (STM), argue that the traditional method has serious drawbacks, including high cost, long duration, release of ideas, and failure to provide solid information. To make it easier, scale down traditional testing to just one particular city or suburb of a city (perhaps the one you live in) to make it affordable. You can make a deal with retailers in your city such that they will display your product and take orders for you in exchange for a store space fee. If you still find this difficult, those who favor STM claim that simulated testing replaces those problems with low cost, short duration, product confidentiality, and reliable, full-scale market results. While specific STMs vary, in a typical one:

- Respondents are screened at a centrally located facility, and only those who satisfy selection criteria for market segmentation are asked to participate.
- Participants are shown commercials or print ads for both the test product and other products, whether competitive or noncompetitive.
- They can then purchase products in either real or simulated store settings. Unpurchased test products may be given to participants as free samples.

- After a set time, participants are contacted again to find out how well the product worked and what incentives they would need to buy it again.

As you may already have realized, STM isn't easy sailing. Some disadvantages of this method are:

- It does not take into account competition, so it is not a true picture of the product's performance in the market. STM just cannot predict as accurately as traditional, full-scale testing.
- Since STM doesn't provide long-term testing, it's difficult for it to predict broad-based consumer product reactions.
- STM destroys the possibility of unbiased product selection amongst competitors by choosing particular customers and then influencing and manipulating them into buying the product being tested.

Because STM must either assume or omit key aspects of real-world marketing, traditional testing that comes as close as possible to full-scale test-marketing gives a more accurate picture.

But, shhhhh . . . Don't tell anyone about the disadvantages of your test marketing. When it comes right down to it, all you want is *sales, no matter how you get them* (of course, within the bounds of the law). I guarantee you that if you can sell more than a couple hundred of your products through your test-marketing efforts, companies will become interested and won't nit-pick about the theoretical disadvantages of your test-marketing scheme (even if you lost money!). Rather, they will see dollar signs in your efforts and will want to license your patent for their own use! If you sell more than 1,000 units on your own, you will most likely be guaranteed in getting the number one company in your inventions' industry to offer you a large contract deal. If you can afford to do test marketing to some degree or level, you will see that your personal returns from your invention are directly proportional to the amount of sales you've managed through the test marketing. This is because the more sales you have, the greater evidence you have to prove your product's potential. With this evidence, you can attract the top companies, and the more top companies you attract, the better your negotiating position with them will be. This becomes very important when it's time to negotiate a big royalty contract.

Customer Feedback

Of course, both approaches to test marketing require a tremendous investment of work and resources and therefore may not be right for you. If that is the case, don't worry, because you still may be able to sell your patent rights without getting sales. To do so, however, you will almost always need proof of positive customer feedback (in addition to your prototype, of course).

If you don't have proof of sale, companies may say, "We're not sure of the market potential of your product," or "We're not sure there is a market for your product." Established companies are typically conservative and only make decisions from hard facts and proven data. Many companies will be skeptical of the advantages claimed by your invention. They may say, "We need to see how people really *feel* about your product." The best way to turn their doubts around is to demonstrate your *positive customer feedback.*

Customer feedback is powerful data. There you were, tinkering in your garage one day, when boredom began to descend. So you just happened to whip up, shall we say, a flexible image magnetostatic ultraviolet transillumination satellite. Not bad for a day's work. Still, you ask yourself, what will other people think of this invention? You realize that you need some immediate customer feedback. So you go see your next-door neighbor, a professional landscaper. Wrong! You might go to that neighbor if you invent a sprinkler head. For a satellite, however, you need NASA.

The point of my little parable? No company will take you seriously unless you have *expert customer feedback* for your invention. Who's an expert? Someone who is a professional in the field of your invention. How do you locate these experts? Easy. Think about where your invention will be used. For example, where would you go for customer feedback on a new state-of-the-art, radar-guided mop you've just invented? Would you approach homemakers in the mop aisle of a local store? Possibly, but this approach is often unsuccessful. Yes, homemakers know their mops; they can probably even let you in on some good mopping secrets. Even so, approaching them could be a hassle and could backfire. Why? Because when people are accosted by a stranger in a store, their guards do go up. They become suspicious, self-interested, and impatient. Usually, they won't take the time to listen to you or to answer your questions. They don't know where the whole ordeal of your questioning is leading, and they do not want to stick around to find out.

When I suggest to you that customer feedback must come from an expert, I mean a *company* that *uses* a product similar to your invention every day. So, for expert hassle-free customer feedback, the best method would be to take the radar mop to a housecleaning company. A company that not only works with a product similar to yours but also depends on it every day should want to try out new products that might be more efficient and easier to use.

For example, I took my FingerTip Soldering Iron to Intel, a company that manufactures breakthrough computer technology, where eager engineers who work daily with soldering irons found my invention extremely useful. The engineers even pointed out a few of the benefits of my invention that I hadn't considered. After all, these were the people who worked with soldering irons for a living—they knew their stuff!

Questionnaires and Customer Feedback

The best way to collect customer feedback data for your invention is to have all your test customers fill out a questionnaire specific to your product. If you get customer feedback in person, they may not always be completely honest in an effort to avoid hurting your feelings. If all you want is positive feedback, then the oral route might be better for you, but the downfall is that you have no documented data handwritten by actual customers. Such written questionnaires can also be an impressive paper mound that you can submit to an interested potential manufacturer of your invention.

After the test customers fill out the questionnaires, it is often a good idea to contact them to invoke a conversation and get a better overall feel for their opinion. In addition, within the questionnaire, you can gain some partial proof of sale by asking the individual or company whether or not they would consider purchasing your invention. You don't actually get the commitment, but these *promised* sales are much easier to get then *actual* sales, and they still pull much in your favor as "proof of market" data for inquiring potential companies who are interested in acquiring your patent rights.

In general, a cleverly written questionnaire:

- Gives the participating company the option of stating that it would buy the product without binding it to a legal agreement—thus alleviating any suspicious feelings of overcommitment
- Fosters participation because it's easy and requires less work on the part of the other party, who might be turned off if asked to write an evaluation of your invention
- Is thought of as accurate, truthful, and less biased, partly because companies use them themselves to obtain product information
- Allows for uniformity, giving participants the same questions in the same order, and doing away with unwelcome comments

Questionnaires often lead to future product study by a potential patent buyer by calling attention to what the company liked best about your invention, and asking it to suggest improvements.

Approaching Companies

The Initial Approach

Before you start approaching companies, you should have completed, or be in the process of completing, the methods laid out in Steps 3 through 5:

- From your patent market research plan, you should know the key players in your industry and where to contact them. You should also have learned which company can best meet your expectations for your product. (Step 3)
- You should have a prototype or model. (Step 4)
- You should have customer feedback and be involved in test-marketing your product. (Step 5)

It's possible to sell your patent without some of those elements, but it is usually difficult. Even if you managed to succeed without all of the recommended elements, it's likely that your negotiating position would be much less favorable. That would leave you with a final royalty deal that would be much less profitable to you. The items discussed in Steps 3 through 5 will give you the knowledge and proof not only to find companies that will buy into your patent, but also to give you a strong and confident negotiating position so that you can get the most profitable royalty contract when it comes down to business.

Before we proceed with Step 6, let me emphasize again that allowing a company to handle your invention (Step 2) can reduce your financial risk and make you a great deal of money. Because winning companies deal daily with large-scale production and distribution, they've already mastered the technique of squeezing maximum profits out of products—and they have the financing to make it work!

No company is going to want your product unless it knows that you and it exist. That means you have to get the right company's attention. There are several ways to approach a major company, but not all of them are worth mentioning. Step 6 cuts through the bologna to teach you only those methods that have been *proven* to work.

One important note: Sending blind submissions to corporations *never* works and will lead you to universal rejection. Most companies won't even look at your inventions or read your letters. You must have personal contact and rapport with a company before you even think about telling them about your idea. The following methods are the most effective ways to get a manufacturer interested.

Trade Shows

Approaching a company for the first time may be an uneasy experience for you, especially when so much is riding on the results. It helps to know there's a single place where you can find many major companies at once: the *trade show*. I can't stress enough how important trade shows can be in your campaign to win over a giant company.

Company employees look forward to attending trade shows so they can get away from stressful deadlines and weighty responsibilities. Most reps are easy-going, taken in by all the excitement, eager to learn about new inventions, and ready to give you their time once you capture their interest.

You can find out where trade shows are held by calling a company that interests you and asking where it goes to show its products. You can also look through *Trade Shows World Wide 1995: International Directory of Events, Facilities, and Suppliers*.

When you attend a trade show, you might want to open a booth of your own. Typically, a space costs $800 to $10,000 to rent, varying on size. This is a small price to pay considering the return you could realize on your investment. Once you've set up your booth, your first move should be to start demonstrating your invention. To get a good spot on a tradeshow floor, you have to go for several years because it works by seniority. But you can make your booth stand out by buying a large one and making it very flashy. Hiring celebrities and models attracts attention. You can also advertise in the tradeshow directory or floor intercom.

A word of caution: At first, *don't allow a company rep to borrow your prototype.* Even if a fascinated crowd has gathered around your booth for a peek at your invention, don't make the mistake of getting caught up in all the hoopla and loaning out your prototype. Even though most reps have honest intentions, a few rotten apples exist—and it only takes one to copy your idea and steal it away from you.

If a rep does ask to "borrow" your prototype, stay cool and be professional. Explain that you have only *one* prototype and you can't afford to let it leave your hands. Try to set up a future time when you can visit the company and give a presentation on your product. If they're interested, they may even offer to pick up the tab for your travel expenses (If not, the expenses would be tax-deductible, like all business expenses). Also, be sure to offer *all* reps additional information on your invention, so they have something to take back and show their company presidents. You will need to prepare this information before the show, and make sure you have plenty of copies on hand. Be sure to include the following:

- A copy of your patent.
- An attractive, accurate color photograph of your invention, on a durable sheet of coated paper. On the reverse side, describe how to use your invention, explain its main advantages, and answer the most frequently asked questions about it.
- A summary of your customer feedback and/or test-marketing results based on your product evaluation questionnaires. Remember, use only expert positive customer feedback and provide proof of sale.

If you don't rent out a booth, or if company representatives aren't visiting your booth, you should pay them all visits at their booths. Stop by their booths and show off your prototype. Then hand out your product information and offer to give a presentation for the key members of the company.

Telephone Conversations

The phone call is the most common way to contact companies—and it can work. But before you pick up that receiver, remember that you'll only have a few minutes at most to make a lasting impression on a busy business professional. So be clever not only about what you say but also about how you say it. Do your utmost to come across as someone who is confident, intelligent, credible, and well-versed in sales techniques. The last thing you want is to have nothing you say come out right. If you're nervous, jot down some notes you can refer to, and practice what you plan to say in advance. When you do call, ask to speak with the "new products manager." If the company is small, your call may be forwarded directly to a vice president or president. To achieve quick results, it's important that you get through to top executives.

So there you are with a leading corporate manager—who is clearly in a hurry—on the other end of the line. What do you say? In a few short sentences, you must sell your idea, explain how your invention fits into their company's plans, and show how it can mean "big bucks" for their company. Here are points you should cover to strengthen your position:

- Mention that you received overwhelming customer feedback and testimony.
- Talk about trade shows and conventions where you've showed-off your product.
- State the main advantages of your invention and point out why they are significant.
- Warn them that some of their competitors are interested in buying your patent from you and that there is widespread interest in your product. (You can name company names if you'd like.)
- Indicate that, based on customer feedback, your prototype has gone through many generations and reached a level of high quality.
- Explain how your invention triumphs over its competition.
- Reveal your test-marketing results, disclosing proof of sale and high product demand and market share.
- Describe your credentials and outline your experience in the field of your invention.
- Ask when you can visit the company to give a product presentation.

- Offer to fax your patent, marketing plan, and any brochures about your invention (this will give you a reason to follow up).
- Let the person you speak with know you're serious about working with the company.

Other Considerations to Bring Up While Speaking to Manufacturers

The best way to arouse a company's curiosity can be to emphasize that your invention has already undergone significant development. Then, if you're turned down in your request for a visit, you can arrange to send your prototype for the company to evaluate.

A company may try to protect itself against litigation, however, by requiring you to waive your rights during the evaluation period. A waiver leaves you with no rights against a company that uses your invention without your permission. The only right you do retain in that situation is your right against patent infringement, which you automatically obtain when the PTO approves your patent.

Obviously, then, I recommend against signing a waiver. To convince the company you're the "real thing," you may want to offer credible references that testify to your honesty. If nothing else seems to work and the company still insists upon a waiver, ask for a certified written document in advance requiring your prototype to be returned to you by a given date. Once you have it, send your prototype by certified mail and get insurance.

Company Presentations

A company presentation should arise out of an initial meeting with *key representatives* through either trade shows or phone calls. Visiting a company should always be your last step—and sometimes it's the only way—to close the sale and convince a company to handle your invention.

Again, a company that has already expressed interest in your invention may be willing to cover your travel costs.

Once you have your foot in the door, be ready for key company players to make on-the-spot decisions about whether they want your invention. And be prepared to give the demonstration of your life! Combine all the materials and techniques you would use in a trade show or phone conversation into a single powerful presentation. And don't forget to invite company reps to handle your prototype for as long as they like, and if they insist on keeping it after you leave, give them a limited time in which they must return it, one or two weeks, and get the promise in writing.

Even the most dynamic presentation, however, gets you only half way to doing the job right, because you still haven't closed the sale. After your presentation, sit down with your original company contact and any other key players and thoroughly address any major concerns about your invention that have come up in your presentation or in earlier discussions. For instance, business executives are inclined to express the following concerns:

1. *Flaws in your prototype.* This should not really become an issue until the company builds the final version. Let the manufacturer know that this is an in-progess model, and describe to them the differences that you would make in the final model.

2. *Necessary modifications of your product that are needed to fit their company personality.* Assure them that you will address these issues if the company doesn't.

3. *Petty disapproval of your product.* This is usually a figment of their imaginations due to the fact that your invention was not invented at that company. Let them know their competitors are interested in your invention, so they should take you seriously, or else they may have to compete with it.

4. *Anxiety over the market potential for your product.* Offer to review your customer feedback and/or test-marketing results with them; this should help allay these concerns.

Overall, your goal is to sidestep all these barriers by reassuring company members that such issues are *minor* concerns that can be *overcome*. Promise to get back to them in a week or two with solutions *in hand* to any problems you can't solve on the spot.

Remember also to keep in regular contact with a company rep, so you can resolve any outstanding issues. If you satisfy all the company's needs and convince it that your product has a *sizable* market, your next task may be to accept a royalty agreement offer!

Dealing with Rejection

As I mentioned in the previous section, some companies may reject your invention simply on the grounds that their people did not think of it first. It's important not to take this kind of rejection personally; companies like these just dislike venturing beyond the boundaries of inside management.

Another common reason for rejection is that a company already handles a *similar* or *competing* product. Again, don't take it personally—no company dares to undermine its own sales efforts. If you find yourself in this situation, switch companies fast! You may find that after there is widespread approval of your product, that same company may change its mind about your invention. After all, it's better for them to acquire your patent than to compete against it!

Your invention may also be rejected because it's not compatible with a company's direction and goals. Again, make sure you research the company you're approaching thoroughly before you propose doing business together.

It's also possible that a company may reject your product because it's already overinvested in itself and can't afford to take on outside inventions. In that case, move on to another company but keep in touch; the company may decide to buy your invention later.

Finally, a company may turn you down because it's unsure of the market for your invention. Here, your test marketing results should help clear up any doubts.

Step 7

Negotiating Agreements

Negotiating Skills

More than 90 percent of all profit-driven patentable inventions, from the high-tech to the simple, become real products as a result of negotiation. That makes good bargaining skills one of your most important assets when it comes time to make the best possible deal for yourself

Like most things, negotiation has a beginning, a middle, and an end. In the beginning phase, the parties seek information about each other's positions in order to identify the issues that separate them. Simply put, they test the waters. In the middle phase of a negotiation, both sides make preliminary offers, swap concessions, and try to find a plan that satisfies their differences. In the final phase, they confirm what they've gained in their negotiations, draft final agreements, and do away with any remaining deadlocks.

If you think this process sounds like too much for you to handle, you're wrong. Mastering the art of negotiation does take some time, but it can be learned with practice.

On the other hand, you may not want to take the risk of negotiating yourself. Professional negotiators, which you can hire for a 5–15% cut, have been known to increase inventors' profits more than 100–200% compared to an inexperienced negotiator. You make the call. Negotiating takes years of experience, so although you need to learn it, it would be foolish to go into a multi-million dollar deal if you were very "green" in experience.

Negotiation Skill 1: Intelligence

What I mean by *intelligence* is simply good common sense. What comprises that magical quality? The ability to acquire and understand information selectively, to analyze it logically, and to arrive at successful conclusions. Only you really know, of course, whether you have what it takes to show good common sense.

Negotiation Skill 2: Knowledge

Knowledge can be more easily acquired than common sense. It includes (1) identifying the main principles that shape negotiation so you can anticipate your opponents' moves and stay one step ahead of them; (2) using tactics to beat your opponents at their own game.

Not to worry—I won't abandon you here! This chapter will take you through the 10 key principles and 9 topnotch tactics of someone who's learned about negotiation the hard way, through trial and error: me. I found that while there are many so-called "principles" and "tactics" of negotiation, only a few actually work. I'll share those principles and tactics with you here.

Negotiation Skill 3: Experience

This third trait is something you'll acquire, by definition, during the negotiation process. You may already have more experience at negotiating than you realize. Remember when you convinced a friend to do things your way, persuaded a car dealer to lower the price, or satisfied a bank that you qualify for a discount home-equity loan? These kinds of experiences have probably made you a better negotiator than you think. So whatever happens, don't panic. Keep in mind that you'll do just fine. For some extra reassurance, try reading Herb Cohen's helpful book, *You Can Negotiate Anything*. Just make sure to avoid books written by academics with scant experience in business negotiation outside the classroom.

Ten Key Negotiation Principles

1. *The first rule is that there are no rules.* Since each negotiation is different—involving particular parties and a specific set of issues—there are no universal rules for the process. The interaction between negotiators does not rely on any absolute guidelines. Just the opposite, negotiators may do anything. That's why the negotiation process can at any moment become baffling and unpredictable, taking you by surprise. It might help to think of negotiation as a big bureaucracy that only spells out prohibitions, not possibilities. That is, it always tells you what you can't do, but never how to get around the rules and reach your goals. Just remember that a successful negotiation calls for cooperation and agreement on both sides. If one party's aims are hopelessly out of synch with the other's, coming to an agreement is about as likely as growing a cactus garden in a rain forest.

2. *It takes two to come to terms.* It stands to reason, therefore, that you can negotiate successfully only by interacting well with the other side. That goes for many aspects of your communication, especially reporting factual development, proving your analysis, and interpreting those facts into a legal basis for a contract. Negotiation, however, is rarely based upon rational discussion alone. Underlying emotional factors always play a key role. To communicate effectively, you must understand the other party's attitudes, motives, and goals, as well as how they affect you. Also, be careful when you make decisions—a poor decision will always come back to haunt you!

3. *Control yourself.* Good negotiators have self-discipline. Although they are partial, they remain objective. That's because they know that personal attacks only add to problems, and that aggression breeds aggression. So avoid losing your cool; it's unprofessional and impedes good decision making. A corollary of this principle is that taking a cynical stance only prompts the other side to do the same. Negotiation works best when it's firm but friendly. Also keep in mind that, if you're going to use promises or "treats," they must be appraised, comprehended, and believed before they can be taken seriously. So it pays to be credible. Wise negotiators neither promise too much nor

threaten too little, and either tactic should be based in the desire to work toward agreement.

4. *Agenda, agenda, agenda.* The agenda set at the start of negotiations affects the outcome of the agreement. Whoever controls the agenda has a better chance of achieving favorable results for several reasons. First, if you set the agenda, you can define and limit the issues in dispute. Second, controlling the agenda allows you to establish priorities so you can move the company's issues to the bargaining table while keeping yours on the back burner. Third, once the other side accepts your agenda, you're in a position to know the key issues in advance, which gives you time to prepare persuasive arguments.

5. *Understand the theory of negotiations.* To be a successful negotiator, you must understand the basic conceptual goal of the process. In any dispute that uses negotiation to resolve issues, each side has a preferred outcome and a bottom line. You might think of the distance between the parties as a continuum of each other's desired outcomes and bottom lines. Your goal as a negotiator, then, becomes twofold: to get your opponent to think that your bottom line is closer to the opponent's preferred outcome than it actually is; and to get your opponent to reassess his or her own bottom line, moving it further away from the desired outcome.

6. *Learn to love compromise.* No issue ever stands alone, for the simple reason that a decision on any single issue always affects others. That's why good negotiators use a strategy of compromise to settle issues of concern and reach their desired goals. Compromise plays an indispensable part in the process of negotiation because no agreement can be reached satisfactorily without it. At its most basic, *compromise* means trading concessions, which in turn have important psychological effects. Concessions establish trust and encourage cooperation through mutual obligation. Generally, the structure and scope of any negotiation reflect the issues involved, which may either address the interests of both parties or provide an advantage for one side at the other's expense. In either case, the issues will have different degrees of importance for each side, making compromise the sine qua non of negotiation.

7. *Beware the critical point.* In every negotiation, the parties establish minimum expectations, which may change as the process goes. This lowest level is called the party's "critical point." It, in turn, sets the limit of each party's bargaining range. Agreement can only occur when each party has attained or surpassed its critical point, which usually happens when the parties believe they've extracted the final concession from each other. If, on the other hand, a party's critical level exceeds what the other party can sacrifice, no agreement will be made. Such may be the case even when both parties want desperately to come to accord. Near the end of a negotiation, one side often reaches its critical point before the other. When this happens, the party that's "behind" cannot make more concessions, while the party that's "ahead" finds itself with even more room to maneuver. In that situation, the responsibility for concluding the agreement falls on the party that has already made satisfactory gains.

8. *Don't be afraid to fall back.* Clever negotiators establish fallback positions as negotiations go along, ranging from their opening stances to their bottom lines. Falling back is the inevitable result of demands and concessions, which you should always plan carefully and whose impact you should assess in advance. As bargaining takes place and concession-trading occurs, the shape of the negotiation alters—which means that either party's bottom line can change. Whether it changes for the better depends on the skill of the negotiator. Unforeseen problems can also arise during discussions. If they do, don't feel obligated to "fix the problem" immediately by conceding. Remember that you'll probably regret on-the-spot decisions later. In other words, don't change your position just because the other party suggests it or persuades you to do so. It's important to bear in mind that every move of either party calls for adapting to new conditions, which, again, should be carefully thought out before they are implemented.

9. *Know the way out.* Good negotiators maintain escape routes for themselves and other parties. If the opposition backs itself into a corner, a smart negotiator will help it find a way out. A gesture of help may also come as a deceptive compromise, which creates the impression that the other party negotiated its way out of difficulty. Never forget that

the most important consideration is for both sides to win, in the sense that they leave the negotiating table with an agreement they can live with. That is, nothing about the agreement will come back to haunt either side. Simply put, negotiation is not a battle that should end with a winner and a loser. This mutual benefit should be reflected in the final agreement, which should summarize clearly what both sides have gained. It's unlikely that an even compromise will be reached, since negotiation rarely results in a 50-50 outcome, but it should be apparent that both parties would have fared worse without negotiation. The outcome of a negotiation seldom reflects the true bargaining strength of either side.

10. *To negotiate is not to agree.* A party's willingness to negotiate does not necessarily indicate its willingness to reach agreement. One side may only be interested in taking the other for all it's worth, for example, by spying to boost its competitive advantage or by using negotiations as a front for its larger strategy of attracting more bidders to the table. Deceptive negotiation is like a grenade with the pin pulled. The longer you hold the grenade in your hand, the greater your chances of having it explode. And when that happens, the consequences can be deadly. No company takes kindly to dishonest negotiations. Once it catches on, you can kiss your chances of working with it again good-bye. And the damage might not be limited to one company—since companies make it a point to know each other's business, word of a deceptive negotiator travels fast. You could lose your credibility in the entire field of business. So avoid taking a chance; deceptive negotiating could backfire and ruin your reputation.

Nine Winning Tactics

1. *Get your negotiating opponent working on your invention.* It's in your interest to have a company invest more and more time in your invention because that will make it want to come to terms with you and to buy into your invention. Time investment is especially important in the early phases of negotiation when a company determines whether it can work with you. If it decides that you're incapable of negotiating

competently, it will end negotiations! So get a company committed to your invention by involving it with engineering, design, test marketing, product evaluation, advertising, and so forth.

2. *Only negotiate with higher-ups.* At some point in negotiations, a company is bound to express disappointment with your progress. Don't let it bluff you! Its disparagement may only be part of its overall strategy to exploit you by making you do as much of its work as possible. Even if you exceed a company's expectations and do everything just right, it will always demand more. Most likely, you'll work with its engineers or managers when negotiations begin. These engineers or managers, often of lower rank in a large company, deliberately set stumbling blocks that can be aggravating, trifling, and painstaking for you to surmount. They may ask you to fix minor flaws in your prototype, for instance, to reduce the manufacturing cost of your product, or to find solutions to potential legal problems. Whatever they throw your way, persist; once you meet with a higher-ranking representative, your problems will disappear! Presidents and CEOs have the authority to let you bypass minor concerns, and they know you've already been through the ringer with their engineers. They don't have time to nit-pick; they just want what's best for the company. And that means they'll personally take care of any problem that arises if they want you and your invention.

3. *Make concessions for gains, not losses.* The single most important advice about giving in to demands is this: don't! Instead, trade concessions on your part for equal concessions on your opponent's part. By making all offers conditional, you gain several advantages. First, you enhance your reputation as an expert negotiator. Second, you let it be known that you can't be cheated. Third, you deter your opponent from seeking too many concessions. Fourth, you achieve favorable results faster. And remember that concession-trading should occur on a range of issues, rather than a single issue, which holds little importance in the overall context of a negotiation. Addressing only one issue at a time may prevent you from getting to other important issues before negotiations sag. So *never* make concessions or changes out of fear, haste, or panic. Instead, use *straw* issues as concessions, saving

your most costly concessions for later. A straw issue has no importance to anyone; you only pretend that it costs you dearly. Your goal
is to get the other side to sympathize with your "losses" by giving in
to your demands.

4. *Allow "mistakes" to get you where you want to go.* This tactic translates to
passing the buck. That is, you can pass some of the concessions you
offered—even though you knew you could not make good on them—
onto the opposing party by playing it dumb. You accepted the compromise because you couldn't resist what the other side offered in
return, only to fall short of your side of the bargain later, forcing your
opponent to take over.

Negotiations with large firms is real hardball. As sad as it is,
many people use lying when they're negotiating to get what they
want. A deal can mean millions of dollars and hundreds of people's
jobs on the line. That's why many top negotiators play dirty. I recommend being a great negotiator and being completely honest. It's
kind of the difference between a good car salesman and a used car
salesman; they both may sell a lot of cars, but their tactics are totally
different.

Before trying this tactic, you should be absolutely certain that it
has a good chance to succeed. The last thing you want is to be stuck
with an impossible promise. To determine whether this plan will
work, ask yourself the following questions. Is my concession something the company already handles daily, making it indispensable for
the company's survival? Am I convinced that the company will be
willing to take over my concession? If you can confidently answer
"yes" to both questions, then go ahead. Just remember that giving in
to the concession is only half the scheme; you still need to toss it back
into your opponent's lap. When reneging on your concession, make
sure you *never* ask the opposing party to take over: Get *it* to ask you.
Explain that when you accepted the terms, you were convinced that
you would be able to live up to your end of the bargain. After trying
and making some progress, however, you eventually realized that
accomplishing the task was harder than you'd imagined and that you
just don't have the resources to finish. The other side will believe you

because you're only one individual, and—most important—it will offer to complete the concession for you.

5. *Create a bargaining climate that gives you the advantage.* It's best to start negotiations with your eyes on the prize, putting any personal feelings aside. Again, it's in your interest to take a firm but friendly stance. Often ignored, however, is the importance of building trust—which means demonstrating your dependability, proficiency, and credibility to your opponent. I'll let you in on a little secret: Too many people do take negotiations personally, or at least they behave as if they do. So I'm going to share with you my six-step process for overcoming any personal tone and keeping the process as objective as possible.

   - State your interests clearly and use evidence to back up your demands.
   - Begin with common ground that favors the interests of both parties.
   - Use the progress made on matters of common ground to defuse, compromise, and move past disagreements.
   - Give the other side a way out if it backs itself into a corner.
   - Restate points of agreement as you go along, making sure that each side understands what's expected of the other.
   - Nail the agreement down by establishing deadlines for parties to perform.

   These steps set the stage for objective negotiating. Let me repeat a final word of caution: *Never* resort to a "take it or leave it" approach.

6. *Guarantee your greatest gain by securing the best offer.* The most important thing to remember as you undertake negotiations is that the other side will take you for all you're worth if possible by offering less. So, as a rule of thumb, do *not* accept first offers; hold out for something better. To elicit that better offer—one that satisfies your requirements—you need only to make it appear that the value of your invention has risen. You may do so by increasing the demand for your invention by starting a bidding war between companies for your invention. To go about this without offending the company you've started negotiating with, get them to invite you to trade shows and to include your invention in their display booth. You can say to them, "I think you don't realize the value of my invention; let's go to a trade show and get some feedback from

your potential customers." Once you set foot on a trade show floor, a bidding war will break out for two reasons. First, and most obvious, is that your invention means profit, which companies desire. Second, because you're already working with a company but you are not yet committed, its sponsorship draws interest from other companies. Some may compete over your invention by bidding for it. The company you began with may start to feel the pressure and ante-up its offer. Or it may persuade you to sign on by speeding up negotiations. Just don't forget to play it safe: You *never* forced it to make a better offer—it was those other companies!

7. *Avoid punishment by changing the subject.* In any negotiation, a time may come when you don't live up to your end of the bargain, and your opponent demands an explanation. How you reply greatly affects your bargaining strength. If you plead guilty and tell the truth, explaining why you couldn't make good on your promise, the opposing party will either understand your position and agree to work out problems with you, *or* stick to its guns and demand fairness. Then, if you can't pay up, you'll face grave consequences set by the other side. Unless you're *absolutely* certain that honesty will prove the best policy, it's usually best to play it smart by pleading innocent. *Never* admit to anything that will only serve to incriminate you. Stall for time instead, so you can keep your promise and meet your opponent's demands. When the other side confronts you, change the subject to avoid the issues at hand *or* address them in a way that focuses on the manner rather than on the substance of the discussion. Tell stories about the field of your invention, or outline new ideas and possible breakthroughs in technology. Question your opponent's progress, commend it for the progress it's already made, or hint of a higher job in the opponent's line of work. You might try to make your case boring, hoping to lose the other side's attention, or you could lapse into technical jargon. You could deluge your opponent with complicated information in hopes of shaking its confidence, or you could request the presence of others in hopes of restructuring your opponent's message.

Disclaimer: I am in no way encouraging anyone to use all these techniques (I do not use certain techniques that make me feel uncomfortable). These are techniques that I have seen work over the years. They are admittedly a little evasive, but when two people are both trying to get what they want, which happen to be completely opposite things, mankind has learned to become a little bit tricky: Use at your own risk!

Whatever you choose, remember you're *only* doing it to buy more time so you can make good on your commitment and come out with flying colors!

8. *Read your opponent's body language.* Almost as important as what the other side says is what it doesn't say. How can you tell whether your opponent is bluffing or serious? Clues often lie in nonverbal messages, or what's commonly called *body language*. Reading other people's signals is not an exact science, because our own emotions inevitably get in the way. But knowing the basics of body language can give you an invaluable skill—and there's no magic trick involved. There are guidelines you can follow.

    First, recognize that every person is different and has a unique body language; learning to read one person doesn't necessarily mean you can use those same patterns to read others more easily.

    Second, start by comparing the reactions of the opposing side when you know it's telling the truth rather than when it's obviously bluffing; the different signals between the two give you an "answer key" that spells out your opponent's real position. Jittery hands may reveal nerves; tense posture: anxiety; fidgeting: preoccupation with other concerns; hand gestures to aid speech: desire to make a point; sitting back: relaxed and ready for you to make your next move; arms crossed: defiance; slouching: boredom, disinterest. Also consider facial expressions. Smiling slightly can indicate agreement; squinting: thinking about all options; perspiring: nervousness about having a bluff called; frowning: disagreement; glaring: anger; tilting head: losing interest; breathing slowly: cautiousness; unblinking: alertness; tight lips: concentration; pause in speech: lack of confidence, searching for a good answer; wide-open eyes: threatened or excited;

dropping lower jaw: positive surprise; staring at wall: disinterest. Posture can also be revealing. Chin in hand may indicate trust or interest; leaning forward: challenging. Also, watch your opponent's eyes. Do they look nervous? Anxious? Smug?

Third, don't be obvious about your observations. If the other side catches on, it could become conscious of its body language and try to change it.

Evaluating body language is never guaranteed to bring success, so treat it judiciously. Because so many other factors can influence a person's gestures and movements, treat body language merely as an aid.

9. *Control the other side by listening.* Have you ever heard the expression, "the more you talk, the deeper you dig your own hole"? Even the best negotiators can trip up here. So don't find yourself wishing too late that you'd kept your mouth shut. Instead, discipline yourself to wait for the right moment to speak. Interrupting your opponent may only lead to noisy debates, with both sides trying desperately to get everything off their chests at once. Waiting to speak also puts you at an advantage because most people—probably including your opponent—enjoy talking, and sooner or later they are bound to slip up and reveal their real bargaining chips. The ideal moment to talk is when the other side has finished outlining its major points but has yet to marshal its strongest arguments. In the interim, you can pick one of your opponent's points that works against you and turn it around in your favor. Let's say that your opponent wants you to correct minor prototype flaws. Agree! Say something like, "I agree that it's vital to have a perfect prototype, especially before word gets out about our invention and competition sets in. Why don't we put this problem behind us as soon as possible by teaming up on small issues to get the jump on competition?" Or try the opposite approach. If your opponent starts to harp on an issue you'd rather forget, stay silent and stop listening. That is, give no sign of encouragement at all, and act as if the issue is a waste of everybody's time. The other side should notice that something has gone awry and change the subject before matters get worse. Unless the issue is a high priority, your opponent should let it slide.

Using Power Words

Use the power of words to control a discussion. In any negotiation, you must get your points across. Even more important, the other side must take you seriously. If you can use words well enough to deliver a powerful message, your opponent is more likely to cooperate and do things your way. The trick is to persuade the other side without provoking its animosity.

Correct Responses

Here is a list of some concepts I've found effective, with examples of how you might use them:

- *Deadline.* "If we don't take action now and get our product out before the first of March, which will leave us with little time, then competing companies will take advantage of how slow we're moving, come out quickly with a similar product, and steal our profits."

- *Surprise.* "You say there's no way your company can manufacture my invention for under $50,000, which exceeds the company's price range. But I have figures right here to show it can be done for $37,000 or less—without jeopardizing quality."

- *Missing link.* "I'm almost finished compiling the test-marketing results you asked for. I just need the executive engineering manager's final signature at Sega, but he's in Chicago and won't be back for two weeks."

- *Limited authority.* "This agreement looks reasonable. But before I can make any commitments, I'll have to get the clause approved by my attorney."

- *Low-balling.* "I realize I quoted you a price of $25,000 and agreed that this offer was acceptable in return for your sponsorship. But the company that's helping me build my prototype just informed me of some unexpected costs that will need to be added to the original amount."

- *Acknowledgment.* "I can understand your concern about high manufacturing costs. Even though we didn't reach our price range, we did make some progress. Besides, the difference will be more than made up as soon as your company starts selling the product."

- *Association.* "I think my invention stands a good chance of captivating the market. I've had nothing but positive customer feedback, unlike anything you've ever heard."
- *Limitation.* "Of course, I would like to build a first-rate prototype—one that will cost me in the neighborhood of $40,000. But with my limited resources, I can only afford $7,000."
- *Snowball effect.* "Since our test-marketing efforts proved rewarding and we've agreed to begin distribution next month, why not include an expanded advertising campaign to capitalize on our product's success?"
- *Fait accompli.* "I realize that you asked last week for the letter of approval from me, and now we're well into the next week. You'll be happy to learn, however, that I've already mailed it to you, and you should have it by tomorrow."

Incorrect Responses

Knowing what to say is only half your strategy; you must also know what *not* to say. Two notorious clichés that you'll probably recognize are virtually guaranteed to derail negotiation. The first takes an unreasonable stance: "Take it or leave it." The second fosters animosity: "If you don't like the offer, you can always leave." Whatever you may have heard in favor of these sorts of statements, they are *never* good tactics, because they leave no way out for your opponent. They only put the other side in the dilemma of having to choose between quitting negotiations and saving face, or accepting your terms and being humiliated.

The Opponent's Advantage

Most major companies that you negotiate with will have one major advantage over you: time. So get ready to feel frustrated; in negotiations, a company will often take its sweet time dealing with you. The negotiation process may seem to drag on forever, with no end in sight. That's because companies are generally in no hurry to complete negotiations—just the opposite. They have more to gain by prolonging the bargaining process. The longer they wait after your patent issue date to come to agreement, the less money they will have to pay you in royalties once sales begin! Remember that the clock is ticking on your invention's royalty life span, which begins when you're issued your patent (Step 1). To some degree, unfortunately, you are at a company's mercy, especially since you depend on it for sales. The trick here is to speed up a company's "time clock" by making them need you more than you need them. To convince a company that they can't afford to pass you up, you need the right attitude—one that's powerful, compelling, and *never* betrays worry. I'm not telling you to stop caring about reaching your goals, just that worrying won't help you get there. On the contrary, it makes you more vulnerable to failure. If you follow the methods I've listed, you can get a company to play right into your hands.

Step 8

Agreements, Contracts, and Licensing

Types of Agreements

To understand how contracts work, you first have to know that there are only two basic types of agreements: *assignment,* or outright sale of your invention; and *licensing,* or leasing your invention in return for royalties. Let's begin by taking a closer look at assignment, and later go on to examine licensing agreements.

Assignment

This type of contract represents a "legal document," recognized by U.S. law, which declares transfer of ownership. In assignment, you sell a company the complete rights to your invention. That means that, once you've sold your patent, you no longer hold any rights to the *make, use,* or *sale* of your invention. Simply put, your invention is no longer yours.

You may be asking yourself, "Why would I sell my invention?" Usually, assignments are made by employees who work for companies that specialize in innovative products. So the real owner is the corporation. Generally, it's true that you'd be better off to license your invention. The times you may want to consider selling your invention are:

- When you need money badly enough that you're willing to settle for less
- When your invention could be eaten alive by competition as soon as it hits the market
- When the market for your invention will take many years (greater than 10) to develop and mature, which means you'd only receive a

significant amount of royalties toward the very end of your patent term

- When your invention is in a "crowded art," where there are many competitors with patents that have only slight differences from yours (otherwise, the corporation that licenses your invention may work around your patent in a couple of years, leaving you with no more royalties for the rest of your patent term!)
- When your invention is so controversial or dangerous that it may offend or hurt some people, drawing widespread criticism against your product

Whatever the case, if you plan to sell out, make sure you do so for the right reasons—your best interests. A word of caution is in order here: *Never* sign your patent rights away until you've received payment in *full*, from either a lump sum or a series of payments, and make sure you are paid by certified check or money order. You don't want to sell your patent only to find out later that the check is no good, leaving you with no money and no patent—and a big legal headache to win back your patent rights.

A modified version of assignment also exists, called *partial assignment*, which means you transfer less than 100 percent ownership. Usually, however, partial assignment only occurs when the assignee (the company or person receiving the transferred ownership) has financed the inventor's product and demands more compensation. Don't forget that assignments are legal ownership agreements; the new owner(s) may resell their invention rights or license it to other corporations.

Figures 8-1 and 8-2 show sample assignment agreements. Which one you use depends on whether you sold your invention after patent issuance (Figure 8-1) or during patent application filing (Figure 8-2). Keep in mind that if you use either of my sample assignments, you may want to change certain provisions to fit your needs. Also, once you've written an assignment document and before you meet with the company, you should consult a patent attorney, who can explain how the agreement will affect your rights.

Figure 8-1. Sample document for assignment of patent

Assignment of Patent

Upon receipt of its value, _____ of _____ (hereinafter Assignor), hereby sells and assigns to _____ of _____ and his/her successors and assigns (hereinafter Assignee) _____ % of Assignors right, title and interest in Patent No. _____ granted on _____ , 20_____ .

Assignor agrees to execute all papers, give any required testimony, and perform other lawful acts, at Assignees expense, as Assignee may require the efforts of Assignor to confirm and enforce the validity of said patent, reissues, and extensions thereof in the future.

In testimony whereof Assignor has hereunto set its hand and seal on the date below.

State _____

ss

County: _____

Date subscribed and sworn before me: _____

(Notary Public)

Figure 8-2. Sample document for assignment of patent application

Assignment of Patent Application

    Upon receipt of its value, _____ of _____ (hereinafter Assignor), hereby sells and assigns to _____ of _____ and his/her successors and assigns (hereinafter Assignee) _____ % of Assignors right, title and interest in and to the invention entitled _____ represented by the application for United States patent with U.S. Patent and Trademark Office Application Number _____ by Assignor, the inventor. These assignment rights include any patents or reissues that may be granted thereon, and any applications which are continuations, continuations-in-part, substitutes, or divisions of said application. Assignor further sells and assigns to Assignee, the above percentage of Assignor's entire right, title and interest of said invention in each and every country foreign to the United States.

    Assignor agrees to execute all papers, give any required testimony and perform other lawful acts, at Assignees expense, as Assignee may require the efforts of Assignor, in an effort to perfect its interest in any resulting patent of the United States and countries foreign thereto, to confirm and enforce the validity of said patent, reissues, and extensions thereof in the future.

    In testimony whereof Assignor has hereunto set its hand and seal on the date below.

State:_____

ss

County:_____

Date subscribed and sworn before me: _____

(Notary Public)

To protect yourself fully, you should always record your assignment with the PTO. I cannot emphasize how vital this procedure is if you want to avoid getting taken. If you don't record your assignment, the assignors can make another assignment to a different assignee who is "unaware" of the first assignment. That second assignee's rights will prevail over yours as first assignee if they record their assignment with the PTO before you do. So recording your assignment immediately prevents unfairness! To record your assignment, simply send it to the PTO (keep a copy) with the service fee (see Appendix C for fees) and ask that it be recorded. The PTO will then stamp your assignment with "recording indicia," which indicates the date and place of recording, and send it back to you. After you get the PTO-stamped document, make a copy for yourself and return the original to the PTO. Lastly, never send in your assignment for "recordal" until you've included the *application number* from your patent application or your *patent number* if your patent's already approved. Those numbers will guarantee that your assignment matches your patent, preventing anybody from claiming otherwise.

Licensing

Under this type of agreement, a company doesn't own your invention; it only *leases* (formally termed *licensing*) your rights to your invention in return for royalties. The three separate rights that you are allowed to license to any entity are the right to make, the right to use, and the right to sell your patented invention. A company then pays you royalties for the *make, use,* or *sale* of your invention. Typically, when you draw up a license agreement, you give all three rights to a corporation because they intend to manufacture (make), test (use), and distribute (sell) your patented product. To what extent a company can use these rights, however, depends on which license is utilized. You need to be aware of three important licenses: *exclusive, limited exclusive,* and *nonexclusive.*

Exclusive

This license gives one company the sole right to fully *make*, *use*, and *sell* your invention. Other companies are prohibited by law from either producing or selling the same invention. Of course, a company favors having an exclusive license because its competition is removed, which gives them a monopoly on your invention! If there's no sales war for your invention between companies, the company you've signed on with capitalizes freely. But what do you get out of it? Nothing more than your usual royalties. And since almost all companies, regardless of their fields, only obtain fractions of their *potential* market shares, if you are tied down by an *exclusive* license, you can't employ other companies to sell your product. You'll never be able to capitalize on your product's *total* market potential. So, unless, a company makes you an offer you can't refuse, or that company owns greater than 90 percent of the total market, *never* agree to an exclusive license. In an exclusive deal you can ask for up-front cash and higher royalties (see licensing agreements).

Limited Exclusive

Unlike an exclusive license, a limited exclusive agreement can give you the freedom to go ahead and allow multiple companies the right to *make*, *use*, and *sell* your invention. In other words, no single company can solely profit from your invention. This means you have the opportunity to reach near your invention's *total* market share by allowing many companies to participate. This doesn't necessarily mean, however, that the company you had originally signed on with will profit less. A limited exclusive agreement is coined *"limited"* because each company's right to the *make*, *use*, and *sale* of your invention is set by factors such as territory, price, or specific markets. You study (research) the firm's market and capabilities, and then you as the investor have to ask for the limits. The manufacturer, of course, is not going to want to be limited. When you *limit* your agreement to any of these three factors or others, a company still holds on to its competitive edge because other companies must also obey any limitations. For instance, if a company is limited to a specific territory, no other companies can sell your invention in the area specified. Or if the company's market share is best defined by price, then it can be agreed upon that no other company can sell your invention under a specific amount.

Some lawyers believe that limited exclusive licenses fall under the class of nonexclusive licenses (see next section), but in actuality they tend to stand in a class of their own. As another example, let's say you've invented a new high-performance engine that uses 10 times less gas than similar engines in its class. General Motors may be interested in buying your invention because of its fuel efficiency, but Ferrari may be interested in making your engine because of its high-performance characteristics. In a case like this, you can make two separate limited exclusive agreements, one with GM, for cars that are under a certain price range, and the other with Ferrari, for cars that are over a certain price range. The two agreements would allow your engine to go into two completely different, noncompetitive markets: general economic automobiles and high-performance exotic cars. Hence, you increase your distribution and maximize your royalty potential.

Before you decide on how specifically to limit your license, be aware of how your decisions will impact your product's goals five years into the future. A limited exclusive agreement may be viewed as a compromise that satisfies both parties, and it is a widely used agreement among inventors.

Nonexclusive

This type of agreement allows you to lease to *all* companies the right to *make*, *use*, and *sell* your invention. The main advantage in obtaining a nonexclusive license is that you now have the opportunity to reach your product's *total* market share potential. You can capitalize completely on your product's worth. Nonexclusive licensing, however, also has its potential grim side. Any company you plan to sign on with will be reluctant to accept such an offer—one that undermines sales. And even if you do manage to convince a company to sign a nonexclusive license, other companies that later become interested in your invention may reject it, based on the fact that it's governed by a nonexclusive license. This could leave your pockets financially dry, especially if you are being passed up by major companies in the field of your invention.

Still, if you find yourself with an invention so amazing that you have several companies bidding for it, this is the time to make the nonexclusive license work for you. After all, the more companies that you can put to work selling your invention, the more money you can make. Before carrying out this plan, be sure that the demand for your invention is high enough that major companies will still sell your invention, regardless of its tie to a nonexclusive license. You can determine this by informing each interested party that another company has made you an offer you can't refuse, particularly because it involves a nonexclusive agreement. If you get a positive response—that is, a matching or better offer—then having a nonexclusive license may be extremely rewarding.

Your aim is to have a company bidding war over your invention. At that point, companies may sign nonexclusives with you because, even with the extra competition, they see the potential to make great profits from your invention.

Drafting Licensing Agreements

When it comes to drafting your own licensing agreement, know that you should thoroughly cover each determinant—pointing out your benefits and the circumstances from which they arise. Figure 8-3 contains a Universal License Agreement that has been reviewed by attorneys for legitimacy. License agreements in general are worth thousands of dollars because of the in-depth legal work involved in constructing them. Because this license is fairly generic, you must tailor it down with the help of your lawyer to meet your specific needs. The following list examines each part of the contract in more detail. Numbers shown in the list correspond with the numbers in Figure 8-3.

Figure 8-3. Sample of universal patent license (exclusive)

1. Parties, Terms, and Parameters:
This agreement is between:

Licensor: _____ , of _____
AND
Licensee: _____ , of _____

Invention Title: _____
Patent Application Ser. # _____
Filing Date: _____
Patent Number: _____
Grant Date: _____

Formula For Computing Licensing Fee:

Licensing Fee $ _____ =

Royalty Rate (%): _____ % MULTIPLIED BY

Est. 1st Yr's Sales (total units): _____ MULTIPLIED BY

Estimated Unit Price $ _____

2. **Background:**

    a. Licensor has developed an invention having the above title and U.S. Patent Serial Number, or Patent Number if already issued, and Licensor warrants that Licensor has full right to grant this license on this invention and Licensor's patent application.

    b. Licensee wishes to acquire the right to make, use, and sell the products embodying the above listed invention and covered by the claims of the Licensor's patent application and any patents issuing thereon (hereinafter "Licensed Product").

3. **Patent License:**

    a. Licensor hereby grants to Licensee an exclusive license to make, use, and sell the Licensed Product. The rights to sell Licensed Product in foreign countries (outside the U.S.) are governed by provision 10. Such patent license shall include the right to grant sublicenses.

    b. Licensor agrees to use its best efforts to finance patent expenses of any U.S. patents in this agreement, and all such patents will be in the name of and remain the property of the Licensor during and following any cancellation of this agreement.

    c. To the best of Licensor's knowledge, his patent or any improvements of such which fall within its legal scope, does not infringe on any other patents.

4. **Defined**

    Net Factory Sales Price: "Net Factory Sales Price" is defined as the Licensee's invoice price, f.o.b. factory, after deduction of regular trade and quantity discounts, but before deduction of any other items, including but not limited to freight allowances, cash discounts, and agents' commissions.

5. Licensing Bonus Fee

    Licensee shall pay to Licensor, upon execution of this Agreement, a nonrefundable Licensing Fee. This Licensing Fee shall also serve as an advance against future royalties. Such Licensing Fee shall be computed as follows: (A) Take the Running Royalty Rate in percent, as stated above. (B) Multiply by Licensee's Estimate of Its First Year's sales, in units of Licensed Product, as stated above. (C) Multiply by Licensee's Estimated Unit Price of Licensed Product, in dollars, as stated above. (D) The combined product shall be the Resultant Licensing Fee, in dollars, as stated above. When licensee begins actual sales of the Licensed Product, it shall certify its Actual Net Factory Sales Price of Licensed Product to Licensor in writing and shall either (1) simultaneously pay Licensor any difference due if the Actual Net Factory Sales Price of Licensed Product is more than the Estimated Unit Price, stated above, or (2) advise Licensor of any credit to which Licensee is entitled if the Actual Net Factory Sales Price of Licensed Product is less than the above Estimated Unit Price. In the latter case, Licensee may deduct such credit from its first royalty remittance to Licensor, under subpart B.

6. Running Royalty

    a. Licensee shall pay to Licensor a Running Royalty, at the rate stated in Part 1. Said Running Royalty shall be computed on Licensee's Net Factory Sales Price of Licensed Product. Such Running Royalty shall accrue when the Licensed Products are first sold or disposed of by Licensee, or by any sublicensee of Licensee. Licensee shall pay the Running Royalty due to Licensor within one month after the end of each calendar quarter, together with a written report to Licensor of the number of units, respective sales prices, and total sales made in such quarter, together with a full itemization on any adjustments. Licensee's first report and payment shall be made within one month after the end of the first calendar quarter following the execution of this Agreement. Such royalty responsibilities extend to all foreign countries pursuant to the provisions in part 10. No royalties shall be paid by Licensee to Licensor until after Licensing Fee under provision 5 as shown above has been earned, but Licensee shall make a quarterly report hereunder for every calendar quarter after the execution hereof, whether or not any royalty payment is due for such quarter.

b. Minimum Annual Royalties

If less than $2,000 (this will vary depending on your product, in general it should be about one-half of the estimated steady sales of the Licensed Products) of royalties has accrued in any royalty quarter, then a minimum quarterly royalty of $2,000 will be paid for that quarter. The $2,000 should be confirmed by Licensee to be the estimated royalties that would be accrued if only half of the estimated sales of Licensed Product for that period were sold. The estimation should be based on future, peak stabilized sales of the Licensed Product.

c. If Minimum Royalty Not Paid

If royalties from sales of Licensed Product are less than the minimum royalty for a particular quarter, Licensee may choose not to pay the minimum quarterly royalty, and if such minimum royalty is not paid within one month after the ending of such a quarter, the license grant described in this Agreement shall be converted to a nonexclusive grant, and Licensor may immediately license others under the above patent.

d. Foreign Payment Permits

If royalty payments are made to Licensor from a foreign country, Licensee assumes the task of procurement of any permits and documents needed in order to make said payments under any exchange regulations.

e. When No Royalties Due

No patent Royalties shall be accrued after the expiration of the last of any patent(s) that issues on Licensor's application.

7. Late Payments

If any payment due under this Agreement is not timely paid, then the unpaid balance shall bear interest until paid at an annual rate of 10%, compounded monthly, until the delinquent balance is paid.

8. Introduction Date

Licensee agrees to introduce the product before __(date)__. In addition, during the term of this agreement, Licensee agrees to assiduously and continuously promote, manufacture, sell, and distribute such product to the best ability and adequately enough to satisfy the Licensed Product's customer demand.

9. Sublicensees

If Licensee grants any sublicenses hereunder, it shall notify Licensor in writing within one month from any such grant and shall provide Licensor with a true copy of any sublicense agreement. Any sublicensee of Licensee under this Agreement shall be bound by all of the terms applying to Licensee hereunder (except the minimum royalties provisions in section 6b) and Licensee shall be responsible for the obligations and duties of any of its sublicensees.

10. Foreign Patent Prosecution

When either party considers it necessary or advantageous to obtain additional foreign patent protection covered by this Agreement (except the U.S.), it shall notify the other party and upon agreement of the other party, Licensor shall, assuming no bar because of prior use or publication in that foreign country, promptly file such foreign application and the expenses thereof shall be shared equally by both parties.

The foreign application (and future patent) as mentioned above shall be bound by all the terms in this Agreement. If Licensee agrees with the filing of the application, but cannot share the expenses due to financial hardship, Licensor may proceed in filing such applications on behalf of Licensee and will debit future royalties equal to one half of such foreign patent prosecution expenses. If neither party has filed an application in a particular foreign country, or the parties have agreed not to file, or such application for foreign patent was discontinued, the royalties for such foreign country shall be paid out to Licensor as if patent protection has been obtained in that foreign country. If one party disagrees with filing such a foreign application, the other party shall have the right to proceed alone at its own expense and obtain full rights to any such foreign patents that may result from foreign patent prosecution, notwithstanding any other provisions of this Agreement. That party then has the right to license, sell, or otherwise exploit the invention (Licensed Product) in those foreign countries where patent protection has been obtained.

If Licensee has not timely requested the filing of a foreign patent application, Licensor is under no obligation to file such foreign application.

11. Samples

Licensee shall annually furnish _____ free samples of any and all Licensed Products, including its packaging.

12. Records

Licensee and any of its sublicensees shall keep full, clear, and accurate records with respect to sales subject to royalty under this Agreement. The records shall be made in a manner such that the royalty reports made pursuant to part 6a can be verified. Licensor, or its authorized agent, shall have the right to examine and audit such records upon reasonable notice during normal business hours, but not more than twice per year. In case of any dispute as to the sufficiency or accuracy of such records, Licensor may have any independent auditor examine and certify such records. Licensee shall make prompt adjustment to compensate for any errors or omissions disclosed by any such examination and certification of Licensee's records. If Licensee's error is greater than $500, Licensee will pay for the cost of the audit.

13. Product Indemnity

a. Licensee hereby assumes all risks associated with the manufacture, distribution, sale, or use of any Licensed Product.

b. Licensee shall defend Licensor against any and all claims or causes of action for death, illness, personal injury or property damage, and possible infringement suits that result from Licensee's and Licensee's Sublicensee's commercial exploitation of Licensed Products, and Licensee shall indemnify Licensor for any and all awards, judgments, settlement payments, and reasonable attorneys' fees and costs incurred by Licensor as a result of any such claim or cause of action.

c. Licensor shall promptly notify Licensee of any such claim or cause of action and assist and cooperate with Licensee in the defense thereof, including the delivery and/or execution of documents and the giving of testimony. Licensee shall have exclusive control over the selection of legal counsel and the course of the defense of any such claim or cause of action. Licensor shall consent to the reasonable settlement of any such claim or cause of action by Licensee.

d. Licensee shall maintain sufficient liability insurance to cover all risks and indemnities assumed by Licensee under Sections a) through b) of this current provision. Upon request of Licensor, Licensee shall provide Licensor with proof of such insurance.

14. Marking

Licensee shall mark all units of Licensed Product that it sells with proper notice of patent marking under 35 U.S.C. Section 287.

15. Termination

This Agreement may be terminated under and according to any of the following contingencies:

a. Default: If Licensee fails to make any payment on the date such payment is due under this Agreement, or if Licensee makes any other default under or breach of this Agreement, Licensor shall have the right to terminate this Agreement upon giving three months' written Notice of Intent To Terminate, specifying such failure, breach, or default to Licensee. If Licensee fails to make any payment in arrears, or otherwise fails to cure the breach or default within such three-month period, Licensor may then send a written Notice of Termination to Licensee, whereupon this Agreement shall terminate in one month from the date of such Notice of Termination. If this Agreement is terminated hereunder, Licensee shall immediately submit a terminal report as described in 6a, and Licensee shall not be relieved of any of its obligations to the date of termination and Licensor may act to enforce Licensee's obligations after any such termination

b. Failure to Introduce/Antishelving: It is agreed that if Licensee does not introduce product before the date in part 8 or Licensee does not sell the Licensed Product for any 100 consecutive days anytime after the introduction date, then Licensor has the option to terminate the Agreement. Licensor must first give notice to Licensee, and if Licensee does not resume producing and selling Licensed Product after 30 days from receipt of such, this agreement will terminate at the end of the 30-day period.

c. Bankruptcy: If Licensee shall go into receivership, bankruptcy, or insolvency, or make an assignment for the benefit of creditors, or go out of business, the Agreement shall be immediately terminable by Licensor by written notice, but without prejudice to any rights of Licensor hereunder.

d. Mutual Consent: The license may be terminated with mutual consent between the Licensor and Licensee.

16. If Infringement Occurs

If either party discovers that the above patent is infringed, it shall communicate the details to the other party. Licensor shall thereupon have the right, but not the obligation, to take whatever action it deems necessary, including the filing of lawsuits, to protect the rights of the parties to this Agreement and to terminate such infringement. Licensee shall cooperate with Licensor if Licensor takes any such action, but all expenses of Licensor shall be borne by Licensor. If Licensor recovers any damages or compensation for any action it takes hereunder, Licensor shall retain 100% of such damages. If Licensor does not wish to take any action hereunder, Licensee shall also have the right, but not the obligation, to take any such action, in which case Licensor shall cooperate with Licensee, but all of Licensee's expenses shall be borne by Licensee. Licensee shall receive 75% of any damages or compensation it recovers for any such infringement and shall pay 25% of such damages or compensation to Licensor, after deducting its costs, including attorney fees.

17. Term

   The term of this Agreement shall end with the expiration of the last of any patent(s) that issues on Licensor's patent application, unless terminated for any purpose set forth in paragraph 15, at which time all rights in said patents shall revert back to Licensor.

18. Notices

   All notices, payments, or statements under this Agreements shall be in writing and shall be sent by first-class certified mail, return receipts requested, postage prepaid, to the party concerned at the above address, or to any substituted address given by notice hereunder. Any such notice, payment, or statement shall be considered sent or made on the day deposited in the mails.

19. Transfer of Rights & Obligations

   The rights of Licensor under this Agreement shall be assignable or otherwise transferable, in whole or in part, by Licensor and shall vest Licensor's assigns or transferees with the same rights and obligations as were held by Licensor. This Agreement shall be assignable by Licensee to any entity that succeeds to the business of Licensee to which Licensed Products relate or to any other entity if Licensor's permission is first obtained in writing.

20. Mediation and Arbitration

   If any dispute arises under this Agreement, the parties shall negotiate in good faith to settle such dispute. If the parties cannot resolve such dispute themselves, then either party may submit the dispute to mediation by a mediator approved by both parties. The parties shall both cooperate with the mediator.

21. Continuing Obligations

   Any rights and obligations under this Agreement that by their nature extend beyond the term of this Agreement, including but not limited to the obligation to maintain confidentiality for trade secrets, shall survive any expiration or termination of this Agreement.

22. Counterparts

    This Agreement may be executed in any number of original counter-parts, and together they shall constitute one Agreement.

23. Severability

    If any provision of this Agreement is found or deemed by a court of competent jurisdiction to be invalid or unenforceable, it shall be considered severable from the remainder of this Agreement and shall not cause the remainder to be invalid or unenforceable. In such event, the Parties shall reform this Agreement to replace such stricken provision with a valid and enforceable provision that comes as close as possible to expressing the intent of the stricken provision.

24. Jurisdiction

    This Agreement shall be interpreted under the laws of Licensor's state, as given in Part 1 above.

25. Waiver, Alteration

    a. The waiver of a breach hereunder may be effected only by a writing signed by the waiving party and shall not constitute a waiver of any other breach.

    b. A provision in this agreement may be altered only by a writing signed by both parties.

26. Signatures

    The terms and conditions herein constitute the entire agreement between the parties and shall supersede all previous agreements, either oral or written, between the Parties hereto with respect to the subject matter hereof. The parties, having carefully read this Agreement and having consulted or been given an opportunity to consult counsel, have indicated their agreement to all of the above terms by signing this Agreement. Each signatory hereto represents that it is authorized to sign this Agreement on behalf of the Party for whom it purports to sign. Licensee and Licensor have each received a copy of this Agreement with both Licensee's and Licensor's original ink signatures thereon.

Date: _____

Print Licensor's Name: _____

Date: _____

Print Licensee's Name: _____

1. This part is a summary of important fact and figure information needed to be referenced in the agreement. The formula on the bottom multiplies three terms in order to calculate the *licensing fee*.

2. This background paragraph outlines the interest of each party.

3. This paragraph specifies the details of the patent grant (exclusive in this case).

4. This is the definition paragraph. *Net sales price* is always a tricky term with multiple meanings that must be nailed down early in the contract in order to avoid confusion or misunderstanding. The definition of *gross sales price* would be the *net sales price* before you subtract out anything. If you can negotiate getting royalties taken off gross sales price, this means more money to you.

5. Licensing bonus fees are customarily paid out to reward inventors for the time, work, and money spent on the development of the invention in the past. In the sample document this figure is based off the estimated first year's sales. It may be simpler just to arbitrarily name an outright sum—say $5,000—for the bonus fee.

6. *Part a* specifies the actual royalty rate you will receive, details of the payment schedule, and the obligation of the Licensee to submit a report with the moneys. *Part b* shows the minimum annual royalty, which is there to keep the manufactures on their toes by giving them

incentive to push your product to the best of their capabilities. *Part c* converts the agreement to a nonexclusive license if Licensee chooses not to pay the minimum royalty. *Part d* explains that the obligation of obtaining foreign permits is in the Licensee's court.

7. Royalties will end at the end of your patent term. You may want to change this provision if you have trade secrets or "know-how" built into your invention. Trade secrets and "know-how" can earn you royalties just as long as such information is kept secret and not leaked out to the public. For example, you invented a new type of food that cures the common cold, but you keep the ingredients secret.

8. This paragraph motivates the corporation to introduce the product as soon as possible. The sooner they do, the sooner your royalties accrue!

9. Your Licensee may want to sublicense some of the manufacturing or marketing of your product to other corporations who have more capabilities in those specific areas. Of course, this is like giving out another license, and you will want to follow this closely. Be wary if your licensee has an interest in dealing with some companies in the Asian regions. Patent regulations in the Eastern countries are very poorly enforced, and you could be setting yourself up for copycat nightmares. Make sure you discuss and highlight your concerns with your Licensee as soon as possible, and keep a close eye on the Sublicensee's operations. You may even want to modify this clause so that the Licensee has to get permission from you before sublicensing.

10. This sets up the guidelines on how foreign patent prosecution will be pursued. Basically there can be mixed agreement and disagreement between the parties regarding the filing of foreign patent applications. Each scenario must be looked at and dealt with individually. Typically, the Licensor will always retain the rights to patents filed in foreign countries, except when the Licensor absolutely refuses to agree to file in a particular foreign country.

11. You're not going to want to have to go to the store and pay for your own invention!

12. This clause provides you with an auditing means if you become suspicious or feel you're being short-changed in royalties. You give yourself

the right to go in and physically check their IRS records for assurance. If a corporation won't agree to putting in this clause for you, they probably aren't trustworthy.

13. This is called an *indemnity clause*. It makes sure that the licensee assumes the responsibility of protecting you in court if someone accidentally maims themself with your invention and then tries to file a civil suit against you. It also allows you to verify that the Licensee carries sufficient liability insurance to cover you.

14. You may want to have your product marked if your patent is pending. Furthermore, if the patent has issued, you need to have the patent number marked on the product.

15. These are some possible termination scenarios. This gives you the option to terminate the agreement in cases of payment default, failure to introduce on time, bankruptcy, antishelving, and mutual consent.

16. This infringement clause lays out the rules of who can sue in cases of infringement. It is important to make sure that the inventor has a right to pursue infringement if the Licensee does not. Most inventors cannot afford the out-of-pocket costs of such an infringement suit (from $50,000 to $100,000). Moreover, some corporations may feel that it's not worth it due to the high costs. The right to file suit by both parties is preserved in this clause.

17. This specifies the term of the patent. It will end after the last patent expires whether it be due to foreign, continuing, divisional, or regular applications.

18. This specifies how information will be communicated.

19. This allows the Licensee to transfer the rights you gave up to others. This mainly applies to corporate buyouts or if the company is changing its direction out of your invention's market. In those cases, it will want to transfer its rights to another company or corporation.

20. In case of disputes, a mutually agreed mediator will be the judge.

21. The corporation should realize that some provisions such as trade secrets and product indemnity are by their nature perpetual obligations.

22. You may need this if there are other papers floating around that apply to the Agreement.

23. This clause allows you to cut out a particular invalid provision without invalidating the whole Agreement.

24. Choose which state laws shall enforce the Agreement. You want the laws of the state in which you reside to apply; therefore, if any disputes arise, they will have to be resolved in your state.

25. This clause makes sure that whatever is agreed upon orally will not be legally binding. Without it, mutual oral consent can be binding in a court of law.

26. This is the final signature/date clause.

Keep in mind that when you do finish drafting your patent license, it is necessary to have a patent attorney look it over—explaining your rights and double-checking your work. If you need more help in drafting licensing agreements, you can call IP&R (in back of book).

When you are finished drafting the agreement, your submission to an interested corporation will start your first round of contract negotiations. You may find that a company will want you to work from a generic royalty agreement that they have specifically used in the past. In that case, they will submit it to you and you can negotiate from there.

The sample license agreement shown in Figure 8-4 is an example of a final royalty contract that was originally submitted to me by the actual corporation. It is a *limited exclusive* license agreement that has also been reviewed by attorneys. To protect the rights of all party members involved, all names and addresses in my limited licensing contract are fictitious.

If you compare it with the sample in Figure 8-3, you will notice that a few provisions from the first license agreement were "negotiated" into the second. When you are working with a company's own generic license agreement, you will typically find it to be lacking in many areas, which gives you less protection. Thus, it is to your advantage to negotiate to include further provisions. In other words, feel free to cut and paste provisions from the sample in Figure 8-3 into the context of *their* license when appropriate.

Figure 8-4. Limited exclusive license agreement

This Agreement made this _____ day of _____ , Nineteen hundred and ninety-five.

BETWEEN:

Steve Barbarich of 1451 Epson Ave., Sunivile, NY 61608; John F. Washington, 3021 Kamerla Ct., Sunivile, NY 98765-0987; Tony James of 9560 Hidille La., Sunvile, NY 98766-7012, hereinafter referred to as Barbarich et al and Lansing Soldering Corporation 3311 M. Limon, Filling IL.

Whereas Barbarich et al are the inventors of a FingerTip Soldering Tool, and holders of U.S. Patent No. 4,651,800 dated Nov. 20, 1993; and whereas Lansing Soldering Corporation is interested in manufacturing and marketing the FingerTip Soldering Tool covered under U.S. Patent #4,651,800, it is therefore agreed as follows:

1. Barbarich et al license to Lansing Soldering Corporation sole and exclusive worldwide rights to manufacture and market products covered by the above patent. These rights are limited to FingerTip Soldering Tools produced and retailed for under $250.00. These rights do not apply to FingerTip Soldering Tools having sophisticated control systems that are retailed for over $250.00 (this number will be adjusted due to inflation over the term of this agreement).

2. Through the expiration of the U.S. Patent #4,651,800, Lansing Soldering Corporation will pay Barbarich et al a royalty of 5% of Lansing's "net U.S. sales" of products covered by U.S. Patent #4,651,800. A royalty will not be paid on subsequent products or inventions developed by Lansing which do not infringe U.S. patent #4,651,800. Products returned to Lansing by its customers, for any reason, such as ones sold on consignment or returned for package refurbishment, shall be subtracted from gross unit sales before computing "net U.S. sales." Starting at the end of month 6, royalty periods are every 6 months as shown below. Lansing will similarly pay a royalty to Barbarich et al equal to 5% of its net sales in foreign countries which Steve Barbarich has filed corresponding foreign patent applications claiming priority from U.S. Patent #4,651,800. All royalty payments to Barbarich et al shall be accompanied

by a written summary report stating the quantity and aggregate net selling price of FingerTip Soldering Tools sold in each country for the corresponding 6 month royalty period.

3. Lansing Soldering Corporation will make an initial bonus of $1,000, and then will pay additional royalty payments according to the minimum schedule below: (Royalty month 1 (one) starts upon completion of all tooling or availability of FingerTip Soldering Irons to ship as finished goods inventory or 6 months from the signing date of the contract, whichever comes first.)

Royalty Month	Minimum Royalty Due at End of Month
6	$ 2,000 (paid to Barbarich et al)
12	$ 2,000 (paid to Barbarich et al)
18	$ 4,000 (paid to Barbarich et al)
24	$ 4,000 (paid to Barbarich et al)
30	$ 4,000 (paid to Barbarich et al)
36	$ 4,000 (paid to Barbarich et al)
42	$ 4,000 (paid to Barbarich et al)
48	$ 4,000 (paid to Barbarich et al)

4. After month 48, minimum royalties continue at $4,000 each 6 months ending with the 6 month period containing the expiration date of the Patent. No patent royalties shall be due after the Patent expires.

5. Royalty payments will be solely payable to and mailed to Steve Barbarich, 1451 Epson Ave, Sunivile, NY 61608. He will distribute the payments as agreed upon by the holders of U.S. Patent #4,651,800. Payments will be made semi-annually on the anniversary date of royalty month 1 (one).

6. If Lansing Soldering Corporation has not made the owed royalty payment and any royalty payment period by thirty (30) days following the end of that period, and provided a delinquency letter has been received by Lansing through registered mail, then, upon the fortieth (40) day of nonpayment, this agreement is terminated. In such case, Lansing remains liable for royalties of 5% of its "net U.S. and foreign sales" for products sold up to the point of termination. In such case, Lansing then

forfeits all patent rights granted by this agreement except it may sell any remaining inventory of the product within 6 months at 5% per unit royalty. This manner of action by Lansing terminates the contract with no further obligations remaining for either party.

6.2 If payments to Barbarich et al do not exceed the minimum royalty payment during two consecutive six month royalty periods, Barbarich et al shall have the right to terminate this agreement by giving written notice to Lansing.

6.3 Lansing and any of its sublicensees shall keep full, clear, and accurate records with respect to sales subject to royalty under this agreement. Barbarich et al, or their authorized agent, shall have the right to examine and audit such records upon reasonable notice but no more than once a year. In case of a dispute as to the sufficiency or accuracy of such records, Barbarich et al, at their expense, may have any independent auditor examine and certify such records and Lansing shall make prompt adjustment to compensate for any errors or omissions disclosed by any such examination. In the event that any payments are not audited within two years of receipt, such audit right will terminate as to that particular payment.

6.4 If Lansing grants any sublicenses hereunder, it shall notify Barbarich et al within one month from any such grant and shall provide Barbarich et al with a true copy of any sublicense agreement. Any sublicensee of Lansing under this agreement shall be bound by all of the terms applying to Lansing in this agreement and Lansing shall be responsible for the obligations and duties of any of its sublicensees.

6.5 Lansing hereby assumes all risks associated with the manufacture, distribution, sale, or use of any Licensed Product. Lansing shall, through its own liability insurance, defend Barbarich et al against any and all claims or causes of action of death, illness, personal injury, or property damage that result from Lansing's and Lansing's sublicensee's commercial exploitation of Licensed Products. Lansing is not responsible for any third party device using or incorporating the FingerTip Soldering Irons

6.6 This agreement contains the complete and final expression of the understandings of the Parties with respect to any matter mentioned herein and may be modified only in writing, said writing to be signed by both Parties making the modification.

7. This agreement shall be governed by the laws of the state of Illinois, of the United States of America.

8. This agreement is binding upon the parties hereto, their heirs, executors, administrators and assigns.

9. In the event of patent infringement by others, Lansing will have first right to institute enforcement proceedings. The proceedings will be at Lansing's expense, and Lansing will recover damages awarded. Barbarich et al agrees to fully cooperate with any such proceeding. If Lansing chooses not to pursue the infringement, or a period of two years of infringement occurs before Lansing takes legal action upon the infringers, Barbarich et al has the right to follow suit on the infringers and recover all resulting damages awarded.

10. This agreement constitutes the complete understanding of intellectual property rights between the above parties and shall initiate the date of the latest signature below and shall end with the last royalty payment according to the above schedule, unless otherwise terminated according to any provisions in this Agreement.

SIGNED:

Steve Barbarich _____   Date: _____

John F. Washington _____   Date: _____

Tony James _____   Date: _____

Lansing Soldering Corp. _____   Date: _____

The following list explains each part of the contract in Figure 8-4 in more detail:

1. This specifies the kind of licensing contract both parties have agreed to. It sets any limitations to your license. For instance, Steve's contract falls under a limited exclusive agreement because it states that "these rights are limited to FingerTip Soldering Tools produced and retailed for under $250.00." In other words, the company is limited by the *price* to the make, use, and sale of Steve's invention. Without this statement, the agreement then becomes an exclusive licensing contract because the first line clearly states that "Lansing Soldering Corporation [has] *sole* and *exclusive* worldwide rights to manufacture and market products covered by the above patent." To make a nonexclusive agreement, you would only need to omit the words *sole* and *exclusive*.

2. This clause sets out the royalty percentage (U.S. and foreign) and links it with the patent number. It also specifies and defines where the royalty is taken out of ("net sales"). A short explanation of how "net sales" is determined is included because the term "sales" alone is a little ambiguous because it could mean either "gross sales" or "net sales." If your negotiating position is strong enough, you can get your royalties taken from "gross sales." This gets you more money because this figure is the total sales before subtracting off discounts, allowances, and returned products. If you have a very strong negotiating position, ask for more than 5 percent royalties. Some inventors have gone up to as high as 8 percent, although 5 percent seems to be the norm. The clause also includes a schedule of how often the royalty payments will be made. Finally, it requires the Licensee to report the details of the sales so that the inventor retains some auditing capability.

3. This clause sets out the minimum royalty payment schedule. It defines an initial up-front bonus payment and a minimum amount of dollars that must be paid biannually no matter how many are actually sold. The initial bonus payment is traditionally given to award inventors for past work, time, and effort spent on developing the invention. Your negotiating position determines how high the numbers are in this payment schedule.

5. This clause sets out how and to whom the royalty payments will be paid out.

6. If Lansing (the Licensee) doesn't make at least the minimum royalty payments in a payment period, the clause provides a means in which the contract is terminated. The Licensee is still responsible for whatever it still owes.

6.2. This clause is to protect the inventor from a corporation that is just "sitting" on the product and not really making much money off it.

6.3. This clause provides the inventor with an auditing means if the inventor becomes suspicious or feels short-changed in royalties. You give yourself the right to go in and physically check their IRS records for assurance. If a corporation won't agree to putting in this clause for you, they probably aren't trustworthy.

6.4. Your Licensee may want to sublicense some of the manufacturing or marketing of your product to other corporations who have more capabilities in those specific areas. Of course, this is like giving out another license, and you will want to follow this closely. Be wary if your Licensee has an interest in dealing with some companies in the Asian regions. Patent regulations in the Eastern countries are very poorly enforced, and you could be setting yourself up for copycat nightmares. Make sure you discuss and highlight your concerns with your Licensee as soon as possible, and keep a close eye on the sublicensee's operations. You may even want to modify this clause so that the Licensee has to get permission from you before sublicensing.

6.5. This is called *an indemnity clause.* It makes sure that the Licensee assumes responsibility of protecting you in court if someone accidentally maims themselves with your invention and then tries to file a civil suit against you.

6.6. This clause makes sure that whatever is said orally after this agreement will not be legally binding. Without it, mutual oral consent can be binding in a court of law. In 1993 Kim Basinger was sued for millions by a production company for orally agreeing to do a Hollywood movie, but then backing out of it later.

7. You want the laws of the state in which you live to govern the contract; therefore, any possible disputes will have to be resolved in your state.

8. Spells out that the agreement is still binding when it transfers ownership.

9. This infringement clause lays out the rules of who can sue in cases of infringement. It is important to make sure that the inventor has a right to pursue infringement if the licensee does not. Most inventors cannot afford the out-of-pocket costs of such an infringement suit (from $50,000 to $100,000). Moreover, some corporations may feel that it's not worth it due to the high costs. The right to follow suit for both parties is preserved in this clause. If you have a stronger negotiating position, you may want to add to the clause a means of recovering resulting damages in the case of the Licensee suing.

10. This is the final signature clause. Keep in mind, however, when you do finish drafting your patent license, it's a necessity to have a patent attorney look it over—explaining your rights and double-checking your work. For help in drafting licensing agreements see the back section of this book: "Inventors' Publishing & Research: Services" or call 1-800-MARKET2 (627-5382). (*Note:* to protect the rights of all party members involved all names and addresses in my limited licensing contract are fictitious.)

Joint Owners' Agreement (JOA)

There are many problems that can arise when a patent has multiple inventors. This is due primarily to federal statute (35 USC Sect. 262), which states that any of the patent joint owners may make, use, or sell the patented invention without the consent or sharing of profits with the other joint owners. This can result in many unfair situations. For example, let's say one of the joint owners works hard for many years to design the invention, build a workable prototype, and develop a market for a particular product while the other just steps in as a competitor and reaps the benefits of the first partner's early work. To prevent this scenario, all of the project's inventors should sign a JOA contract. It essentially reverses statute 35 USC Sect. 262 by.

1. Ensuring that if one of the joint owners decides to sell the patented product, that owner must pay each of the other joint inventors a reasonable royalty.

2. Ensuring that all parties share profits proportionately (in a licensing or assignment situation) according to their interests and expenditures in the product. Essentially, you split up the percentages of ownership of the patent among the joint owners, depending on who deserves the most.

3. Prohibiting one party from exploiting the patent without majority consent.

4. Providing a method for settling possible disputes (mediation, arbitration).

Figure 8-5 shows a standard blank JOA. The JOA can be completed any time after the patent application is turned in. You are allowed to make changes or add to the JOA to suit your specific purposes.

The JOA is a written agreement among the joint owners and should not be filed with the PTO. Just make sure that each joint owner keeps an original signed copy that has been signed by all the other owners.

Figure 8-5. Joint owners' agreement

This agreement is made by and between the following parties who, by separate assignment or as joint applicants, own the following respective shares of the invention and patent application identified below:

_____ %   of _____

_____ %   of _____

_____ %   of _____

Invention Title: FingerTip Soldering Tool

Patent Application Ser. Nr.: _____

Filed: _____

The parties desire to stipulate the terms under which they will exploit this invention and patent application and therefore agree as follows:

1. No Action Without Everyone's Consent: None of the parties to this agreement shall license this invention or application, other than normal prosecution, without the written consent and cooperation of the other party or parties (hereinafter "parties") to this agreement, except as provided below. Any action so taken shall be committed to writing signed by all of the parties, or as many parties as consent, with copies to all other parties.

2. Decisions: In case any party is considering licensing the invention or patent application, the parties shall consult on such opportunity and a majority decision shall control unless the minority has reason to believe, in the case of licensing, that a more profitable opportunity for licensing can be feasibly obtained within a year from that debating time. In this case, a mutually acceptable arbiter shall be chosen who will listen to both sides and specifically determine if the minority's concerns about more profitable opportunities is legitimate. If the arbiter decides for the minority party, the minority shall control; otherwise the majority controls. In the event the parties are equally divided, the matter shall be also submitted to an impartial, mutually acceptable arbiter, whose decision shall control. If no arbiter can be agreed upon, then the parties shall each select a representative and the parties' representatives shall select the arbiter. After a decision is so made, all parties shall abide by the decision and shall cooperate fully by whatever means are necessary to implement and give full force to such decision. However, if there is time for any parties to obtain a better or different offer, they shall be entitled to do so and the decision shall be postponed for up to three months to allow such other parties to act.

3. Proportionate Sharing: The parties to this agreement shall share, in the percentages indicated above, in all income from, liabilities, and expenditures agreed to be made by any decision under Part 2 above in connection with the invention or patent application. In case a decision is made to make any expenditure, as for foreign patent application filing, exploitation, prototype building, etc., and a minority or other parties

opposes such expenditure or is unable to contribute a proportionate share, then the others shall advance the minority or other parties' share of the expenditure. Such others shall be reimbursed by the minority or other parties by double the amount so advanced from the minority or other parties' proportionate share of any income received, provided such income has some reasonable connection with the expenditure. No party shall be entitled to reimbursement or credit for any labor except external labor due to prototyping the invention (up to five prototypes a year) or other labor agreed upon in advance by all the parties hereto.

4. If Any Parties Desire to Manufacture, Etc.: Any party in this agreement can sell the product or service embodying the above invention without consent of the other parties under Part 1 above. The cost of the product shall include, in addition to normal profit, labor, commission, and/or overhead, etc., provision for a reasonable royalty, which shall be paid for the term of the above patent application. Such royalty shall be fair and reasonable and must be agreed upon within the range of 3 percent to 5 percent of the said cost of the product. Such royalty shall be distributed to all of the parties hereto according to their proportionate shares and on a quarterly basis, accompanied by a written royalty report and sent within one month after the close of each calendar quarter.

5. In Case of Dispute: In case any dispute or disagreement arises out of this agreement or in connection with the invention or patent application, the parties shall confer as much as necessary to settle the disagreement; all parties shall act and compromise to at least the degree a reasonable person would act. If the parties cannot settle their differences on their own, they shall submit the dispute to mediation by an impartial third party or professional mediator agreed to by all of the parties. If the parties cannot agree on a mediator, or cannot come to an agreement after mediation, then they shall submit the matter to binding arbitration with a mutually acceptable arbitrator or the American Arbitration Association. The arbitrator shall settle the dispute in whatever manner he or she feels will do substantial justice, recognizing the rights of all parties and commercial realities of the marketplace. The parties shall abide by the terms of the arbitrator's

decision and shall cooperate fully and do any acts necessary to implement such decision. The costs of the arbitrator shall be advanced by all of the parties or in accordance with Part 3 above and the arbitrator may make any allocation of arbitration costs he or she feels is reasonable. By signing below, the parties assert that they have reviewed, understand, and agree to the terms set forth in this agreement.

_____   Date: _____

_____   Date: _____

_____   Date: _____

Royalties

Determining the Amount of Royalties

When you are trying to determine how big a royalty check you feel you deserve, you should be warned that there's no set amount for any product. Because all inventors value their innovations differently, your product's worth is really up to the negotiating parties. You can ask the company you are working with what kind of royalties they have given to inventors in the past to get a rough idea of where you're heading. Generally though, royalties run from 3 to 5 percent for items that:

- Are assembled in mass quantities (greater than one million per year) on intense production assembly lines
- Are in highly competitive markets
- Carry a low retail price (less than $10.00)

Royalty rates start at 5 percent and can move as high as 10 percent for items that carry a relatively high profit margin. In some cases, technologically advanced items or product breakthroughs may reach as high as 50 percent. Typically, however, the higher the quantity produced, the lower the royalty percentage.

Despite these figures, you won't know for sure how much to expect until you've begun negotiating over royalties. The real secret to increasing your royalties lies in your ability to convince the opposing party that you deserve more. Here is a list of crucial factors that you will want to use as bargaining chips to persuade the opposing party to increase your royalties:

1. Your *relative bargaining strength*. Are you in a position to demand more, or does it seem that you need the company more than it needs you?

2. The anticipated amount of *net profits* the Licensee believes it will achieve, as a result of your product doing well on the marketplace. The Licensee will always play down this figure.

3. The *advantages* your product offers over its competition, and why it stands a good chance of dominating its competition, if any.

4. The *commercial performance* of past inventions that resemble yours, particularly in terms of public acceptance and net profits.

5. The potential *market share* of your product's overall worth.

6. The *amount of work, time, and money you've saved the company* in actively participating in its research and development.

7. The *degree of respect and the level of expertise* you've gained in the field of your invention.

8. The *low cost of manufacturing your invention* compared to similar or competing products. The company selling your invention will have low overhead.

Royalty Payments

When it comes time to collecting royalties, every inventor takes careful consideration about how they will be paid. What type of royalty will you get? Before you sign any paperwork, you need to be aware of the four types of royalties: *gross sales*, *net sales*, *fixed sum per unit*, or *selling price*. To determine which type will be best for you, try to envision how your product will do 10 years down the road. What seems like a tantalizing royalty offer today may turn out to be horribly unprofitable if your invention stops selling a few years ahead.

Percent of Gross Sales

This type of royalty is based upon you receiving a *percentage* of your product's *total* sales, **not** reduced by customer discounts, returns, allowances, or any other adjustments. By far, this kind of agreement is the best offer you may come across—a royalty that doesn't make you pay for product *deductions* out of your own pocket. However, trying to convince a company to pay out royalties based on gross sales is no easy task. In most cases, it is only possible when one or more of these factors are true:

1. The inventor has spent a great deal of time, money, and work in getting the invention under way.

2. The inventor has manufactured the product, thus greatly reducing the risk to a company that plans to distribute it.

3. The inventor signs an exclusive licensing contract with a company that controls only an average portion of the product's *total* market share.

4. The inventor experiences an extraordinary towering demand for the product—it's a breakthrough of some sort that people are desperately waiting for.

Under most typical circumstances, however, companies will usually shun such agreements. After all, they would have to reach into their pockets to make up for the difference caused by any deduction. Look at it this way: Unless there's an irrefutably enormous demand for your invention, don't even fuss with pursuing a gross sale royalty.

Percent of Net Sales

This is the most common method of royalty payment. Gross sales are reduced by returns, allowances, customer discounts, or any other deductions (specified in the license) to arrive at *net sales*—which you receive a percentage from. I recommend this type of royalty because it permits both parties to capitalize without the expense of the other. One word of caution: *Never* allow a company simply to use the word *deduction* to determine its net sales. You should demand that all *deductions* are to be specified in the license. The last thing you want is to be held accountable for an inequitable deduction, such as freight costs. Some common deductions are returns, bad debt, credit card charges, and freight. Other deductions such as packaging costs or advertising costs are uncommon and you should demand to have those removed from the definition of a deduction.

Fixed Sum Per Unit

Another possibility is simply to take a fixed sum for every product sold no matter what the selling price of the product is. This may work to your advantage if there is a trend toward the reduction of your product's selling price. On the other hand, if the Licensee decides to make more expensive versions of your products, you're stuck with the lower amount. In that case, you would have been better off with a royalty based on percent of net or gross sales.

Percent of Profit (1/3 to 1/2)

Some companies may offer you royalties based on the profit made from the sale of your patented product. Some typical offers may lie in the range from one third to one half of the profit. It's almost always safer to take a percentage of *sales* rather than *profit* because in the case of sales, even when the company isn't making much profit from the product, you're still getting paid a consistent royalty from sales. On the other hand, if you know the company's profits are going to be high, you may take the risk in making a profit deal with the company.

In practicality, a "1/3 profit royalty" deal and a "5 percent sales royalty" deal are very similar. The number 5 in "5 percent royalties off of sales" has been historically used based on the average overhead and profit typically experienced by companies with successful products. Typically, only 10 to 15 percent of the total sales of a successful product is profit. The other 85 to 90 percent go toward company overhead, expenses, cost of product, and so forth. So if a company gives you 5 percent royalties, what they are really giving you is approximately 30 to 50 percent of their profit (10 to 15 percent profit divided by the 5 percent royalty). This means that, in essence, the two methods are derived from the same reasoning. The idea is to give the inventor a good portion (30 to 50 percent) of the profit coming in from the patented product. However, as I warned earlier, you should remember that profit is usually more erratic than sales, which leaves you at more risk if you decide to go this route.

Also be aware that some companies may try to cheat on a profit deal by taking their losses from other parts of their company and claiming it onto your product. Ensure that you have access to company books so that you can audit them if necessary. Be suspicious if they have sold enormous quantities of your product but paid back very little royalties to you.

Choosing Between Selling or Licensing Your Invention

In today's world of fast-breaking technologies, many inventors consider the prospect of giving their invention up for sale. Suppose you're offered a lump sum of money for the *entire* rights of your patent. Should you take the offer? It depends on your circumstances. (Review the section on *assignments*, pages 137–141.)

If you have convinced yourself beyond a doubt that selling your invention serves your best interests, you need to think about how much you should receive. When determining this amount—the price it takes for you to part with your invention—compare a *quarter* of your *entitled* royalty earnings to your *buyout* price. If the difference between the total of your *entitled* royalty earnings and the total *buyout* price is a figure you can't risk losing, then by all means don't sell out!

Here's an example:

Suppose you file a *regular* patent application in 1997. One year later (1998), your patent *issues*. After two years from your patent *issue date* (2000), a company begins selling your invention, which you've licensed to them. A total of three years has elapsed since the date you've filed a patent application, which started your royalty life period. This leaves you with 17 years of entitled royalties (the 20-year maximum minus three years).

Now let's assume that during this seventeen-year royalty period, the company's *average* sale price for your invention is $25.00, along with its annual sales that reach an *average* 100,000 units. Plus, your royalty rate is 5 percent. At the end of 2000 (year 1), your royalty check would equal $125,000:

(0.05 x 25.00 = $1.25) x (1 x 100,000 = 100,000) = $125,000

At the end of 2016 (year 17), you will have collected a *total* of $2,125,000.

(0.05 x 25.00) x (17 x 100,000) = $2,125,000

You need now only calculate the buyout price—which reasonably should be a *quarter* of your *entitled* royalty earnings: $531,250.

(0.25 x $2,125,000 = $531,250)

In this case, the difference between your *entitled* royalty earnings and the *buyout* price is $1,593,750.

($2,125,000 – $531,250 = $1,593,750)

Coming up with an accurate *difference*—one that's a *realistic* figure—may prove to be difficult or even impossible. Due to the many inconstant variables involved, this calculation can *never* be entirely accurate. One part of the equation is straightforward—the money you are offered for your invention. The second part of the equation, which involves your entitled royalty earnings, depends on the following:

- Which license you advocate utilizing (exclusive, limited exclusive, or nonexclusive).

- The *class* of royalties you believe you'll receive (net sales, gross sales, selling price, or fixed sum per unit).
- The period of time between when you begin selling your product to the end of your patent life term. Typically, inventors don't begin marketing their products until several years from their *regular* patent applications file date, especially first-time inventors.
- The *adjusted* sales performance of your product during its patent life term, taking into consideration its *introduction* years when your product becomes known to the public, its *peak* years when your product earns maximum sales, and its declining years when it exhausts the marketplace.
- How well your product will stand up against similar and/or competing products.

As you can see, deciding to sell out is no bowl of cherries. You'll need to make intelligent choices, unbiased predictions, and conservative estimations. Also, if you think the decision of selling out is tough, just wait until you start looking for a buyer—it's nothing compared to what you'll have to go through to convince someone that the risks of buying your invention are undeniably outweighed by its potential profits.

Step 9

Improving the Strength of Your Patent

It happens all too often: Just when inventors are starting to collect royalties from their patent, a competitor finds a way to "work around" the patent, flooding the market with cheaper products that are strikingly similar to the original, and consequently cheating the inventors out of the millions that should have been theirs! Unfortunately, if someone finds such a "work-around" to your patent, what they're doing is perfectly legal. Don't wait to find yourself sitting around crying over the unfairness of the situation. Instead, take preventative measures now, and this scenario will never happen!

A factor that really determines how easy it is for copycats to work around your patent is called the *strength* of the patent. The principle factor that determines the strength of your patent lies in how novel and unobvious your invention really is. Let's say you've come up with a product to which there is nothing even similar: an electronic box that lets two individuals communicate by transcribing their thoughts onto a computer terminal. Because of its uniqueness, your patent will be very strong. On the other hand, let's say your patent is based solely upon the modification of a prior product that is in a crowded art: a central processing unit that is similar to the ones made by Intel, in the crowded computer industry. In this case, you may have a weak patent.

Whether your patent is strong or weak, you want to protect your investment as much as possible or you could lose millions in royalties.

Taking the time to deter copycats is a relatively simple procedure when you think about the huge losses you might incur if you don't do anything at all. The following sections explain some methods you can use to strengthen your patent and beat the copycats.

Method 1: Try to Work Around Your Own Invention

This may sound funny at first, but it is actually the best way to stop the copycats. Your goal is to file another patent application that includes all of the possible work-arounds or modifications to your patented invention that you can think of. Essentially, the work-arounds can be slight derivations, spin-offs, or even large modifications to your patented product that you think would still be worthwhile inventions to produce. Don't make the deviations so great that the new product idea suffers from a lack of concept or lacks the advantage that your patented product originally benefited from.

Let's look at how I did this with my soldering tool. The advantage was that this invention allowed the user to work with the same hand on which the heating tool was placed. It was granted a patent because it satisfied an unappreciated need that no other product satisfied. As a work-around, I tried to come up with new, entirely different ways of satisfying that need. I created a variety of designs that would also satisfy that "same hand" advantage, such as using an attachment to connect the tool to the wrist, arm, two fingers, and so forth. Then I filed all these designs as separate applications.

Don't hesitate to file more than one design in a single patent application. If it turns out that more than one design is patentable in the future, the PTO will allow you to file *divisional patent applications* later to separate the ideas.

For the mere price of filing for a patent application, you can explore the possibilities of working around your patent before copycats take you to the cleaners. If the PTO rejects all of your work-arounds, you should recognize that this further fortifies their view of the strength of your original patent. And if your work-arounds do go through, you should be pleased to know that *you* can own the patents to your work-arounds, and that you've kept them out of the hands of your copycat competitors.

Method 2: File for a Re-Issue Application

Within two years after your patent has been issued, you have the right to *broaden* your legal claims in your patent, thus increasing the legal scope of your invention. You can do this by filing a special type of application, called a *re-issue application*, and paying the appropriate normal application filing fee. If you feel you (or a lawyer) can increase the scope of your invention by rewording your claims, it may be worth dollars to you in the future. The catch here is that the wording in your new claims cannot go beyond what has been implied or inferred in the other sections of your patent. If they do, then you may want to try working around your own invention (Method 1) instead.

Method 3: Include Trade Secrets in Your Patent

Trade secrets are the best form of protection in the world because nobody can ever copy you. Coca-Cola is an example of a trade secret that nobody has been able to copy for almost a century. You don't have to disclose your ingredients. A trade secret may serve you even better than a patent—at least, as long as it remains a secret. Who needs a patent if you have a great secret? It's the ultimate protection, but risky because someday if somebody is crafty enough to figure out your secret, you're unprotected, unless you filed a patent. The problem arises when you file a patent you have to disclose to the detail all of the parts of your invention. So you're better off keeping it a secret if you're sure know will be able to "reverse-engineer" your idea. A trade secret may be enough protection for you if the sale of your invention is low-key, or in a niche market oriented through direct marketing or stores in small, out-of-the way cities. However, although you can sue someone you've employed or entrusted who purposely steals or leaks out a trade secret, *once the secret is leaked out to the public, anyone can legally use it*. A patent, on the other hand, seals your right to monopolize and enforce your rights upon anyone. If your product is a big-ticket item, you are better off getting a patent.

You might also want to work your trade secrets into your patent.

In general, you cannot include secrets in a patent because once your patent is published, it becomes public information. However, the PTO does provide means to include *trade secret descriptions that don't include information in determining patentability of your product.* This is tricky since a trade secret typically is the heart of your invention. Despite all of this, the *Manual of Patent Examining Procedure* (MPEP) mentions that you can submit trade secrets in such a manner, by "appropriate deletions of nonmaterial portions of the information. This should be done only where there will be no loss of information material to patentability under 37 CFR 1.56 or 1.555." In other words, if you or your lawyer (whoever writes the claims) can leave out specific words in your claims but still adequately describe your product and process, you may be able to leave a trade secret out of the patent text and then submit separately what the PTO calls a "Trade Secret Document" or "Proprietary Information." See section 724.02 in the MPEP for further details if you are interested in trying this.

Be careful about relying on trade secrets instead of patents because modern technology has made it easy to reverse-engineer practically anything, no matter how complex or miniature it may be. Reverse-engineer means to start from the end result and be able to completely work backward to figure out the inner working or composition of the invention. It is in fact scientifically easier to dissect or reverse-engineer an invention than it is to build one.

Method 4: Don't Include "Patent Number" Marking on Your Invention

Some companies don't include the patent number marking on their products. The marking makes it very convenient for a copycat to take down the exact number of the patent, order a copy of it, and then try to work around it. Even without the patent number, copycats can still do a patent search and locate your product, but this requires a bit more work and may turn off some copycats. However, if you don't include the patent number on your invention, you can only sue a possible infringer of your patent starting from the first date you contacted the infringing company Patent holders can sue from the date the infringer starts selling their invention, as long as the patent holder's patent has been issued (and is not in a pending state).

Method 5: Protest a Patent Application

If you are aware of a patent application that someone has filed to try to work around your patent, you may file a protest with the PTO (Title 37 CFR 1.291). In the protest, you can use arguments such as these:

1. The proposed work-around invention is something that has been in public use or on sale for more than one year in this country (one year rule: Title 35 102(b)).

2. You have information that the applicant abandoned the invention or did not personally invent the work-arounds that the application is for.

3. You have information relating to their lack of disclosure.

4. You have proof that the applicant's main intention is to work around your patent so that they don't have to pay you royalties.

5. You have information indicating "fraud" of some sort related to their work-around application.

6. You have other information demonstrating that their application lacks compliance with the statutory requirements for patents.

When submitting a protest, you do need to know and have read all the information concerning the patent. But how do you get this information if patent applications are held in secrecy? For one, you must at least know that there is an application filed with a product similar to yours and have an idea of which corporation is responsible for it. You may then send the PTO a "petition for access" for the application, laying out all the reasons why you desire and deserve such access. Be prepared to come up with some creative grounds in your petition because the PTO doesn't normally rule in favor of such petitions. You must send two copies of the petition to the Commissioner of the PTO because they need to send one copy to the applicant. See a patent attorney for details.

Usually, if you know about the existence of an application, it is because you are in close touch with the "grapevine" and rumors being passed around in your industry. If you do decide to file a protest, don't protest any attributes of the applicant's work-around invention that might also apply to yours; the PTO might reexamine your patent and find it invalid.

What to Do if Someone Worked Around Your Patent

If a competitor has worked around your patent in some way, there are still a couple of options you can pursue. First, your patent may dominate over their patent. The PTO may have let their patent through due to an innovation in its modification, even though your broader patent exists. This is a complicated issue, and you should see a patent lawyer if you believe the two patents interact in this way. You may be entitled to royalties from their product's success.

For a stiff fee (over $2,000), you can file with the PTO a request for re-examination of the claims in the work-around patent. In a re-examination, the PTO will take another close look at the invention's patentability and possibly invalidate the patent if your arguments are strong and valid. Your re-examination request will not be accepted unless you have prima facie (majority) evidence that points to a "substantial new question of patentability." (In cases of rejection, you are entitled to a partial refund of the fee.) All of your arguments and evidence for invalidating the claims of the competitor's patent must be derived from prior art references and publications. In other words, you must provide published facts and references that may show that the PTO made a mistake by originally allowing the patent application to pass its statutory requirements.

What to Do if Someone Copied Without a Patent

In many cases copycats simply try to manufacture and sell your inventions without a patent and without your permission. In this case, you can sue them for infringement (see Step 8 for details). Unfortunately, the reason that copycats risk such infringement is because they know that court expenses for infringement suits can range from $20,000 to millions, depending on what's at stake, and that it may not be profitable for your licensee company (which is legally using your patent) to sue them. For example, if your product only makes $40,000/year in profit, then it would take at least two years of profit just to take care of your court expenses. Now if the competition really wants to get dirty, several of them can start making your product at around the same time. Now it definitely isn't worth it for your licensee company to sue, but it *is* worth it for you to sue (that is, if you can afford it!). If you end up with a messy scenario such as this, try to find a patent lawyer who works on a contingency fee basis (collects later); otherwise, it will probably be impossible to afford.

You should always be wary about sharing your information with others, even if you do have a patent. Many Asian countries are infamous for their copycat factories and tactics and can tap into your success at the drop of a dime. The worst part is that even if you have foreign patents, in some countries such as China, they are barely enforced. China has one of the biggest copycat markets for music tapes and CDs in the world, selling copied CDs illegally for just a few dollars. Nintendo, the world leader in video games, lost millions of dollars because several businesses popped up in China whose sole purpose was to copy and illegally sell Nintendo video games. (They sold them at private computer stores!!) Nintendo had to spend millions of dollars before the Chinese government finally enforced its patent laws.

It gets worse. The president of an American company that bought my inventions had an amusing story about an Eastern copycat that started producing one of their products. Someone had stolen the mold to create the products and brought it back to Asia. The mold was a little worn out and had a few scratches due to wear and tear. Later on, after some investigation, a few of the molds that the copycats built were located in Asia. These molds were copied to such detail that they even included the same exact *scratches* on the outside!

Step 10

Product Differentiation

Expand Your Horizons and Protect Your Interests

Once you have successfully sold or licensed one of your patents, you may want to work on product differentiation to further increase your future royalties and benefits. Your goal is to create spin-offs or improvements to your invention that could be added to your licensee corporation's product line to supplement sales of your original invention. If your ideas are different enough, they may be patentable. Even if they are not, because your original patent generally covers it, these derivative products may be worthwhile to pursue. Corporations may find them appealing enough to add to their product lines (requiring them to kick back even more royalties to you!). In fact, if you license out a successful patent to a particular corporation, you can almost guarantee that the corporation will try to come up with modifications or next-generation improvements to your original invention in the future. Why not beat them to it?

Some of the invention ideas you designed to protect you from copycats (Step 9) may be applicable here if they are valuable enough inventions to pursue on the market. This chapter focuses on two types of derivative products: spin-offs and modifications.

Spin-offs

Creating a spin-off involves applying the *objects and advantages* of your original patent invention to a completely different product or use. Spin-offs of this type are often considered patentable because you end up with a new product or use. Your spin-off may not be patentable if the manner in which you applied your original concepts is considered obvious by the PTO. Colored lightbulbs for the use of "party lights" that come in red, blue, or green are a good example of a spin-off to an existing product. Another example would be to make a hair clipper for people and adapt it for the use of pets.

If you feel your spin-off idea may not be strong enough to warrant a patent, you may want to try to modify or improve some of the other common features of the invention. This gives your invention more chances of standing out from other products.

Coming up with creative thoughts that lead to spin-off ideas may be difficult, but there are some guidelines that may help you:

1. Instead of trying to come up with a totally new product right off the bat, first list the objects and advantages of your invention on paper.

2. Now research the full product lines of your licensee corporation (of your original patent) or its competitors to get a feel for what other product derivatives exist in your general area.

3. Next, one by one, go through these other competitive products and see if you can apply or adapt any of your major objects and advantages (from your original patent) to these other products. If you can, you may quickly find yourself with two or three spin-off ideas.

4. Take the initial steps to protect your new ideas.

5. Since you are already familiar with your general area, you should be able to sell your new spin-off ideas with much less effort.

It is important to always keep in close contact with the licensee corporation of your original patent. When you come up with spin-off ideas, you will find that they are often willing to take a serious look at them—especially if your original invention is making money for them. And supplementing their product line can only mean more royalties for you.

Modifications

The second way to derive new products is through modification or improvement of your original patented invention. To get an idea of what you can add, look at the many features that competitive products offer and simply add those to yours. Now, not only do you have the advantages of your originally patented invention, which no one else has the right to use, but you also have included the advantages or features of other competitive products. Since many of the additive features on competitive products are common to the industry (e.g., adding a light to a mining helmet design), you should be able to include them without running into infringement problems.

You'll find out just how innovative your improvements are when you file another patent application claiming your new improved product. If the PTO believes you've added enough modifications or improvements to make your new invention "unobvious" over the original, they will issue you an improvement patent. On the other hand, if your new invention is ruled as obvious over your old, you will probably not get another patent. In this case, you may still find the derivative product useful enough to profit from.

# Appendix A

Inventor's Assistance Organizations

Appendix A has been taken from the *Inventor Assistance Source Directory* and has been reprinted here courtesy of Pacific Northwest Laboratory. Contact these firms and clubs and you will find workshops and meetings between inventors bring valuable experience and information to the table.

ALABAMA

David L. Day
Program Coordinator
Alabama Technology Assistance
    Program
1717 11th Avenue So., Ste. 419
Birmingham, AL 35294
(205) 934-5395
fax (205) 934-7645

Raymond W. Hembree
Economic Dev. Chief
U.S. Small Business Administration
Business Development
2121 Eighth Ave. No., Ste. 200
Birmingham, AL 35203-2398
(205) 731-1338
fax (205) 731-1404

John Sandefur
State Director
Alabama SBDC
Medical Towers Building
1717 11th Ave., Ste. 419
Birmingham, AL 35294
(205) 934-7260
fax (205) 934-7645

ALASKA

Jan Fredericks
State Director
University of Alaska
SBDC
430 W. 7th Ave., Ste. 110
Anchorage, AK 99501
(907) 274-7232
fax (907) 274-9524

Al Jorgensen
President
Inventors Institute of Alaska
P.O. Box 876154
Wasilla, AK 99687
(907) 376-5114

John W. Sibert, Ph.D.
Exec. Director
AK Science/Technology Foundation
550 W. 7th Ave., Ste. 360
Anchorage, AK 99501
(907) 272-4333
fax (907) 274-6228

Mike Sims
Director of Business Development
Kenai Peninsula Borough
Economic Development District, Inc.
110 S. Willow, Ste. 106
Kenai, AK 99611
(907) 283-3335
fax (907) 283-3913

Robert Williams
Z.J. Loussac Public Library
Serials/Acquisitions Dept.
3600 Denali St.
Anchorage, AK 99503-6093
(907) 261-2970
fax (907) 562-1244

Robin Zerbel
Manager
World Trade Center Alaska
421 West First Avenue, Ste. 300
Anchorage, AK 99501
(907) 278-7233
fax (907) 278-2982

ARIZONA

Paul A. Baltes
Director
Engineering Profess. Development
University of Arizona
Box 9, Harvill Bldg.
Tucson, AZ 85721
(602) 621-5104
fax (602) 621-1443

Dr. Robert J. Calcaterra
President/CEO
Arizona Technology Incubator
1535 N. Hayden Rd.
Scottsdale, AZ 85257-3773
(602) 990-0400
fax (602) 970-6355

Michael York
Director
Gateway Community College
Small Business Development Center
108 N. 40th St.
Phoenix, AZ 85034
(602) 230-7308 ext. #109
fax (602) 392-5329

ARKANSAS

Garland E. Bull
President
Inventors Congress, Inc.
P.O. Box 411
Dandanelle, AR 72834
(501) 229-4515

Guy Enchelmayer
Director
E. AR. Bus. Incubator System
5501 Krueger Dr.
Jonesboro, AR 72401
(501) 935-8365
fax (501) 931-5133

CALIFORNIA

Newton E. Ball
Principal Engineer
Orbic Controls
Box 23827
Pleasant Hill, CA 94523
fax (510) 944-4987

Terry Chappell
Santa Cruz IWIEF Chapter
730 Encino Dr.
Aptos, CA 95003
(408) 662-1936
fax (408) 662-1936

John Christensen
President
Central Valley
Inventor's Association, Inc.
P.O. Box 1551
Manteca, CA 95336
(209) 239-5414

Marvin Clark
President
Antelope Valley IWIEF Chapter
4444 E. Ave. R, Sp. 127
Palmdale, CA 93550
(805) 273-0144

E. Joseph Cossman
President
Cossman International, Inc.
P.O. Box 4480
Palm Springs, CA 92263
(760) 320-7717
fax (760) 320-9247

Jacques Dulin
Director
Pillsbury, Madison & Sutro
Ten Almaden Blvd., Ste. 800
San Jose, CA 95113-2266
(408) 977-0120
fax (408) 977-0129

Joe Edmonds
Director
Black Inventors Technical Resources
P.O. Box 6402
Torrance, CA 90504
(310) 323-4668
fax (310) 323-4668

Sherm Fishman
Executive Director
Small Entity Patent Owners Assn.
295 Stevenson Dr.
Pleasant Hill, CA 94523
(510) 934-1331
fax (510) 934-1132

David Alan Foster
President
Total Multimedia
299 West Hillcrest Dr., Ste. 200
Thousand Oaks, CA 91360
(805) 497-4053

John Gee
Director
NASA - Ames Technology
Commercialization Center
155-A Moffett Park Dr., Ste. 104
Sunnyvale, CA 94089
(408) 734-4700
fax (408) 734-4946

Stephen Paul Gnass
Publisher
Invention Connection
P.O. Box 93669
Los Angeles, CA 90093-0669
800-458-5624
fax (213) 962-8588

Albert P. Halluin
Partner
Pennie & Edmonds
2730 Sand Hill Rd.
Menlo Park, CA 94025
(415) 854-3660
fax (415) 854-3694

Danny Holmes
President
Idea to Market Network
P.O. Box 12248
Santa Rosa, CA 95406
800-ITM-3210
fax (707) 584-4161

Greg W. Lauren
Coordinator
San Diego Inventors Group
11190 Poblado Rd.
San Diego, CA 92127
(619) 673-4733
fax (619) 451-6154

Daniel Leckrone
Chairman
Technology Properties, Ltd.
4010 Moorpark Ave., Ste. 215
San Jose, CA 95117
(408) 243-9898
fax (408) 296-6637

Robert Lewis
Inventors Helper Industries
4480 Treat Blvd., Ste. 310
Concord, CA 94521
(510) 676-4975
fax (510) 535-0450

George D. Margolin, Ph.D.
President
Margolin Development Company
Inventive Product Development
P.O. Box 2846
Newport Beach, CA 92663
(714) 645-5950
fax (714) 645-5974

John Moreland
Assistant Editor
Dream Merchant Magazine
2309 Torrance Blvd., Ste. 201
Torrance, CA 90501
1-800-35-DREAM
fax (310) 328-1844

Michael Odza
Publisher
Technology Access Report
16 Digital Dr., Ste. 250
Novato, CA 94949
(800) 733-1556
fax (415) 883-6421

William W. Otterson
Director
CONNECT UC/San Diego Ext.
Technology/Entrepreneurship
U.C.S.D. Extension - 0176
La Jolla, CA 92093-0176
(619) 534-6114
fax (619) 552-0649

Dr. Marshal E. Reddick
Director
Institute of Entrepreneurship
California State Univ. Los Angeles
5151 State University
Los Angeles, CA 90032
(213) 343-2971

Martha Regan
Vice President
Inventors New Venture Alliance
P.O. Box 371148
Montara, CA 94037
(510) 726-1945
fax (510) 726-1945

James F. Riordan
President
The James F. Riordan Co., Inc.
3110 Camerosa Circle
Cameron Park, CA 95682
(916) 676-4729

Charles Robbins
Director
Sawyer Inventive Resource Center
520 Mendocino Ave., Ste 210
Santa Rosa, CA 95401
(707) 524-1773
fax (707) 524-1772

Gene Scott
President
Macro - Search Corp.
2082 Business Center Dr. #225
Irvine, CA 92715
(714) 253-9930
fax (714) 253-0951

Robert M. Sperry, Esq.
Patent Attorney
Private Patent Practice
23390 Ostronic Dr.
Woodland Hills, CA 91367
(818) 225-1011
fax (818) 340-4629

Robert L. Stark
Invention Workshop
Univ. Southern California
Far West Tech Transfer Center
3716 S. Hope St., Rm. 200
Los Angeles, CA 90007
(213) 743-6132
fax (213) 746-9043

Alan Tratner
President
(805) 962-5722
fax (805) 899-4927

Alan A. Tratner
International President
Inventors Workshop
International Education Foundation
7332 Mason Avenue
Canoga Park, CA 91306-2822
(818) 340-4268
fax (818) 884-8312

Lawrence J. Udell
Executive Director
Center for New Venture Alliance
California State University
Hayward, CA 94542-3066
(510) 881-3805
fax (510) 727-2039

Maggie Weisberg
Editor
Lightbulb Journal
1029 Castillo St.
Santa Barbara, CA 93101-3736

Chuck Wolfe
Principal
Credo, Wolfe & Associates
2801 Moorpark Ave., Ste. 2
San Jose, CA 95128-3103
(408) 345-0288
fax (408) 345-0282

Dr. A. Wortman
President
ISTAR Inc.
406 Alta Ave.
Santa Monica, CA 90402-2714
(310) 394-7332
fax (310) 394-7332

COLORADO

Karl J. Dakin, PC
Dakin Law Tech, LLC
384 Iverness Dr. So., Ste. 205
Englewood, CO 80112
(303) 779-1992
fax (303) 779-9784

John T. Farady
President
Affiliated Inventors Found. Inc.
902 N. Circle Dr., #208
Colorado Springs, CO 80909-5002
(719) 380-1234
fax (719) 635-1578

Joanne Hayes
Publisher
Inventors' Digest
4850 Galley Rd., Ste. 209
Colorado Springs, CO 80915
(719) 573-4540
fax (719) 573-4679

Harold Linke
Club Administration
30317 Lewis Ridge Rd.
Evergreen, CO 80439-8725

President
Colorado Biomedical Venture Center
1610 Pierce St.
Denver, CO 80214
(303) 237-3998
fax (303) 237-4010

Dr. Patrick MacCarthy
Professor
Colorado School of Mines
Dept. of Chemistry & Geochemistry
Golden, CO 80801
(303) 273-3626
fax (303) 273-3629

Michael R. McKensie
Director
CO Inventors Council, Inc.
P.O. Box 88
Holyoke, CO 80734
(303) 854-3851

Charlene Sims
Rocky Flats Local Impacts Initiative
Business Development Center
5460 Ward Rd., Ste 205
Arvada, CO 80002
(303) 940-6090

Cornelia A. Snyder
President
Rocky Mountain Inventors Congress
P.O. Box 4365
Denver, CO 80204
(303) 674-5338

Teri Wenz
CU Business Advancement Centers
335 S. 43rd St.
Boulder, CO 80303
(303) 499-8114

CONNECTICUT

Barbara Burnes
Principal
InoNet, Inc.
187 South Salem Rd.
Ridgefield, CT 06877
(203) 438-1661
fax (203) 221-7060

Lorraine M. Donaldson, Esq.
Attorney
Patent & Licensing Group of New
    England
10 Bay St., Ste. 112
Westport, CT 06880
(203) 454-3540
fax (203) 222-8608

Jack Lander
Program Director VP
Innovators Network of Greater
    Danbury
37 Seneca Rd.
Danbury, CT 06811
(203) 797-8955

Stanley Mason
President
SIMCO, Inc.
61 River Rd.
Weston, CT 06883
(203) 227-0041
fax (203) 222-1890

John P. O'Conner
State Director
CT Small Business Dev. Center
U of CT Allyn Larabee Brown Bldg.
U-9r, Route 44
Storrs, CT 06269-5094
(203) 486-4135
fax (203) 486-1576

DELAWARE

Susan Rhoades
Tech. Specialist
Delaware Economic Development
   Office
99 Kings Highway, P.O. Box 1401
Dover, DE 19903
(302) 739-4271
fax (302) 739-5749

Clinton Tymes
SBDC State Director
University of Delaware
005 Purnell Hall
Newark, DE 19716
(302) 831-2747
fax (302) 831-1423

DISTRICT OF COLUMBIA

Donald Kelly
Director
Patent Examining Group
Patent & Trademark Office
U.S. Department of Commerce
Washington, DC 20231
(703) 308-0975
fax (703) 305-3463

Terry Levinson
U.S. Department of Energy
1000 Independence Ave. CE 521,
   5E052
Washington, DC 20585
(202) 586-1478
fax (202) 586-8134

Levi Lipscomb
Acting Director
Howard University
SBDC
2600 6th St. NW., P.O. Box 748
Washington, DC 20059
(202) 806-1550
fax (202) 806-1777

Jill MacNeice
Washington Editor
Tech Access Report
5723 Nebraska Ave. NW
Washington, DC 20015
(202) 244-4191

Ruth Nyblod
Admin. for Proj. XL
Office of Public Affairs
Patent & Trademark Office
Washington, DC 20231
(703) 305-8341
fax (703) 308-5258

Bill Scheirer
Economist
U.S. Small Business Administration
2328 19th NW
Washington, DC 20009
(202) 205-6977
fax (202) 205-7064

Herbert C. Wamsley
Exec. Director
Intellectual Property Owners Assoc.
1255 23rd St. N.W., Ste. 850
Washington, DC 20037
(202) 466-2396
fax (202) 466-2893

FLORIDA

William R. Bowman
Vice President
The Inventors Club
WSRE-TV
1000 College Blvd.
Pensacola, FL 32504
(904) 484-1224
fax (904) 484-1255

Dr. W. Les Cahoon
Area Director
STAC @ USF
COE, ENB 118
4202 E. Fowler Ave.
Tampa, FL 33620-5350
(813) 974-4222
fax (813) 974-3369

Jerry Cartwright
State Director
Florida SBDC Network
19 West Garden St.
Pensacola, FL 32501
(850) 595-6060
fax (850) 444-2070

Brent Gregory
Research Economist
Florida Department of Commerce
107 West Gaines St.
Tallahassee, FL 32399-2000
(904) 487-3134
fax (904) 487-6516

Jim Hahn
Associate Director
Small Business Development Center
P.O. Box 161530
Orlando, FL 32816-1530
(407) 823-5554
fax (407) 823-3073

Anne E. Klenner
CEO
Klenner International
P.O. Box 1748
Ormond Beach, FL 32175
(904) 673-4339
fax (904) 673-5911

Eugene H. Man, Ph.D.
President/CEO
Center for Health Technologies, Inc.
1150 N.W. 14th St., Ste. 105
Miami, FL 33136-2112
(305) 325-2733
fax (305) 325-2698

Joseph Mason, Jr.
Reg. Patent Attorney
Mason & Associates, P.A.
18167 U.S. Hwy 19 North, Ste. 150
Clearwater, FL 34624-6566
(813) 538-3800
fax (813) 538-3820

Dr. Gary Nelson
Executive Vice Pres.
Edison Inventors Association, Inc.
P.O. Box 07398
Ft. Myers, FL 33919
(813) 275-4332

Pamela H. Riddle
Director
FL Product Innovation Center
2622 NW 43rd St., Ste. B3
Gainesville, FL 32606-7428
(904) 334-1680
fax (904) 334-1682

Ronald E. Smith, Esq.
Reg. Patent Attorney
Mason & Associates, P.A.
17757 U.S. Hwy 19 N., Ste. 500
Clearwater, FL 34624
(813) 538-3800
fax (813) 538-3820

Robert Wheeler
President
Tampa Bay Inventors Council
P.O. Box 2254
Largo, FL 34646
(813) 596-3384

Betty White
Dir. Public Affairs
Inventors Society of South Florida
P.O. Box 4306
Boynton Beach, FL 33424
(561) 736-6594

William Whitman
President
Thermal Storage Systems, Inc.
2517 Trinidad St.
Sarasota, FL 34231
(813) 921-0517

Jerry Zajic
Tech Specialist
PSPI, Inc.
15 Dahoon Court South
Homosassa, FL 34446-8922
(904) 382-1535

GEORGIA

Donna Brown
Program Specialist
University of Georgia SBDC
1180 E. Broad St.
Athens, GA 30602-5412
(706) 542-6804
fax (706) 542-6776

Ronald L. Henderson
Dir. Grants Management
U.S. Department of Energy
Atlanta Support Office
730 Peachtree St. NE, Ste. 876
Atlanta, GA 30308
(404) 347-7139
fax (404) 347-3098

Alexander T. Marinaccio
Chairman
Inventors Clubs of America, Inc.
P.O. Box 450261
Atlanta, GA 31145-0261
1-800-336-0169
fax (404) 355-8889

Mary-Frances Panettiere
Head, Tech Resources
Georgia Institute of Technology
Library and Information Center
Atlanta, GA 30332-0900
(404) 894-4508
fax (404) 894-8190

W.C. Stillwagon
President
CAN DO Industries, Inc.
7610 Ball Mill Rd.
Atlanta, GA 30350
(770) 396-1401
fax (404) 671-1070

HAWAII

Barbara Kim Stanton
Executive Director/CEO
High Tech. Devel. Corp.
300 Kahelu Ave., Ste. 35
Honolulu, HI 96789
(808) 539-3806
fax (808) 539-3611

IDAHO

Rick Ritter
Executive Director
Idaho Innovation Center
2300 N. Yellowstone
Idaho Falls, ID 83401
(208) 523-1026
fax (208) 523-1049

Betty Capps
Regional Director
Idaho State University
Small Business Development Center
2300 North Yellowstone, Ste. 121
Idaho Falls, ID 83401
(208) 523-1087
fax (208) 523-1049

Gerald Fleischman, P.E.
Bioenergy Specialist
State of Idaho
Dept. of Water Resources
Box 83720
Boise, ID 83702-0098
(208) 327-7959
fax (208) 327-7866

State Director
Idaho Small Business Development
    Ctr.
State Office - Boise State Univ.
1910 University Dr.
Boise, ID 83725
(208) 385-1640
fax (208) 385-3877

Burt Knudson
Technical Services Consultants
ISBDC Technology Consultant
ISBDC Technology Connection
1910 University Dr.
Boise, ID 83725
(208) 385-3870
fax (208) 385-3877

Helen M. LeBoeuf-Binninger
Regional Director
Idaho SBDC
Lewis-Clark State College
500 - 8th Avenue
Lewiston, ID 83501
(208) 799-2465
fax (208) 799-2878

John Lynn
Regional Director
Idaho Small Business Devel. Center
North Idaho College
1000 W. Garden
Coeur d Alene, ID 83814
(208) 773-9807
fax (208) 777-8123

Ken J. Pedersen
Patent Attorney
404 S. 8th St., Ste 310
Boise, ID 83702
(208) 343-6355
fax (208) 385-9768

James R. Steinfort
Director
Technical & Industrial Extens. Serv.
Boise State University
1910 University Dr.
Boise, ID 83752
(208) 385-3689
fax (208) 385-3877

ILLINOIS

Bruce R. Baumeister
President
Innovation Development Corporation
P.O. Box 1185
Calumet City, IL 60409
(708) 891-0316
fax (708) 891-0316

David L. Gulley, Ph.D.
Senior Associate
Great Cities Coordinating Office
University of Illinois at Chicago
1737 West Polk St., Ste. 310
Chicago, IL 60612-7227
(312) 996-4995
fax (312) 413-0238

Ken Kirkland
Director
Northern Illinois University
Tech. Commercialization Office
DeKalb, IL 60115-2874
(815) 753-1238
fax (815) 753-1631

Roger Luman
Director
Business and Technical Assistance
   Centers
Bradley University
Peoria, IL 61625
(309) 677-2852
fax (309) 677-3386

Jim Mager
Director
Office of Technology & Commerce
Southern Illinois Univ. at Edwardsville
Campus Box 1108
Edwardsville, IL 62026
(618) 692-2166
fax (618) 692-2555

John W. Morehead
President
Technology Search International, Inc.
500 East Higgins Rd.
Elk Grove Village, IL 60007-1437
(708) 593-2111
fax (708) 593-2182

Thomas E. Parkinson
Director
Evanston Business & Tech Center
1840 Oak Ave.
Evanston, IL 60201
(708) 866-1817
fax (708) 866-1808

Nicholas G. Parnello
President/Founder
American Inventors Council
P.O. Box 4304
Rockford, IL 61110
(815) 968-1040
fax (815) 962-1495

Barbara Spiegel
Administrator
Northwestern University
Technology Transfer Program
633 Clark St.
Evanston, IL 60208-1111
(847) 467-2979

Daniel D. Voorhis
Director
Western Illinois University - SBDC
Seal Hall 214
Macomb, IL 61455
(309) 298-2211
fax (309) 298-2520

INDIANA

Robert Humbert
President
Indiana Inventors Association
5514 South Adams
Marion, IN 46953
(765) 674-2845

W.S. Johnson
Director
Indiana University
Indust. Res. Liaison Program
One City Centre, Ste. 200
Bloomington, IN 47404
(812) 855-6294
fax (812) 855-8270

Stephen Thrash
Executive Director
Indiana Small Business
    Development Network
One N. Capitol, Ste. 420
Indianapolis, IN 46204
(317) 264-6871

Daniel Yovich
Professor
Inv. & Entrep. Soc. of IN
P.O. Box 2224
Hammond, IN 46323
(219) 989-2354
fax (219) 989-2750

IOWA

John Beneke
Director
Iowa Lakes SBDC
Gateway North Highway 71 North
Spencer, IA 51301
(712) 262-4213
fax (712) 262-4047

Clark Marshall
Director
Iowa Small Bus. Develop. Center
Gateway North
Spencer, IA 51301
(712) 262-4213
fax (712) 262-4047

Benjamin C. Swartz
Director
Drake University, SBDC
INVENTURE Program
2507 University Ave.
Des Moines, IA 50311
(515) 271-2655
fax (515) 271-4540

KANSAS

Clyde C. Engert
President
Innovative Technology Enterprise
    Corp.
112 W 6th St., Ste 408
Topeka, KS 66603
(913) 233-9102
fax (913) 296-1160

Tom Hull
State Director
Kansas SBDC
Wichita State University
1845 Fairmount
Wichita, KS 67260-0148
(316) 689-3193
fax (316) 689-3647

C. Dale Lemons
Executive Director
Pittsburg State University
Business & Technology Institute
Pittsburg, KS 66762-7560
(316) 235-4920
fax (316) 232-6440

Arlene Moore
Doc. Patent Librarian
Wichita State University
1845 Fairmount
Wichita, KS 67260-0068
(316) 689-3155
fax (316) 689-3048

KENTUCKY

Ken Blandford
Mgmt. Consultant
University of Louisville
SBDC
Burhans Hall - Shelby Campus
Louisville, KY 40292
(502) 588-7854
fax (502) 588-8573

Janet Holloway
State Director
University of Kentucky
Kentucky SBDC
225 Bus. & Econ. Bldg.
Lexington, KY 40506-0034
(606) 257-7668
fax (606) 258-1907

Vance A. Smith
Attorney
Bluegrass Inventors Guild
P.O. Box 43610
Louisville, KY 40253-0610
(502) 423-9850
fax (502) 423-1452

LOUISIANA

John Baker
State Director
Northeast Louisiana University
Louisiana SBDC
700 University Ave.
Monroe, LA 71209
(318) 342-5506
fax (318) 342-5510

Charles D'Agostino
Exec. Director
Louisiana State University
LA Business & Technology Center
South Stadium Dr.
Baton Rouge, LA 70803-6100
(504) 334-5555
fax (504) 388-3975

Laverne Jasek
Econ. Dev. Spec.
Louisiana Dept. of Economic Dev.
P.O. Box 94185
Baton Rouge, LA 70804-9185
(504) 342-5371

Robert Montgomery
Patent Agent & Pres.
Southern Technology Development
109 Brownlee Ave.
Broussard, LA 70518-3021
(318) 837-4042
fax (318) 837-5552

MAINE

James S. Ward
University of Maine
Department of Industrial Cooperation
5711 Boardman Hall
Orono, ME 04469-5711
(207) 581-1488
fax (207) 581-1484

MARYLAND

John Boucher
Chairman of Commun.
Innovators Network
2106 Salisbury Rd.
Silver Springs, MD 20910
(301) 585-1885

Kate Hayes
Coordinator
Technology Transfer Info. Cntr.
National Agricultural Library
10301 Baltimore Blvd.
Beltsville, MD 20705-2351
(301) 504-6875
fax (301) 504-7098

George P. Lewett
Director
NIST
OTEA
Building 411, Rm. A115
Gaithersburg, MD 20899-0001
(301) 975-5500
fax (301) 975-3839

MASSACHUSETTS

Jack Brady
President
Worcester Area Inventors
65 Windsor St.
Worcester, MA 01605
(508) 757-6178

Steve Chamuel
President
HighTech Design
26 Murray St.
W. Peabody, MA 01960
(508) 535-2543

John Ciccarelli
State Director
Small Business Development Center
205 School of Management, UMass
Amherst, MA 01003
(413) 545-6301
fax (413) 545-1273

Donald L. Gammon
President
Inventors Assoc. of New England
115 Abbot St.
Andover, MA 01810-4835
(978) 474-0488
fax (978) 474-0488

Donald Job
President
Innovative Products Research
    & Services
393 Beacon St.
Lowell, MA 01850
(978) 934-0035
fax (978) 934-0035

Donald Job
President
Enbede Co.
P.O. Box 335
Lexington, MA 02173
(781) 934-0035
fax (781) 934-0035

Edward Kahn
President
EKMS, Inc.
100 Inman St.
Cambridge, MA 02139
(617) 864-4706
fax (617) 864-7956

Bill Wolf
Executive Director
Technology Capitol Network
201 Vassar St.
Cambridge, MA 02139
(617) 253-8214
fax (617) 258-7264

MICHIGAN

Charles Blankenship
President
Economic Development Corp.
P.O. Box 387
Traverse City, MI 49685
(616) 946-1596
fax (616) 946-2565

Barbara B. Eldersveld
InnCom
P.O. Box 507
Ypsilanti, MI 48197
(313) 963-0616
fax (313) 963-7606

J. Downs Herold
Dir. of Liaison
University of Michigan
College of Engineering
2901 Hubbard
Ann Arbor, MI 48109-2016
(313) 747-0041
fax (313) 747-0036

Thomas Kubanek
Econ. Dev. Dir.
Manistee County Economic
Development Office
375 River St., Ste. 205
Manistee, MI 49660
(616) 723-4325
fax (616) 723-1488

Sarah McCue
Communications Mgr.
Michigan SBDC
2727 Second Ave.
Detroit, MI 48201
(313) 964-1798
fax (313) 964-3648

Joe Nies
Director
Industrial Development Center
311 Houghton St.
Ontonagon, MI 49953
(906) 884-2795

Thomas Schumann
Program Director
Technology Transfer Center
Ferris State University
1020 E. Maple St.
Big Rapids, MI 49307
(616) 592-3774
fax (616) 796-1448

MINNESOTA

Bill Baker
Director
Inventors & Designers Ed Association
P.O. Box 268
Stillwater, MN 55082
(612) 430-1116

Bill Baker
Inventor's Network
23 Empire Dr., Ste 105
St. Paul, MN 55103
612-602-3175

Ruth Bernstein
President
Inventors' Network
818 Dunwoody Blvd.
Minneapolis, MN 55403
(612) 933-8911

Andrew Berton
President
Excel Development Group Inc.
1721 Mount Curve Ave.
Minneapolis, MN 55403-1017
(612) 374-3233
fax (612) 377-0865

Wes Cutter
Vice President
Nordic Track
Product Planning & Development
104 Peavey Rd.
Chaska, MN 55318
(612) 368-2777
fax (612) 368-2781

Sara Madsen
MIC Coordinator
Minnesota Inventors Congress
805 E. Bridge
P.O. Box 71
Redwood Falls, MN 56283
(507) 637-2344
fax (507) 637-5929

Michael & Lynn Marra
Marra Design Associates, Inc.
7007 Dakota Ave.
Chan Hassen, MN 55317
(612) 937-8141
fax (612) 934-1180

Kathy McDonald
Coordinator
Metro ECSU Young Inventors Fair
3499 Lexington Ave. No.
St. Paul, MN 55126
(612) 490-0058
fax (612) 490-1920

Mark Mueller
Director
Minnesota Technology, Inc. Reg. Ofc.
Center for Economic Devel. - UMD
Ste. 140, Olcott Plaza, 820 N. 9th St.
Virginia, MN 55792
(218) 741-4241
fax (218) 741-4249

Randall Olson
Executive Director
Minnesota Project Innovation, Inc.
111 Third Ave. So., Ste. 100
Minneapolis, MN 55401-2551
(612) 338-3280
fax (612) 338-3483

Paul G. Paris
President
Society of MN Inventors
20231 Basalt St.
Anoka, MN 55303
(612) 753-2766

Mike Tikkanen
Past President
Minnesota Entrepreneurs Club
1000 LaSelle Ave.
Minneapolis, MN 55403-2005
(612) 533-1932
fax (612) 533-1865

Wade Van Valkenburg
President
Accessible Technologies, Inc.
494 Curfew
St. Paul, MN 55104
(612) 659-0569
fax (612) 645-3675

Roger Zhan
President of the Minneapolis
   Entrepreneurs Club
(612) 330-0963

Member Svcs. Coord.
The Collaborative
10 S. 5th St., Ste. 415
Minneapolis, MN 55402
(612) 338-3828
fax (612) 338-1876

MISSISSIPPI

Dr. William Blair
President
Society of MS Inventors
P.O. Box 13004
Jackson, MS 39236-3004
(601) 982-6229
fax (601) 982-6610

Raleigh Byars
State Director
Mississippi SBDC
Ste. 216, Old Chemistry Bldg.
University, MS 38677
(601) 232-5001
fax (601) 232-5001

J.W. Lang
Director
Small Business Development Center
Meridian Community College
Meridian, MS 39307
(601) 482-7445
fax (601) 482-5803

Bobby Lantrip
Mgr. Tech Services
Mississippi SBDC
Ste. 216, Old Chemistry Bldg.
University, MS 38677
(601) 232-5001
fax (601) 232-5001

Gordon Tupper
President
Delta Inventors Society
P.O. Box 257
Stoneville, MS 38776
(601) 686-3350
fax (601) 686-4045

Noel Estel Wilson, Jr.
Managing Dir.
Mississippi State University
Small Business Development Center
P.O. Box 5288
Mississippi State, MS 39762
(601) 325-8684
fax (601) 325-8686

MISSOURI

Dr. John Amos
Professor
University of Missouri - Rolla
Center for Technology Dev.
Bldg. 1, Nagogami Terrace
Rolla, MO 65401
(314) 341-4559
fax (314) 341-4992

Nick Arends
Business Counselor
Univ. of Missouri-Columbia SBDC
Mid-Missouri Inventor Assoc.
1800 University Place
Columbia, MO 65211
(314) 882-7096
fax (314) 882-9931

Gene J. Boesch
Managing Director
St. Louis Technology Center
P.O. Box 12405
St. Louis, MO 63132
(314) 432-4204
fax (314) 432-1250

Fred Goss
Tech Project Manager
Center for Tech. Transfer/Econ. Dev.
University of Missouri - Rolla
Rolla, MO 65401
(314) 341-4559
fax (314) 341-6495

H.S. Duke Leahy
Washington University
Campus Box 1054
1 Brookings Dr.
St. Louis, MO 63130
(314) 935-5825
fax (314) 935-5862

Mark Manley
Engineer
Center for Technology
Grinstead 80 CMSU
Warrensburg, MO 64093
(816) 543-4402

Bernard L. Sarbaugh
Coordinator for Tech
Central Missouri State University
Grinstead 80
Warrensberg, MO 64093
(816) 543-4402
fax (816) 543-8159

Lisa Sireno
Assistant Director
Missouri Innovation Center
5650 A. S. Sinclair Rd.
Columbia, MO 65203
(573) 446-3100

Ed Stout
Mid-America Inventors
1746 Levee Rd.
North Kansas City, MO 64116
(816) 221-2442
fax (816) 221-3995

Jerry Udell
Innovation Institute
Route 2, Box 184
Everton, MO 65646
(417) 836-6302
fax (417) 836-6337

Gary J. Weil
Vice President
EnTech Engineering, Inc.
1846 Craig Park Court
St. Louis, MO 63146
(314) 434-5255
fax (314) 434-3270

MONTANA

Bob Campbell
Western Regional Dir.
Montana Entrepreneurship Center
The University of Montana
Ste. 204, McGill Hall
Missoula, MT 59812
(406) 243-4009
fax (406) 243-4030

Fred E. Davison
President
Creativity, Innovation, Productivity,
    Inc.
RR #1, Box 37
Highwood, MT 59450
fax (406) 733-5031

David P. Desch
Sr. Investments Mgr.
Montana Science & Tech. Alliance
46 N. Last Chance Gulch, Ste. 2B
Helena, MT 59620
(406) 449-2778
fax (406) 442-0788

Clarence A. Emerson
Acting President, Montana Inventors
    Assoc.
President of King Tool
5350 Love Lane
Bozeman, MT 59715
(406) 586-1541
fax (406) 585-9028

Roger N. Flair
Montana State University
Research & Devel. Institute
1711 West College
Bozeman, MT 59715
(406) 587-4479
fax (406) 587-4480

Teri Foley
Business Development Center
305 W. Mercury St.
Butte, MT 59701
(406) 723-4061

W. T. George
Pre-Patent Assistant
Yellowstone Inventors Assoc.
3 Carrie Lynn
Billings, MT 59102
(406) 259-9110

Howard E. Haines
Bioenergy Eng. Spec.
Montana Dept. of Nat. Resour. & Cons.
Energy Division
1520 E. 6th Ave., P.O. Box 202301
Helena, MT 59620-2301
(406) 444-6697
fax (406) 444-6721

Bruce Hofmann
Bus. Develop. Coord.
Montana Tradeport Authority
2722 3rd Ave. N., Ste. 300 W
Billings, MT 59101-1931
(406) 256-6871
fax (406) 256-6877

Al Jones
1929 Clubhouse Way #6
Billings, MT 59105
(406) 259-1251

Ann Keenan
Sr. Reg. Director
Montana Entrepreneurship Center
Montana State University
Reid Hall
Bozeman, MT 59717
(406) 994-2024
fax (406) 994-4152

Dave Krueger
Reg. Dir., Billings
Montana Entrepreneurship Center
Montana State University - Billings
Cisel Hall
Billings, MT 59101
(406) 657-2813
fax (406) 657-2327

NEBRASKA

Robert Bernier
State Director
University of Nebraska at Omaha
Nebraska Business Devel. Centers
1313 Farnam St., Ste. 132
Omaha, NE 68182
(402) 554-2521
fax (402) 554-3747

Herbert Hoover
Info. Specialist
University of NE-Lincoln
UN Engineering Extension
W191 Nebraska Hall
Lincoln, NE 68588-0535
(402) 472-5600
fax (402) 472-2410

Jackie Johnston
Memb. Serv. Director
Association of SBDCs
1313 Farnam St., Ste. 132
Omaha, NE 68182-0472
(402) 595-2387
fax (402) 595-2388

Ron Tillery
President
The Development Council
1007 Second Ave., P.O. Box 607
Kearney, NE 68848
(308) 237-9346
fax (308) 237-3103

NEVADA

Don Costar, Pte
Founder
Nevada Inventors Association
P.O. Box 9905
Reno, NV 89507-0905
(702) 322-9636
fax (702) 322-0147

Sharolyn Craft
Director
Nevada Sm. Bus. Devel. Ctr
University of Nevada Las Vegas
4505 Maryland Pkwy., Box 456011
Las Vegas, NV 89154-6011
(702) 895-0852
fax (702) 895-4095

Dr. Thomas Gutherie
President/CEO
So. Nevada Certified Development Co.
2770 S. Maryland Pkwy. Ste. #212
Las Vegas, NV 89109
(702) 732-3998
fax (702) 732-2705

John Kleppe, Ph.D., P.E.
President, NITEC
c/o TMCC Institute for Bus. & Ind.
4001 S. Virginia St.
Reno, NV 89502
(702) 829-9000
fax (702) 829-9009

Sam Males
State Director
SBDC
University of Nevada, Reno (032)
College of Business Admin.
Reno, NV 89557
(702) 784-1717
fax (702) 784-4337

Rolin Stutes
President
Nevada Inventors Association
P.O. Box 3121
Carson City, NV 89702-3121
(702) 877-1161
fax (702) 849-3342

NEW HAMPSHIRE

Robert T. Ebberson
Manchester SBDC & Training
    Programs Office
1000 Elm St., 8th Floor
Manchester, NH 03101-1730
(603) 624-2000
fax (603) 634-2449

Stephanie Henkel
Senior Editor
Sensors
174 Concord St.
Peterborough, NH 03458
(603) 924-9631
fax (603) 924-7408

Gene R. Talsky
President
PROMARK Consulting Services
P.O. Box 5249
Hanover, NH 03755
(603) 643-3043
fax (603) 643-3043

Richard Thompson
I.D.E.A.
Star Route Box 98
Meridan, NH 03770
(603) 469-3304
fax (603) 469-3305

David S. Urey
Licensing Consultants
TechWorks
15 Kancamagus Estates, P.O. Box 337
Conway, NH 03818-0337
(603) 447-6331
fax (603) 447-6331

NEW JERSEY

Randy Harmon
Help Desk Manager
NJSBDC/Rutgers Grad. School of
    Mgmt.
Technology Help Desk
180 University Ave.
Newark, NJ 07102
(201) 648-1597
fax (201) 648-1596

Sheila Kalisher
President
National Society of Inventors
P.O. Box 434
Cranford, NJ 07016
(973) 994-9282

Alyson Miller
Asst. State Director
NJ Small Bus. Devel. Center
180 University Ave.
Newark, NJ 07102
(201) 648-5950
fax (201) 648-1110

NEW MEXICO

James M. Geenwood
Exec. Dir.
Los Alamos Economic Development
    Corp.
P.O. Box 715
Los Alamos, NM 87544
(505) 662-0001
fax (505) 662-0099

Allan Gutjahr
Vice President
Research & Economic Development
New Mexico Tech
College Avenue
Socorro, NM 87801
(505) 835-5646
fax (505) 835-5649

Richard Reisinger
Dir. Product Development
Technology Ventures Corporation
4919 Marble NE
Albuquerque, NM 87110
(505) 246-2882
fax (505) 246-2891

Howard L. Smith
Interim Dean
Anderson School of Management
The University of New Mexico
Albuquerque, NM 87131-1221
(505) 277-6471
fax (505) 277-7108

Dr. Averett Tombes
VP Res. & Econ. Dev.
New Mexico State University
Box 30001, Dept 3RED
Las Cruces, NM 88003
(505) 646-2022
fax (505) 646-6530

NEW YORK

Jeffrey Bass
Director of Strategic Business
    Planning
Margolin, Winer & Evens
400 Garden City Plaza
Garden City, NY 11530
(516) 747-2000
fax (516) 747-6707

Harvey Heit
Small Business Development Center
  - Brooklyn
111 Livingston St., Rm. 208
Brooklyn, NY 11201
(718) 596-7081
fax (718) 596-6989

Donna Hopkins
Patents Librarian
New York Public Library
5th Avenue & 42nd St.
New York, NY 10018
(212) 930-0917

Phil Knapp
NY Society of Prof. Inventors
116 Stuart Ave.
Amityville, NY 11701
(516) 598-3228
fax (516) 598-3241

Jeffrey Kohler
Director
Aztech, Inc.
1576 Sweet Home Rd.
Amherst, NY 14228
(716) 636-3628
fax (716) 636-3630

Richard Labs
Research Director/CL&B
Technology Business Advisory Group
100 Kinloch Commons
Manlius, NY 13104-2484
(315) 682-8502
fax (315) 682-8508

Paul W. Larrabee
Tech. Info. Assoc.
New York State Energy Authority
2 Empire State Plaza, Ste. 1901
Albany, NY 12223-1253
(518) 465-6251
fax (518) 432-9474

Brian McLaughlin
Informations Svc. and Research
P.O. Box 95
Syracuse, NY 13210
(315) 476-7359

NY Society of Prof. Inventors
SUNY Farmingdale
Lupton Hall
Farmingdale, NY 11735
(516) 420-2397

Tom Reynolds
Director
SUNY Institute of Technology
Small Business Devel. Center
P.O. Box 3050
Utica, NY 13504
(315) 792-7546
fax (315) 792-7554

Leo Smith
President
Smith Engineering
114-56 142nd St.
Jamaica, NY 11436
(718) 529-3434

Earl Wells
InfoEd
453 New Karner Rd.
Albany, NY 12205
(518) 464-0691
fax (518) 464-0695

Paul White
OM
Patent Research Services
P.O. Box 68
Dix Hills, NY 11746
1-800-835-0880
fax 1-800-633-3292

Paul White
OM
Inventor's Helper
P.O. Box 68
Dix Hills, NY 11746
1-800-633-9727
fax 1-800-633-3292

William Wild
Director
West. NY Tech. Devel. Center
200 Harrison St.
Jamestown, NY 14701
(716) 661-3336
fax (716) 483-4470

NORTH CAROLINA

Scott R. Daugherty
State Director
NC SBDC
4509 Creedmoor Rd., #201
Raleigh, NC 27612
(919) 571-4154
fax (919) 571-4161

Brent Lane
President
NC Technological Development
    Authority, Inc.
2 Davis Dr., P.O. Box 13169
Research Triangle Park, NC 27709
(919) 990-8558
fax (919) 990-8561

Deborah McKenna
Technology Counselor
Small Business Technical
    Development Center
34 Wall St., Rm. 707
Asheville, NC 28801
(704) 285-0021
fax (704) 285-0021

Edward P. White
Consultant
907 Linden Rd.
Chapel Hill, NC 27514-7742
(919) 929-7283
fax (919) 933-9233

NORTH DAKOTA

Warren Enyart
CEO
Technology Transfer, Inc.
1833 East Bismarck Expressway
Bismarck, ND 58504
(701) 221-5346
fax (701) 221-5320

Garrison Area Improvement
 Association
P.O. Box 445
Garrison, ND 58540
(701) 463-2631
fax (701) 463-7487

Bruce Gjovig
Director
Center for Innov. & Bus. Devel
Box 8372, UND Station
Grand Forks, ND 58202
(701) 777-3132
fax (701) 777-2339

Wally Kearns
State Director
ND/SBDC
University of North Dakota
118 Gamble Hall, Box 7308
Grand Forks, ND 58202
(701) 777-3700
fax (701) 777-3225

Chuck Pineo
ERIP/SBIR Prog. Mgr.
Center for Innovation & Business Dev.
Box 8372 - UND Station
Grand Forks, ND 58202
(701) 777-3132
fax (701) 777-2339

OHIO

Director
Invention Connection of Cleveland
P.O. Box 360804
Cleveland, OH 44136
(216) 226-9681

Dinah Adkins
Executive Director
National Business Incubation Assn.
20 E. Circle Dr., #190
Athens, OH 45701
(614) 593-4331
fax (614) 593-1996

Charles Alter
Director of Business Development
Edson Industrial Systems Center
1700 N. Westwood Ave., Ste. 2286
Toledo, OH 43607-1207
(419) 531-8610
fax (419) 531-8465

Robert E. Bailey
Director
Ohio Technology Transfer Research
    Resource Program
Rm. 216 Bevis Hall
1080 Carmack Rd.
Columbus, OH 43210
(614) 292-5485
fax (614) 292-1893

Fred Carr
Director
University of Akron
Center for Economic Education
213 Crouse Hall
Akron, OH 44325-4210
(216) 972-7762
fax (216) 972-6990

Ron Docie
President
Hopewell Coop., Inc.
73 Maplewood Dr.
Athens, OH 45701-1910
(614) 594-5200
fax (614) 594-4004

Mike Kingsbourgh
President
Inventors Society at Northwest, OH
617 Croghan St.
Fremont, OH 43420
(419) 332-2221
fax (419) 334-6164

Michael Lacivita
President
Youngstown - Warren Inventors
    Assoc.
3220 Eldora Dr.
Youngstown, OH 44511
(216) 792-4880

Mike Lehere
NORSAC
SBIR Assistance Center
58 W. Center St.
Akron, OH 44308
(216) 375-2173
fax (216) 762-3657

Ned Oldham
President
Akron/Youngstown Inventors
1225 W. Market St.
Akron, OH 44313
(216) 864-5550
fax (216) 867-7986

Michel Perdreau
Dir./Member Services
National Business Incubation Assn.
20 E. Circle Dr., #190
Athens, OH 45701
(614) 593-4331
fax (614) 593-1996

Jerry Semer
Attorney at Law
617 Croghan St.
Fremont, OH 43420
(419) 332-2221
fax (419) 334-6164

Ronald J. Versic
Chairman
Inventors Council of Dayton
Young Inventors Committee
P.O. Box 630
Dayton, OH 45459-0630
(937) 439-4497
fax (937) 439-1704

Calvin Wight
1496 Lakewood Ave.
Lakewood, OH, 44107

OKLAHOMA

Ken F. Addison, Jr.
Oklahoma Inventors Congress
P.O. Box 27850
Tulsa, OK 74149-0850
(918) 245-6465
fax (918) 245-2947

Zelda J. Anderson
Owner/Manager
Marketing/Business Assistance
P.O. Box 1474
Broken Arrow, OK 74013
(918) 258-8420

Bill Gregory
Coordinator
Inventors Resource and Technology
   Center, OSBDC
100 S. University Ave., Rm. 106
Enid, OK 73701
(405) 242-7989
fax (405) 237-2304

Terry Henneke
Bid Asst. Coordin.
O.T. Autry Area Vocat. Tech. School
1201 West Willow
Enid, OK 73703
(405) 242-2750
fax (405) 233-8262

Mark Kachigian
President
Head & Johnson PA
228 W. 17th Place
Tulsa, OK 74119
(918) 587-2000
fax (918) 587-5603

Tom Mosley, Jr.
Dir. Tech Transfer
Zuzak Corporation
5460 S. Garnett, Ste. A
Tulsa, OK 74146
(918) 663-0155
fax (918) 622-6755

Julian Taylor
President
Invention Development Society
8230 SW 8th St.
Oklahoma City, OK 73128
(405) 787-0145
fax (405) 789-8198

Betty Wright
Childrens Inventors Coordinator
Oklahoma Student Inventors
    Exposition
8230 S.W. 8th St.
Oklahoma City, OK 73128
(405) 787-0145

OREGON

John Bayer
President/Principal
MarketLink Strategies
P.O. Box 42182
Portland, OR 97242
(503) 232-1514
fax (503) 234-3731

John A. Beaulieu
President
Oregon Resource and Technology
Development Fund
1934 N.E. Broadway
Portland, OR 97232-1502
(503) 282-4462
fax (503) 280-6080

David Fanning
Esquire/Attorney
Kolisch, Hartwell, Dickinson,
    McCormack & Heuser, P.C.
520 S.W. Yamhill St., Ste. 200
Portland, OR 97204
(503) 224-6655
fax (503) 295-6679

Arthur Ferretti
President
Unitor Corporation
P.O. Box 309
Silverton, OR 97381
(503) 873-7746
fax (503) 873-7746

Dr. Brecharr Hemmaplardh
President
Theodore Texas & Associates
P.O. Box 4633
Portland, OR 97208
(503) 244-6447
fax (503) 246-4859

Phyllis Lohse
Business Consultant
2123 SW Greene
West Linn, OR 97068-4107
(503) 655-3410
fax (503) 657-5138

Robert L. Newhart II
Director
Business Development Center
Central Oregon Community College
2600 NW College Way
Bend, OR 97701-5998
(503) 383-7290
fax (503) 383-7503

Barbara O'Neill
Oregon State Library
Patent & Trademark Depository
State Library Building
Salem, OR 97310
(503) 378-4239
fax (503) 588-7119

Pete Taylors
Program Director/Saturday Academy
Oregon Graduate Institute
P.O. Box 91000
Portland, OR 97291-1000
(503) 639-8701
fax (503) 690-1470

PENNSYLVANIA

Charles Coder
Director
Bucknell University SBDC
Product Development Center
126 Dana Engineering Building
Lewisburg, PA 17837
(717) 524-1249
fax (717) 524-1768

Jay W. Cohen
President
American Society of Inventors
P.O. Box 58426
Philadelphia, PA 19102
(215) 546-6601

Gregory L. Higgins, Jr.
State Director
Pennsylvania SBDC
423 Vance Hall, 3733 Spruce St.
Philadelphia, PA 19104-6374
(215) 898-1219
fax (215) 573-2135

Robert K. Jordon
Founder
Northwestern Inventors Council
Gannon University
Erie, PA 16541
(814) 871-7619
fax (814) 455-2631

Robert S. Krutsick
Exec. Vice President
University City Science Center
3624 Market St.
Philadelphia, PA 19104
(215) 387-2255
fax (215) 382-0056

Jay Schenck
PENN Tap
Penn State Behrend College
Station Rd.
Erie, PA 16563-0101

Dr. Louis Schiffman
President
Techni-Research Assoc., Inc.
P.O. Box T
Willow Grove, PA 19090-0922
(215) 657-1753
fax (215) 576-7924

Henry Skillman
American Society of Inventors
1601 Market St., Ste. 720
Philadelphia, PA 19103

Henry Skillman
Treasurer
American Society of Inventors
Box 58426
Philadelphia, PA 19102
(215) 563-4100

Dr. Bruce M. Smackey
Inventors Assistance
Lehigh University
621 Taylor St.
Bethlehem, PA 18015
(215) 758-3446
fax (215) 758-4499

Richard Stollman
President
Domestic & International Tech Ltd.
115 West Ave.
Jenkintown, PA 19046
(215) 885-7670
fax (215) 884-1385

RHODE ISLAND

Domenic Bucci
Rhode Island Solar Energy Assoc.
42 Tremont St.
Cranston, RI 02920-2543
(401) 942-6691

Douglas Jobling
State Director
SBDC
Bryant College
1150 Douglas Pike
Smithfield, RI 02917
(401) 232-6111
fax (401) 232-6416

Claudia Terra
Executive Director
Rhode Island Partnership for Science
   & Technology
7 Jackson Walkway
Providence, RI 02903
(401) 277-2601
fax (401) 277-2102

SOUTH CAROLINA

William Chard
Assoc. V.P. Research
Battelle Liaison
Clemson University
300 Brackett Hall Clemson Univ.
Clemson, SC 29634-5705
(803) 656-1296
fax (803) 656-0202

Judy Clements
Operations Manager
University of South Carolina/Aiken
   Private Investor Network
171 University Pkwy.
Aiken, SC 29801
(803) 648-6851
fax (803) 641-3362

Dallas Garrett
Southeast Manufacturing Tech Center
1201 Main St., Ste. 2010
P.O. Box 1149
Columbia, SC 29202
(803) 252-6976
fax (803) 252-0056

John Lenti
State Director
SC SBDC
College of Business Administration
University of South Carolina
Columbia, SC 29208
(803) 777-4907
fax (803) 777-4403

Dennis Rogers
Director
O'Connell Econ. Ent. Institute
University of South Carolina/Aiken
171 University Pkwy.
Aiken, SC 29801
(803) 648-6851
fax (803) 641-3362

Johnny Sheppard
President
Carolina Inventors Council
2960 Dacusville High Way
Easley, SC 29640
(803) 859-0066

Dr. N. M. Vyas
Assoc. Director
Economic Enterprise Institute
University of South Carolina/Aiken
171 University Pkwy.
Aiken, SC 29801
(803) 648-6851
fax (803) 641-3445

Ronald A. Young
Vice President
Enterprise Development Inc. of SC
P.O. Box 1149
Columbia, SC 29202
(803) 252-8806
fax (803) 252-0053

SOUTH DAKOTA

Duane Sander
Dean
College of Engineering-SDSU
CEH 201 Box 2219
Brookings, SD 57007-0096
(605) 688-4161
fax (605) 688-5878

Steven Wegman
Engineer
SD Public Utility Commission
State Capitol Bldg., 500 E. Capital
Pierre, SD 57501
(605) 773-3201
fax (605) 773-3809

TENNESSEE

Director
The University of Tennessee
Research Corporation
415 Communication Bldg.
Knoxville, TN 37996-0344
(615) 974-1882
fax (615) 974-2803

Tom Bowie
Consultant
Tennessee SBDC
320 So. Dudley
Memphis, TN 38104
(901) 527-1041
fax (901) 527-1047

Dewey Feezell
President
Tennessee Inventors Assoc.
P.O. Box 11225
Knoxville, TN 37939
(615) 483-0151
fax (615) 974-5492

Dennis A. Grahl
Martin Marietta Energy Systems, Inc.
Office of Technology Transfer
P.O. Box 2009
Oak Ridge, TN 37831-8242
(615) 576-0378
fax (615) 574-9241

Sharon Taylor-McKinney
Business Consultant
TN SBDC/SW
320 S. Dudley
Memphis, TN 38104
(901) 527-1041
fax (901) 527-1047

TEXAS

Mary Abrahams
Program Coordinator
Center for Entrepreneurship
Baylor University
P.O. Box 98011
Waco, TX 76798
(817) 755-2265
fax (817) 755-271

Daniel Altman
President
Venture Assistance
Forensic & Small Business Srvcs.
5807 S. Braeswood Blvd.
Houston, TX 77096
(713) 729-1129
fax (713) 729-1129

Tim Bigham
Principle Researcher
Information Insights
1418 Fairwood Rd.
Austin, TX 78722
(512) 451-8871
fax (512) 451-1885

Curtis E. Carlson, Jr.
Director
U.S. Department of Energy
Dallas Support Office
1420 W. Mockingbird Lane, Ste. 400
Dallas, TX 75247
(214) 767-7245
fax (214) 767-7231

Jan G. Casner
Richardson ISD
c/o 15611 Overmead Circle
Dallas, TX 75248
(214) 448-2850
fax (214) 448-2848

Jan Chisham
155503 Champaign Ct.
Tomball, TX 77537-6164
281-351-1316
jc@nol.net
www.flash.net/~cgenius/naie/
www.choicemall.com/naie

Ned Conley
Conley, Rose & Tayon
1850 Texas Commerce Tower
600 Travis St.
Houston, TX 77002-2912
(713) 238-8000
fax (713) 238-8008

Wessie Cramer
Executive Director
Network of American Inventors and
    Entrepreneurs
11371 Walters Rd.
Houston, TX 77067
(281) 351-1316
fax: (281) 351-1606

Russell D. Culbertson
Patent Attorney
Shaffer & Culbertson
1250 Capital of TX Hy. S.
Building 1, Ste. 360
Austin, TX 78746
(512) 327-8932
fax (512) 327-2665

Bruce Davis
Toy & Game Inventors of America
5813 McCart Ave.
Ft. Worth, TX 76133
(817) 292-9021
fax (817) 346-8697

Jill Fabricant, Ph.D.
Director
NASA - Johnson Technology
    Commercialization Center
2200 Space Park Dr., Ste. 200
Houston, TX 77058
(713) 335-1250
fax (713) 333-9285

Worth Hefley
President
Amarillo Inventors Assoc.
P.O. Box 15023
Amarillo, TX 79105
(806) 376-8726
fax (806) 376-7753

Lynn W. Hollingsworth
General Partner
Best Concept P.D. Co.
1212 Collinwood West Dr.
Austin, TX 78753
(512) 834-7886

John Kirk, Jr.
Shareholder
Jenkens & Gilchrist
1100 Louisiana, Ste. 1800
Houston, TX 77002
(713) 951-3300
fax (713) 951-3314

Susan Macy
Director
University of Houston
SBDC-Texas Product Dev. Cntr.
1100 Louisiana, Ste. 500
Houston, TX 77002
(713) 752-8440
fax (713) 756-1515

Mike Mead
President & Founder
Entrepreneurs Online
10550 Richmond Ave., Ste. 200
Houston, TX 77042
(713) 784-8822
fax (712) 735-2900

John Moetteli, P.E., M.A.
Owner
Da Vinci Design
15207 McConn
Webster, TX 77598
(713) 280-9473
fax (713) 280-9152

David F. Montgomery
Director
Texas Tech Univ.
Small Business Develop. Center
2579 S. Loop 289
Lubbock, TX 79423
(806) 745-1637
fax (806) 745-6207

Mrs. Eloyd Murphy
President
Texas Inventors Assoc.
PO Box 311
Arlington, TX 76004
(817) 265-1540

David Ostfeld
Partner
Chamberlain, Hrdlicka, White,
    Williams & Martin
1400 Citicorp Center - 1200 Smith St.
Houston, TX 77002
(713) 658-2505
fax (713) 658-2553

Jamin Patrick
Director
Austin Technology Incubator
8920 Business Park Dr.
Austin, TX 78759
(512) 794-9994
fax (512) 794-9997

Bernarr Pravel
Partner
Pravel, Hewitt, Kimball & Krieger
1177 West Loop South, 10th Floor
Houston, TX 77027
(713) 850-0909
fax (713) 750-0165

Kenneth A. Roddy
Patent Agent
2916 West T.C. Jester, Ste. 108
Houston, TX 77018
(713) 686-7676
fax (713) 957-4344

J. Nevin Shaffer, Jr.
Patent Attorney
Shaffer & Culbertson
1250 Capital of TX Hy. S.
Building 1, Ste. 360
Austin, TX 78746
(512) 327-8932
fax (512) 327-2665

Brian P. Shannon
President
Ultimate Concepts, Inc.
P.O. Box 740304
Houston, TX 77274-304
(713) 873-6338
fax (713) 778-9092

Pamela Speraw
Director
Bill J. Priest Inst. for Econ. Dev.
Technology Transfer Center
1402 Corinth
Dallas, TX 75215
(214) 565-5852
fax (214) 565-5881

UTAH

G. Michael Alder
Director
Business Creation
324 S. State St., Ste. 500
Salt Lake City, UT 84114-7380
(801) 538-8770
fax (801) 538-8773

Sterling Francom
Cntr. for Entrepreneurship Training
P.O. Box 30808
Salt Lake City, UT 84130-8080
(801) 967-4558
fax (801) 967-4017

David Morrison
Patents Librarian
Marriott Library
University of Utah
Salt Lake City, UT 84112
(801) 581-8394
fax (801) 585-3464

David Nimkin
Utah Small Business Dev. Center
102 West 500 South #315
Salt Lake City, UT 84101
(801) 581-7905
fax (801) 581-7814

Stephen Reed
Director
Weber State University
Technology Assistance Center
Ogden, UT 84408-1801
(801) 626-6309
fax (801) 626-6987

Dennis Rigby
Proc. Outreach Spec.
S.E.U.A.L.G.
P.O. Box 1106
Price, UT 84501
(801) 637-5444
fax (801) 637-5448

Jim Sonntag
Patent Attorney
420 E. South Temple, #345
Salt Lake City, UT 84111
(801) 359-3762
fax (801) 359-3763

Karen Stewart
Marketing Director
CEDO
777 S. State St.
Orem, UT 84058
(801) 226-1521
fax (801) 226-2678

Josie Valdez
SBA (Small Business Administration)
125 South State St.
Salt Lake City, UT 84138
(801) 524-3209
fax (801) 524-4160

Jake Vandermeide
Chairman
Science, Technology & Innovation
State Office
P.O. Box 11
West Jordan, UT 84084
(801) 569-2973

Mike Warren
Utah Small Business Dev. Center
102 West 500 South #315
Salt Lake City, UT 84101
(801) 581-7905
fax (801) 581-7814

John Winder
President
Intermountain Society of Inventors
    and Designers
9888 Darin Dr.
Sandy, UT 84070
(801) 571-2617

J. Winslow Young
Reg. Patent Attorney
P.O. Box 1088
Centerville, UT 84014-5088
(801) 292-1248

VERMONT

Curt Carter
Dev. Programs Coord.
State of Vermont
Agency of Devel. & Comm. Affairs
Montpelier, VT 05609
(802) 828-3221
fax (802) 828-3258

Hervey Scudder
Sales Development
The Catalyst Group
P.O. Box 1200
Brattleboro, VT 05302-1200
(802) 254-3645
fax (802) 254-3645

VIRGINIA

Dinesh Agarwal
Partner
Shlesinger, Arkwright & Garvey
3000 South Eads St.
Arlington, VA 22202
(703) 684-5600
fax (703) 836-5288

Stephen Clark
Reg. Patent Agent
916 W. 25th St.
Norfolk, VA 23517
(804) 625-1140
fax (804) 625-5917

Paul Hesse
Sr. Technical Spec.
EREC Energy Efficiency
Renewable Energy Clearinghouse
P.O. Box 3048
Merrifield, VA 22110
(800) 523-2929

Wanda Hylton
Virginia Tech Graduate Center
2990 Telestar Court
Falls Church, VA 22042
(703) 698-6016
fax (703) 698-6062

Charles A. Kulp
Director
Small Business Development Center
918 Emmet St. North, Ste. 200
Charlottesville, VA 22903-4878
(804) 295-8198
fax (804) 295-7066

Bill Martin
N.C.I./E.R.E.C.
8260 Greensboro Dr., Ste. 325
McLean, VA 22102
(703) 903-0325
fax (703) 903-9750

Mike Miller
NJ Comm. on Science and Tech.
4156 Elizabeth Lane
Annadale, VA 22003
(703) 425-4825
fax (703) 425-6736

Martha Morales
Associate Exec. Dir.
AIPLA
2001 Jefferson Davis Hwy., Ste. 203
Arlington, VA 22202
(703) 415-0780
fax (703) 415-0786

Cathy Renault
Dir. Entrep. Devel.
Technology Commercialization
Cntr. for Innovative Tech.
CIT Bldg, Ste. 600, 2214 Rock Hill Rd.
Herndon, VA 22070
(703) 689-3000
fax (703) 689-3041

Sally Rood
Associate Director
National Technology Transfer Center
Wheeling Jesuit College
2121 Eisenhower Ave., Ste. 400
Alexandria, VA 22314
(703) 518-8800
fax (703) 518-8986

B. Edward Shlesinger, Jr.
Senior Partner
Shlesinger, Arkwright & Garvey
3000 South Eads St.
Arlington, VA 22202
(703) 684-5600
fax (703) 836-5288

WASHINGTON

Wiboon Arunthanes, Ph.D.
Asst. Prof. Mktng.
Washington State University, Tri-
    Cities
100 Sprout Rd.
Richland, WA 99352-1643
(509) 375-9207
fax (509) 375-5337

Dallas Breamer
President
Tri-Cities Enterprise Assoc.
2000 Logston Blvd.
Richland, WA 99352
(509) 375-3268
fax (509) 375-4838

Barbara Campbell
Director
NASA - Northwest Office RTTC
12318 NE 100th Place
Kirkland, WA 98033
(206) 827-5136
fax (206) 827-5430

James M. Canode
Project Director
The Business Consortium, Inc.
P.O. Box 599
Wilbur, WA 99185
(509) 647-2000
fax (509) 647-2001

John Lindsay
President/CEO
TRIDEC
901 N. Colorado
Kennewick, WA 99336
(509) 735-1000
fax (509) 735-6609

George Linsteadt
Federal Laboratory Consortium
Management Support Office
P.O. Box 545
Sequim, WA 98382-0545
(206) 683-1005
fax (206) 683-6654

Steven Loyd
Western Investment Network
P.O. Box 13310 Burton Station
Vashon Island, WA 98013
(206) 441-3123
fax (206) 463-6386

JoAnna Slaybaugh-Taylor
Innov. & Tech. Dev. Spec.
SBDC
Innovation Assessment Center
    Program
135 Kruegel Hall
Pullman, WA 99164-4727
(509) 335-1576
fax (509) 335-0949

Harriet B. Stephenson, Ph.D.
Albers School of Business &
    Economics
Seattle University
Broadway and Madison
Seattle, WA 98122-4460
(206) 296-5702
fax (206) 296-5795

Robert Storwick
Patent Attorney
Graybeal, Jackson, Haley & Johnson
777 108th Ave. NE, Ste. 2460
Bellevue, WA 98004-5117
(206) 455-5575
fax (206) 455-1046

Peter Stroosma
Skagit Valley College
SBDC
2405 College Way
Mount Vernon, WA 98273
(206) 428-1282
fax (206) 336-6116

Lynn Trzynka
Small Business Development Center
Western Washington University
309 Parks Hall
Bellingham, WA 98225-9073
(206) 650-3899
fax (206) 650-4844

Jim Van Orsow
IAC Director
Washington State University
Innovation Assessment Center
180 Nickerson St., #207
Seattle, WA 98109
(206) 464-5450
fax (206) 464-6357

Margaret Wagner-Dahl
Acting Director
University of Washington JD-50
Office of Technology Transfer
1107 N.E. 45th St., Ste. 200
Seattle, WA 98105
(206) 543-3970
fax (206) 685-4767

WEST VIRGINIA

Hazel Kroesser
State Director
WV Small Business Devel. Center
950 Kanawha Blvd. East
Charleston, WV 25301
(304) 558-2960
fax (304) 558-0127

WISCONSIN

Technology Deployment Fund
Wisconsin Dept. of Development
P.O. Box 7970
Madison, WI 53707
(608) 267-9383
fax (608) 267-2829

Debra Malewicki
Program Manager
Wisconsin Innovation Service Ctr.
UW-Whitewater
402 McCutchan Hall
Whitewater, WI 52190
(414) 472-1365
fax (414) 472-1600

WYOMING

Kay Stucker
U.S. Small Business Administration
P.O. Box 2839
Casper, WY 82602
(307) 261-5761
fax (307) 261-5499

Scott Warner
Asst. Mgr./Org. Coord Discovery Lab
West Inventors Council
109 Engineering Research
P.O. Box 6101
Morgantown, WY 26506-6101
(304) 293-3612
fax (304) 293-3472

FOREIGN COUNTRIES

Dr. Meki Solomona
Director
Economic Dev. Planning Office
American Samoa Government
Pago Pago, American Samoa, 96799
American Samoa
(684) 633-5155
fax (684) 633-4195

Susan Best
Project Director
Women Inventors Project
1 Greensboro Dr., Ste. 302
Etobicoke, Ontario M9W 1C8
Canada
(416) 243-0660
fax (416) 243-0688

Terry Collins
Consultant
Nova Scotia Dept. of Economic Dev.
1800 Argyle, P.O. Box 519
Halifax, Nova Scotia B3J 2R7
Canada
(902) 424-7382
fax (902) 424-5739

Mark Ellwood
President
Inventors Alliance of Canada
47 Kenneth Avenue
Toronto, Ontario M6P 1J1
Canada
(416) 762-3453
fax (416) 762-3301

Jeff Galenzoski
President
B.C. Inventors Society
P.O. Box 5086
Vancouver, BC V6B 4A9
Canada

Stephen Guerin
Inventor/Owner
Guerin Science & Technology
1060 Walden Circle Unit 11
Mississauga, Ontario L5J 4J9
Canada
(905) 855-5357

Bob Huehn
Senior Analyst
Canadian Industrial Innovation
    Centre
156 Columbia St. West
Waterloo, Ontario N2L 3L3
Canada
(519) 885-5870
fax (519) 885-5729

Vince Kehoe
Intell. Prop. Analyst
Concept Licensing Corporation
1518 Dome Tower 333-7 Avenue SW
Calgary, Alberta T2P 2Z1
Canada
(403) 265-3011
fax (403) 266-4091

Mrs. Chips Klein
Co-Director
The Women Inventors Project, Inc.
1 Greensboro Dr., Ste. 302
Etobicoke, Ontario M9W 1C8
Canada
(416) 243-0668
fax (416) 243-0688

Ralf Koechling
President
Copyrights, Inventions & Patents
    Association of Canada
1518 Dome Tower, 333-7 Ave. SW
Calgary, Alberta T2P 2Z1
Canada
(403) 265-3011
fax (403) 266-4091

Ms. Teri Lydiard
Tech Transfer Officer
University/Industry Liaison
Simon Fraser University
Burnby, BC V5A 1S6
Canada
(604) 291-5844
fax (604) 291-3477

Luc E. Morisset
Director
Canadian Centre for Ind. Inn.,
    Montreal
Evaluation and Technology Transfer
75 Port Royal East, Ste. 600
Montreal, Quebec H3L 3T1
Canada
(514) 383-7712
fax (514) 383-7040

Gregor Reid
Dir. Res. Services
The University of Western Ontario
London, Ontario N6A 5B8
Canada
(519) 661-2161
fax (519) 661-3907

Gary Svoboda
Manager
Canadian Industrial/Innovation Ctr.
156 Columbia St. West
Waterloo, Ontario N2L 3L3
Canada
(519) 885-5870
fax (519) 885-5729

Richard Valee
President
Inventors Society of Nova Scotia
1046 Barrington St., Ste. 106
Halifax, Nova Scotia B3H 2R1
Canada
(902) 421-1250
fax (902) 429-9983

Chris Webb
Director
Canadian Young Inventors Fair
    Society
Box 12151
1220 - 808 Nelson St.
Vancouver, BC V6Z 2H2
Canada
(604) 689-3626
fax (604) 684-4589

Joseph E. La Ville
Owner/Manager
Solarville
P.O. Box 1167
Agana, 96910
Guam
(671) 472-8131
fax (671) 472-8131

Juan Rivera Bigas
Executive Director
Puerto Rico Products Association
P.O. Box 363631
San Juan, 00936-3631
Puerto Rico
(809) 753-8484
fax (809) 753-0855

Jose Romaguera
Executive Director
PR-SBDC
Box 5253, College Station
Mayaguez, PR 00681
Puerto Rico
(809) 834-5556
fax (809) 832-5550

Boris Plahteanu, Ph.D.
Prof. Dr. Eng.
National Inventics Institute of Jassy
P.O. Box 727
Iasi-3, RO-6600
Romania
(40) 98-146577
fax (40) 98-147923

Vladimir Yossifov
Head
World Intellectual Property Organ.
Devel. Co-op. Program Support
34 Chemin des Colombettes
1211 Geneva 20,
Switzerland
(022) 730-9111
fax (022) 733-5428

Sources of Capital/ Aid for Inventors and Small Businesses

There are many federally funded and nonprofit programs devoted to helping small businesses and inventors. All inventors are entrepreneurs in a way because they've dreamed about commercializing their ideas. This book has been dedicated to showing inventors how to go through the full process of marketing their inventions and patents through licensing or outright buyout. But to do this, you will be going through the same initial steps as any small business entrepreneurs whose intentions are to carry out the future business all on their own. With this in mind, it would be a good idea to apply for at least a fictitious name since most of the programs listed in the following sections are designed to give money and aid to small businesses or inventors with business intentions. The more serious you appear, the more likely that they will help you.

Government Funded Programs

National Institute of Standards and Technology (NIST)

The NIST was established by Congress "to assist industry in the development of technology . . . needed to improve product quality, to modernize manufacturing processes, to ensure product reliability . . . and to facilitate rapid commercialization . . . of products based on new scientific discoveries." They are under the U.S. Department of Commerce, with a $609 million budget and more than thirty-two hundred scientists, engineers, technicians, and support personnel.

The NIST offers a range of aid and grants through the following programs:
- ATP - Advanced Technology Program
- MEP - Manufacturing Extension Partnership
- ERIP - Energy Related Inventions Program
- InnConn - Innovative Concepts Program

Advanced Technology Program (ATP)

The ATP provides technology development funding in an effort to accelerate the development and commercialization of promising, high-risk technologies with substantial potential for enhancing U.S. economic growth. This money is granted through cooperative research agreements to single businesses or industry-led joint ventures. Applicants must share the costs of ATP projects.

Awards to individual companies are limited to $2 million over three years and can be used only for direct R&D costs. Awards to joint ventures can be for up to five years; joint ventures must provide more than 50 percent of the resources for the project. The ATP does not fund product development. It will support development of laboratory prototypes and proof of technical feasibility but not commercial prototypes or proof of commercial feasibility.

The ATP selects specific projects through a rigorous competitive process that includes evaluation of both the technical and business merits of a project. Some past award winners have been:
- Development of thick-film processing technology for radio-frequency equipment
- Development of technology to "clean" semiconductor wafer of trace metals and particles
- New design for high-precision, multi-axis machine tools
- Improvement in scientific understanding for relationship between processing, part geometry, microstructure, and part performance for fiber-reinforced molded parts
- Creation of generic software technology to restore, enhance, or digitally reformat moving pictures
- Application of newly developed production technologies to fabricate high-efficiency long-lived blue-green lasers and LEDs

- Development of the methodology for producing animal-derived extracellular matrix materials as prosthetic materials to support the regeneration of tissues and glands

Contact:
Advanced Technology Program
1-800-ATP-FUND
fax: (301) 926-9524
e-mail: atp@micf.nist.gov

Manufacturing Extension Partnership (MEP)

The MEP is a nationwide network of organizations to support U.S.-based manufacturers in increasing their competitiveness nationally and internationally through ongoing technological advancement. NIST is building and coordinating the partnership to help smaller manufacturers tap into regional and national sources of information, knowledge, and insight into the use of modern manufacturing and production technologies. By 1997, there are supposed to be more than one hundred manufacturing extension centers nationwide.

These partnerships include four major elements:

1. Regionally based Manufacturing Technology Centers (MTCs), providing hands-on technical assistance to small and mid-sized manufacturers—linked to Small Business Development Centers

2. Smaller, satellite operations called Manufacturing Outreach Centers

3. The State Technology Extension Program (STEP), providing grants to help states build the infrastructure needed for technology transfer efforts

4. The Links Program to pull together—both electronically and otherwise—not only the NIST-affiliated offices but also all other federal, state, local, and university technology transfer entities into one national network

From January 1989 through June 1991, client companies estimated that the MTCs helped them save a total of $139 million—eight times more than the federal investment of $18 million during that time.

Companies That Have Used MEP

- Newburgh Molded Products: used new processing technology to increase its production volume by two-thirds.
- Kintz Plastics: bought new automation equipment to cut its production time for making steel and aluminum molds from eight weeks to eight days.
- Brimfield Precision: saved more than $200,000 on the purchase of a new computer-aided design and manufacturing system after trying out several systems at an MTC and choosing a less expensive system than the one they previously thought necessary.
- New York Vitamin Manufacturer: sped up the production and cut its time for filling back orders by more than 50 percent.

MEP & MTC Contacts

General Information:
Phil Nanzetta
Manufacturing Extension Partnership
(301) 975-5020
fax: (301) 963-6556
e-mail: mepinfo@micf.nist.gov
B115 Polymer Building

John J. Chernesky
California MTC
13430 Hawthorne Blvd.
Hawthorne, CA 90250
(310) 355-3060

George H. Sutherland
Great Lakes MTC
Prospect Park Building
4600 Prospect Ave.
Cleveland, OH 44103-4314
(216) 432-5300

Paul E. Clay, Jr.
Mid-America MTC
10561 Barkley, St. 602
Overland Park, KS 66212
(913) 649-4333

Michael A. Taback
Midwest MTC
2901 Hubbard Rd.
Ann Arbor, MI 48105
(313) 769-4377

Mark Tebbano
Northeast MTC
385 Jordan Rd.
Troy, NY 12180-8347
(518) 283-1010

Jim Bishop
Southeast MTC
P.O. Box 1149
Columbia, SC 29202
(803) 252-6976

Jan Pounds
Upper Midwest MTC
111 3rd Ave., S., Suite 400
Minneapolis, MN 55401
(612) 338-8822

Energy-Related Inventions Program (ERIP)

The ERIP is a national program established for the research and development of all potentially useful energy sources and energy use technologies. The U.S. Department of Energy (DOE) conducts the program. Essentially, the ERIP encourages innovation in the development of energy technology. Particular attention is given to inventions submitted by independent inventors and small businesses.

Since the program began in 1975, more than 31,000 inventions have been submitted to NIST for evaluation. More than 625 of these submissions were recommended to DOE, with more than 450 receiving funding. The average grant is about $89,000, with the maximum award ever given being just under $100,000.

When NIST receives your application, they screen your invention for acceptance into the program. This takes about four weeks. If accepted, it goes to the first stage of evaluation, which takes place under NIST staff discretion. This usually takes between 16 and 20 weeks. If your invention is considered technically feasible and commercially practical, and has strong potential for saving or producing energy, it is rated "promising" and moved to the second stage of evaluation, which takes between eight and 11 weeks.

In the second stage, your invention is passed onto the DOE. Your ERIP coordinator (from the DOE) will ask you to submit a preliminary proposal describing the support you need. Then the coordinator will use your proposal, NIST's recommendations, and a market assessment of the invention to decide how to fund and support your invention.

Time of Evaluation:
Screening Process - 4 weeks
First Stage Evaluation - 16-20 weeks
Second Stage Evaluation- 8-11 weeks

To submit an invention/contacts, write to:
Office of Technology Evaluation & Assessment
National Institute of Standards and Technology
Gaithersburg, MD 20899

Ask for an Evaluation Request Form (Form 1019). Fill out the form and return it with a description of your invention and the material needed to support your claims. You should describe the invention completely on paper. Use drawings where applicable; they do not have to be professionally done. You should state claims clearly. Point out how the invention is unique, and how performance and costs are an improvement over competing items. You should discuss how the invention will affect national energy goals. Support your claims with calculations or test data. Remember, qualified engineers will be using these data to evaluate your invention. Do not submit models or samples of materials unless the office specifically asks you to do so during the evaluation. Anyone can submit an invention to NIST, and there is no fee or obligation by the inventor.

Innovative Concepts Program (InnConn)

The Innovative Concepts Program (InnConn) is run by the Department of Energy (DOE) through the Office of Technical and Financial Assistance. Like ERIP, InnConn supports energy-related ideas, but InnConn provides assistance much earlier in the invention process. They provide assistance and grants so that innovators can explore their concepts. The program provides seed money to allow innovators to determine if their ideas are technically and economically feasible. InnConn also provides valuable nonfinancial support by helping innovators find technical partners, commercial sponsors, and new sources of funding. One example of this support is a technology fair, at which the innovators are given a chance to present their initial findings to a wide audience of private and commercial investors.

Since the Innovative Concepts Program began in 1983, 70 projects have been funded, of which 55 have been completed. Of those completed, 45 percent have received funding from other sources to continue the work, leading to numerous journal articles, master's and Ph.D. theses, and patents. Many projects have found commercial applications. The awards for doing the "concept research" are typically between $15,000 and $20,000.

This program is intended to support novel ideas for energy efficiency that are significant departures from existing technologies. It is not intended for incremental improvements or promotion of existing technologies. Well-developed inventions that are past the conceptual stage should apply to ERIP rather then InnConn.

Contacts:
Lisa Barnett, Program Manager
U.S. Department of Energy
Forrestal Building, CE-521
1000 Independence Ave., SW
Washington, DC 20585
(202) 586-1605

Raymond L. Watts, K6-54
Pacific Northwest Laboratory
Box 999
Richland, WA 99352
fax: (509) 372-4369

Private Organizations

Service Corps of Retired Executives (SCORE)

SCORE is a 13,000 member volunteer organization sponsored by the U.S. Small Business Administration (SBA). The program matches business-hardened and experienced counselors with owners and managers of small businesses who need expert advice but lack the financial resources to pay for it. SCORE volunteers help small business owners and managers identify basic management problems, determine causes, analyze problems, and help find solutions to problems identified and solved by the counselors long ago.

Contact:
1-800-310-HELP

PTO Fees

If you have questions for the PTO or would like to request any of the forms listed here, contact the PTO at (703) 305-8510, or by fax at (703) 305-8525.

Application Fees

Code	37 CFR Sec.	DESCRIPTION	Oct 1995
101	1.16(a)	Basic Filing Fee	$730
201	1.16(a)	Basic Filing Fee (Small Entity)	$375
102	1.16(b)	Independent Claims	$78
202	1.16(b)	Independent Claims (Small Entity)	$39
103	1.16©	Claims in Excess of 20	$22
203	1.16©	Claims in Excess of 20 (Small Entity)	$11
104	1.16(d)	Multiple Dependent Claims	$250
204	1.16(d)	Multiple Dependent Claims (Small Entity)	$125
105	1.16(e)	Surcharge - Late Filing Fee	$130
205	1.16(e)	Surcharge - Late Filing Fee (Small Entity)	$65
106	1.16(f)	Design Filing Fee	$310
206	1.16(f)	Design Filing Fee (Small Entity)	$155
107	1.16(g)	Plant Filing Fee	$510
207	1.16(g)	Plant Filing Fee (Small Entity)	$255
108	1.16(h)	Reissue Filing Fee	$750
208	1.16(h)	Reissue Filing Fee (Small Entity)	$375
109	1.16(I)	Reissue Independent Claims	$78
209	1.16(I)	Reissue Independent Claims (Small Entity)	$39
110	1.16(j)	Reissue Claims in Excess of 20	$22
210	1.16(j)	Reissue Claims in Excess of 20 (Small Entity)	$11

114	1.16(k)	Provisional Application Filing Fee	$150
214	1.16(k)	Provisional Application Filing Fee (Small Entity)	$75
127	1.16(l)	Surcharge - Incomplete Provisional App. Filed	$50
227	1.16(l)	Surcharge - Incomplete Prov. App. Filed (Small Entity)	$25
115	1.17(a)	Extension - First Month	$110
215	1.17(a)	Extension - First Month (Small Entity)	$55
116	1.17(b)	Extension - Second Month	$380
216	1.17(b)	Extension - Second Month (Small Entity)	$190
117	1.17©	Extension - Third Month	$900
217	1.17©	Extension - Third Month (Small Entity)	$450
118	1.17(d)	Extension - Fourth Month	$1,400
218	1.17(d)	Extension - Fourth Month (Small Entity)	$700
119	1.17(e)	Notice of Appeal	$290
219	1.17(e)	Notice of Appeal (Small Entity)	$145
120	1.17(f)	Filing a Brief	$290
220	1.17(f)	Filing a Brief (Small Entity)	$145
121	1.17(g)	Request for Oral Hearing	$250
221	1.17(g)	Request for Oral Hearing (Small Entity)	$125

Petition Fees

Code	37 CFR Sec.	DESCRIPTION	Oct 1995
122	1.17(h)	Petition - Not All Inventors	$130
122	1.17(h)	Petition - Correction of Inventorship	$130
122	1.17(h)	Petition - Decision on Questions	$130
122	1.17(h)	Petition - Suspend Rules	$130
122	1.17(h)	Petition - Expedited License	$130
122	1.17(h)	Petition - Scope of License	$130
122	1.17(h)	Petition - Retroactive License	$130
122	1.17(h)	Petition - Refusing Maintenance Fee	$130
122	1.17(h)	Petition - Refusing Maintenance Fee-Expired Patent	$130
122	1.17(h)	Petition - Interference	$130
122	1.17(h)	Petition - Reconsider Interference	$130
122	1.17(h)	Petition - Late Filing of Interference	$150

122	1.17(h)	Petition - Refusal to Publish SIR	$130
122	1.17(i)	Petition - For Assignment	$130
122	1.17(i)	Petition - For Application	$130
122	1.17(i)	Petition - Late Priority Papers	$130
122	1.17(i)	Petition - Suspend Action	$130
122	1.17(i)	Petition - Divisional Reissues to Issue Separately	$130
122	1.17(i)	Petition - For Interference Agreement	$130
122	1.17(i)	Petition - Amendment after Issue	$130
122	1.17(i)	Petition - Withdrawal after Issue	$130
122	1.17(i)	Petition - Defer Issue	$130
122	1.17(i)	Petition - Issue to Assignee	$130
122	1.17(i)	Petition - Accord a Filing Date under §1.53	$130
122	1.17(i)	Petition - Accord a Filing Date under §1.62	$130
122	1.17(i)	Petition - Make Application Special	$130
138	1.17(j)	Petition - Public Use Proceeding	$1,430
139	1.17(k)	Non-English Specification	$130
140	1.17(l)	Petition - Revive Abandoned Application	$110
240	1.17(l)	Petition - Revive Abandoned Application (Small Entity)	$55
141	1.17(m)	Petition - Revive Unintentionally Abandoned Application	$1,250
241	1.17(m)	Petition - Revive Unintentionally Abandoned Application (Small Entity)	$625
112	1.17(n)	SIR - Prior to Examiner's Action	$870
113	1.17(o)	SIR - After Examiner's Action	$1,740
126	1.17(p)	Submission of an Info Disclosure Statement (§1.97)	$220
123	1.17(q)	Petition - Correction of Inventorship (Prov. App.)	$50
123	1.17(q)	Petition - Accord a Filing Date (Prov. App.)	$50
146	1.17®	Filing a Submission after Final Rejection (1.129(a))	$750
246	1.17®	Filing Submiss. after Final Reject. (1.129(a)) (Small Entity)	$375
149	1.17(s)	Per Add'l Invention to be Examined (1.129(b))	$750
249	1.17(s)	Per Add'l Invention to be Examined(1.129(b)) (Sm Entity)	$375

Issue Fees

Code	37 CFR Sec.	DESCRIPTION	Oct 1995
142	1.18(a)	Utility Issue Fee	$1,250
242	1.18(a)	Utility Issue Fee (Small Entity)	$625
143	1.18(b)	Design Issue Fee	$430
243	1.18(b)	Design Issue Fee (Small Entity)	$215
144	1.18©	Plant Issue Fee	$630
244	1.18©	Plant Issue Fee (Small Entity)	$315
122	1.20(b)	Petition - Correction of Inventorship	$130

Copies and Service Fees

Code	37 CFR Sec.	DESCRIPTION	Oct 1995
561	1.19(a)(1)(i)	Copy of Patent	$3
562	1.19(a)(1)(ii)	Patent Copy-Overnight Deliv. to PTO Box or Overnight Fax	$6
563	1.19(a)(1)(iii)	Patent Copy Ordered by Exp. Mail or fax-Exp. service	$25
564	1.19(a)(2)	Plant Patent Copy	$12
565	1.19(a)(3)(i)	Copy of Utility Patent or SIR in Color	$24
566	1.19(b)(1)(i)	Certified Copy of Patent Application as Filed	$15
567	1.19(b)(1)(ii)	Cert. Copy of Patent Application as Filed, Expedited	$30
568	1.19(b)(2)	Copy of Patent-Related File Wrapper/Contents	$150
569	1.19(b)(3)	Copies of Office Records, per Document	$25
570	1.19(b)(4)	For Assignment Records, Abstract of Title and Cert.	$25
571	1.19©	Library Service	$50
572	1.19(d)	List of Patents in Subclass	$3
573	1.19(e)	Uncert. Statement-Status of Maintenance Fee Payment	$10
574	1.19(f)	Copy of Non-U.S. Patent Document	$25
575	1.19(g)	Comparing and Certifying Copies, per Doc, per Copy	$25
576	1.19(h)	Duplicate or Corrected Filing Receipt	$25

Maintenance Fees

Code	37 CFR Sec.	DESCRIPTION	Oct 1995
183	1.20(e)	Maintenance Fee - 3.5 Years	$990
283	1.20(e)	Maintenance Fee - 3.5 Years (Small Entity)	$495
184	1.20(f)	Maintenance Fee - 7.5 Years	$1,990
284	1.20(f)	Maintenance Fee - 7.5 Years (Small Entity)	$995
185	1.20(g)	Maintenance Fee - 11.5 Years	$2,990
285	1.20(g)	Maintenance Fee - 11.5 Years (Small Entity)	$1,495
186	1.20(h)	Surcharge - Maintenance Fee - 6 Months	$130
286	1.20(h)	Surcharge - Maintenance Fee - 6 Months (Small Entity)	$65
187	1.20(i)(1)	Surcharge - Maintenance after Expiration- Unavoidable	$660
188	1.20(i)(2)	Surcharge - Maintenance after Expiration- Unintentional	$1,550
111	1.20(j)	Extension of Term of Patent	$1,060

PTO Agent Examination and Other Fees

Code	37 CFR Sec.	DESCRIPTION	Oct 1995
609	1.21(a)(1)	Admission to Examination	$310
610	1.21(a)(2)	Registration to Practice	$100
611	1.21(a)(3)	Reinstatement to Practice	$15
612	1.21(a)(4)	Certificate of Good Standing	$10
613	1.21(a)(4)	Certificate of Good Standing, Suitable Framing	$20
615	1.21(a)(5)	Review of Decision of Director, OED	$130
616	1.21(a)(6)	Regrading of Examination	$130
607	1.21(b)(1)	Establish Deposit Account	$10
608	1.21(b)(2)	Service Charge below Minimum Balance	$25
608	1.21(b)(3)	Service Charge below Minimum Balance	$25
577	1.21©	Filing a Disclosure Document	$10
578	1.21(d)	Box Rental	$50
579	1.21(e)	International Type Search Report	$40
580	1.21(g)	Self-Service Copy Charge	$.25
581	1.21(h)	Recording Patent Property	$40

583	1.21(i)	Publication in the OG	$25
585	1.21(k)	Unspecified Other Services	Actual Cost
584	1.21(j)	Labor Charges for Services	$30
588	1.21(o)	Terminal Use APS-TEXT	$40
592	1.21(k)	Terminal Use APS-CSIR (per hour)	$50
586	1.21(l)	Retaining Abandoned Application	$130
617	1.21(m)	Processing Returned Checks	$50
587	1.21(n)	Handling Fee - Incomplete Application	$130
590	1.24	Coupons for Patent and Trademark Copies	$3
589	1.296	Handling Fee - Withdrawal SIR	$130
150	1.445(a)(1)	Transmittal Fee	$220

Foreign Application Processing/P.C.T. Fees

Code	37 CFR Sec.	DESCRIPTION	Oct 1995
151	1.445(a)(2)(i)	PCT Search Fee - No U.S. Application	$660
153	1.445(a)(2)(ii)	PCT Search Fee - Prior U.S. Application	$430
152	1.445(a)(3)	Supplemental Search	$190
190	1.482(a)(1)(i)	Preliminary Exam Fee	$470
191	1.482(a)(1)(ii)	Preliminary Exam Fee	$710
192	1.482(a)(2)(i)	Additional Invention	$140
193	1.482(a)(2)(ii)	Additional Invention	$250
956	1.492(a)(1)	Preliminary Examining Authority	$680
957	1.492(a)(1)	Preliminary Examining Authority (Small Entity)	$340
958	1.492(a)(2)	Searching Authority	$750
959	1.492(a)(2)	Searching Authority (Small Entity)	$375
960	1.492(a)(3)	PTO Not ISA nor IPEA	$1,010
961	1.492(a)(3)	PTO Not ISA nor IPEA (Small Entity)	$505
962	1.492(a)(4)	Claims - IPEA	$94
963	1.492(a)(4)	Claims - IPEA (Small Entity)	$47
970	1.492(a)(5)	Filing with EPO/JPO Search Report	$880
971	1.492(a)(5)	Filing with EPO/JPO Search Report (Small Entity)	$440
964	1.492(b)	Claims - Extra Individual (Over 3)	$78
965	1.492(b)	Claims - Extra Individual (Over 3) (Sm. Ent)	$39
966	1.492©	Claims - Extra Total (Over 20)	$22

967	1.492©	Claims - Extra Total (Over 20) (Sm. Ent)	$11
968	1.492(d)	Claims - Multiple Dependents	$250
969	1.492(d)	Claims - Multiple Dependents (Sm. Ent)	$125

Surcharges/Correction/Miscellaneous Fees

Code	37 CFR Sec.	DESCRIPTION	Oct 1995
145	1.20(a)	Certificate of Correction	$100
147	1.20©	Reexamination	$2,390
148	1.20(d)	Statutory Disclaimer	$110
248	1.20(d)	Statutory Disclaimer (Small Entity)	$55
154	1.492(e)	Surcharge	$130
254	1.492(e)	Surcharge (Small Entity)	$65
156	1.492(f)	English Translation - After 20 Months	$130
361	2.6(a)(1)	Application for Registration, per Class	$245
362	2.6(a)(2)	Amendment to Allege Use, per Class	$100
363	2.6(a)(3)	Statement of Use, per Class	$100
364	2.6(a)(4)	Extension for Filing Statement of Use, per Class	$100
365	2.6(a)(5)	Application for Renewal, per Class	$300
366	2.6(a)(6)	Surcharge for Late Renewal, per Class	$100
367	2.6(a)(7)	Publication of Mark under §12(c), per Class	$100
368	2.6(a)(8)	Issuing New Certificate of Registration	$100
369	2.6(a)(9)	Certificate of Correction of Registrant's Error	$100
370	2.6(a)(10)	Filing Disclaimer to Registration	$100
371	2.6(a)(11)	Filing Amendment to Registration	$100
372	2.6(a)(12)	Filing Affidavit under Section 8, per Class	$100
373	2.6(a)(13)	Filing Affidavit under Section 15, per Class	$100
374	2.6(a)(14)	Filing Affidavit under Sections 8 & 15, per Class	$200
375	2.6(a)(15)	Petitions to the Commissioner	$100
376	2.6(a)(16)	Petition to Cancel, per Class	$200
377	2.6(a)(17)	Notice of Opposition, per Class	$200
378	2.6(a)(18)	Ex Parte Appeal to the TTAB, per Class	$100
379	2.6(a)(19)	Dividing an Application, per New Application Create	$100
461	2.6(b)(1)(i)	Copy of Registered Mark	$3

462	2.6(b)(1)(ii)	Copy of Reg Mark, Overnight Del. to PTO Box or fax	$6
463	2.6(b)(1)(iii)	Copy of Reg Mark Ordered via Exp Mail or fax, Exp Svc	$25
466	2.6(b)(2)(i)	Certified Copy of TM Application as Filed	$15
467	2.6(b)(2)(ii)	Certified Copy of TM Application as Filed, Expedited	$30
468	2.6(b)(3)	Certified or Uncertified Copy of TM-Related File Wrapper/Content	$50
464	2.6(b)(4)(i)	Cert. Copy of Registered Mark, Title or Status	$10
465	2.6(b)(4)(ii)	Cert. Copy of Registered Mark, Title or Status - Exp	$20
469	2.6(b)(5)	Certified or Uncertified Copy of TM Records	$25
481	2.6(b)(6)	Recording Trademark Property, per Mark, per Document	$40
482	2.6(b)(6)	For Second and Subsequent Marks in Same Document	$25
470	2.6(b)(7)	For Assignment Records, Abstracts of Title and Cert	$25
488	2.6(b)(8)	Terminal Use X-SEARCH	$40
480	2.6(b)(9)	Self-Service Copy Charge	$0.25
484	2.6(b)(10)	Labor Charges for Services	$30
485	2.6(b)(11)	Unspecified Other Services	Actual Cost

Inventors' Publishing and Research

- We find manufacturers and earn you royalties
- Free advice
- Free royalty estimates for new patents
- Proven track record
- Experienced agents

- Worldwide manufacturing contacts
- We take pride in representing your US Patent
- An aggressive six-month placement program
- Negotiating and licensing expertise

We Find Manufacturers So You Can Earn Royalties

Inventors' Publishing and Research (IP&R) specializes in the effective promotion of inventions and patents to an international network of manufacturers. Founded by an inventor, IP&R's goal is to get your invention through the doors of major corporations, present your invention to key executives in the industry, and license your invention for up-front money and royalties from manufacturers.

The Best Track Record in the Industry

No other company can claim such a successful track record because no one else has it. The word is out: It is publically documented that you're approximately 50 times more likely to get your product on the market with IP&R than with invention companies who advertise on TV and radio.

Lost Time Equals Lost Royalties

Every day you wait means potential lost royalty paychecks that you could be receiving today. The time that transpires after your patent is filed can never be recovered. IP&R has an aggressive marketing strategy that has proven to be effective for promoting inventions to manufacturers within a six-month period (average time).

International Network of Manufacturers

Our network of manufacturers and connections around the world is extremely large and actively growing. Many of our corporate connections will not deal with inventors, but work only through qualified agents, like ourselves. IP&R not only has the contacts, but also has the power to get in because we have:

CREDENTIALS

- ✓ Experience
- ✓ Effective Sales Promotions
- ✓ Reputable Agents
- ✓ A Proven Track Record
- ✓ Licensing Contacts
- ✓ A Personal Approach
- ✓ Tradeshow Presence

"I had difficulties getting a manufacturer interested in my invention, but after IP&R's help, everything turned completely around! Now I made a deal for $820,000 up front with a manufacturer."

—BORIS KHUDENKO, OWNER OF 12 US PATENTS

What Kinds Royalties Can I Expect to Earn?

The national average for a royalty is about five percent. IP&R's average royalty is roughly seven percent! It takes years of experience to learn how to negotiate with major corporations. IP&R brings all this experience to the table when we work for you. The ability to negotiate a higher percentage such as seven or eight percent depends on a number of complex factors that must be skillfully handled.

A Shot Heard Round the World

With IP&R's aggressive marketing approach, we personally contact a large number of manufacturers (simultaneously) within a short period of six months. Our approach gets the quickest results and provides maximum impact, creating a national "buzz" for your invention. This sparks simultaneous interest and excitement from manufacturers. Ultimately, this has the potential for creating multiple bids and offers for your invention.

Licensing: The Top of the Mountain

IP&R knows the rules and sophisticated formulae for calculating royalties. Wouldn't you agree guessing a figure or "taking a stab in the dark" would be terribly foolish? Do you know how to negotiate minimum annual royalties? IP&R is experienced and qualified to represent you fully!

SERVICES PROVIDED BY IP&R

✓ Patent Work	✓ Prototyping, Engineering	✓ Test Marketing
✓ Distributor Marketing	✓ Market Research	✓ Package Design
✓ Publicity Campaigning	✓ Tradeshow Representation	✓ Negotiation
✓ Product Endorsements	✓ Store Feedback	✓ Licensing

"By maximizing your chances in finding a manufacturer, you are maximizing your chances of earning a future royalty income. I know what it is like to earn them. You have an invention with great potential, but how can you convince the world? You can personally speak to me or my Director of Product Selection."

—STEVEN S. BARBARICH, PRESIDENT OF IP&R

The History of IP&R: Honesty and Dedication to the American Inventor

Founded by successful inventor Steven S. Barbarich, Inventors' Publishing and Research prides itself on effective, honest promotion of inventions. Mr. Barbarich licensed his first invention for Atari computers at the age of 16. Since then, he has helped commercialized dozens of inventions.

After his many successes, Mr. Barbarich founded IP&R in an effort to team up with inventors and help make their dreams become a reality. In additional to being an international agent, Mr. Barbarich tours the country giving speeches to non-profit inventors' groups and SBA associations. All this done to support inventors and the thriving community from which new ideas become tomorrow's reality.

Call TOLL FREE and personally speak to one of our product agents:
1-800-MARKET2 (627-5382)

Mailing address: **Inventors' Publishing**
P.O. Box 881536
San Francisco, CA 94188

www.inventorspublishing.com